GW00635172

Essential Kinesiology Techniques for Muscle Testing Practitioners

By Terry Larder

Essential Kinesiology Techniques for Muscle Testing Practitioners

ISBN: 978-1-910181-78-2

Published August 2020

Printed and Published by Anchorprint Group Limited

www.anchorprint.co.uk

Copyright © Terry Larder

Special Note:

These techniques and procedures are for the purpose of information and research only. Neither the author nor publisher presents any part of this work as a diagnosis or prescription for any ailment for which medical attention should be sought.

All rights reserved.

No part of this publication may be reproduced, stored in a retrieval system, transmitted or utilised in any form or by any means, electronic, mechanical, photocopying, recording or otherwise, without written permission from the copyright holder.

Foreword from the Kinesiology Association (UK)

The Kinesiology Association (KA) is delighted to be working in alliance with Terry Larder the principle of The Classical Kinesiology Institute. When we decided to develop our own Curriculum for a brand-new KA Diploma Course it was serendipitous that at the time Terry was planning to produce this book, her definitive Kinesiology guide.

Over her many years as a Kinesiologist and Trainer, Terry has always had a passion for wanting to know the provenance of the methods she uses. The production of this book has allowed her to reference, from numerous sources, many of the techniques taught at diploma level so we now have the definitive text book a Professional Diplomates in Kinesiology.

This book is the cornerstone for the training of new students who aspire to become professional members of the Kinesiology Association.

This body of work is also an excellent reference manual for any established Kinesiologists who want to ensure they are using the techniques correctly, because we all know how information can easily become distorted over time.

This new and comprehensive book will help to underpin one of the KA's aims and objectives - To advance and promote high standards of ethics, training and practice for KA practitioners.

Established in 1988 the KA (previously known as the Association of Systematic Kinesiology) is the UK's largest membership organisation with around 500 members and provides them with on-going support, guidance and training.

The Kinesiology Association Trustees

Kinesiology
Association
YOUR BODY IN BALANCE

The KA is a registered Charity (No. 299306) and a Company Limited by Guarantee (No. 2235125).

Registered Office: 15 Cygnet Drive, Durrington, Wiltshire, SP4 8LQ. Telephone: 01980 881646

Email: admin@kinesiologyassociation.org   Website, www.kinesiologyassociation.org

Table of contents

Acknowledgements

There are so many people who have inspired me with their research, many of whom sadly I don't even know their names. First, I must acknowledge the researchers who I know have contributed incredible kinesiology techniques that have helped thousands of people. In this book I have referenced as many of them as I could find. These include the late George Goodheart, Dr Walter Schmitt, the late Carl Ferreri, Christopher Astill-Smith and of course Dr Sheldon Deal, without whom, this book would not have been possible. Dr Deal's yearly UK seminars have been a rich source of information for this book. I would especially like to thank him, and all the Applied Kinesiology graduates whose research he shared with us.

Additionally, my very genuine thanks and gratitude go to:

Marie Cheshire who meticulously transcribed 15+ years of Dr Deal's seminars; her work made my book achievable.

Knowlative for their rich website resource where I could check and research techniques. They also very generously gave their permission for the use of their illustrations, some of which are used in this book.

Dr Sally Prestwich and Linda Belcher for their generosity in sharing their notes and spending their valuable time with me in discussion.

Chris Halls for his eagle eye, piercing questions, and exceptionally helpful editing suggestions – his family can have him back now!

Emma, Sarah and Simon White for being my models and taking photographs.

The UK's Kinesiology Association who have been a great encouragement during this project.

Richard Linnett from Anchor Print Group who breathed life into the book. He's been an absolute pleasure to work with.

All of my students who over the past 30 years have inspired me to write this book as a legacy to the muscle response testing community.

The late Dr Rodney Adeniyi-Jones and Sherridan Stock who have been my mentors over the years.

Last but not least, my long-suffering supportive husband David who, right from the beginning in 1985, has given me the space and encouragement to become the practitioner I wanted to be.

Prologue

James Green, the Herbalist, says that herbal medicine-making is like dancing. "It's easy, it's natural and undeniably delightful", he says. Interlacing the many techniques that we discover through muscle response testing and gliding from one to another, reminds me of a dance too! Each dance is different, depending on who we are dancing with, i.e. which person we are interacting with. As with dancing, once you find the rhythm of the music you'll never want to stop. After nearly 40 years, I still find it fun. Each interaction with a client brings a new connection with them, sharing the simple pleasures of exploring with them their body's subtle cues, discovering underlying causes of their distress, and entertaining them during the process so that they long to come back for more.

"The term 'expert' is derived from the verb root meaning 'to try', 'to risk', 'to press forward'. We all do that with every new thought and experience we create. Living a life qualifies each of us as an expert. We don't have to agree with each other for things to work, merely appreciate one another and enjoy our differences as the 'Medicine Show' proceeds from stage to stage in your home (or in your clinic)" (Green, 2002)

As well as introducing you to a wealth of techniques to add to your 'toolbox', I want to give you some fundamentals of good practice to help you start as you mean to go on. Don't wait until your 'dancing' is fluent before you work with people, the only way you'll get better is by taking a risk – pressing forward and creating kinesiology experiences. The more you enter the dance, the more fluent you'll become!

> **" This book is for those who have been introduced to foundation level kinesiology and wish to add to their skills and for kinesiologists everywhere who want to refresh, learn something new, and add to their repertoire of techniques. "**

Glossary

TERM	EXPLANATION
AHP	Acupressure Holding Points or Meridian Energy Interchange (MEI) points.
AIM	Accurate Indicator Muscle; A muscle that is strong in the clear and will unlock with a magnet.
ANALOGUE MUSCLE TEST	Developed by the late Alan Sales, who augmented research from Richard Utt and others. The muscle is tested through its whole range of motion under pressure, rather than performing a static test. This gives a holographic readout of the relationship between the muscle's associated meridian/organ and the rest of the body systems/meridians. A lot more information can be gathered using this test.
ANCHOR	Testing an AIM, the lesion is challenged once more after the protocol is complete. This allows the brain to recognise the new signal and the changes that have just taken place. Since everything that we do is prompting the brain to implement a new instruction, we always anchor every procedure we carry out so that the message is abundantly clear.
BLANKET TEST	A test that tells the tester that there is an imbalance in a particular area, but further testing needs to be done to isolate the problem. Examples of blanket tests include chakra imbalances, or a TMJ imbalance.
CHALLENGE	The lesion/point only shows when the tester touches it or presses it.
CIRCUIT RETAINING MODE	Another name for 'pause lock'.
CL/CIRCUIT LOCATE	Either the client or the tester can activate the point/lesion.
G1 – GAMMA I MUSCLE TEST	Eccentric muscle contraction; this is when the tester asks the client to hold and the client contracts the muscle in response. The lesion making the muscle weak will be from the neck down. The way to remember this is "Tester Initiated, Lower Spine" (TILS).
DYNAMIC/REBOUND CHALLENGE	"A mechanical challenge where one or more structures of the body are actively or passively moved and then released before or whilst testing an IM" a quote from (Wolfgang Gerz MD). A rebound challenge is used in the investigation of most cranial faults and vertebral misalignment. The direction of the rebound challenge that changes the IM indicates the direction in which the correction is made.

G2 – GAMMA II MUSCLE TEST	Concentric contraction of the muscle; this is when the tester responds to the client who starts the muscle contraction first. The lesion making the muscle weak will be from the neck up. The way to remember this is "Client Initiated, Supra Spine" (CISS).
HIGH GAIN TECHNIQUE	Occasionally imbalances fail to show up, even if the practitioner is aware that there could be a problem in the area being tested. Sometimes the response to a CL or challenge can cause the body to recruit extra energy to body circuits because it sees the test as exceptionally stressful. Indicator muscles can go hypertonic, for example. High gain techniques are ways that the kinesiologist can 'cajole' the body into expressing itself.
HYPERTONIC	The muscle is too tight and will not unlock with a north pole magnet or pinching together the muscle's spindle cells. This muscle state is not suitable to use as an accurate indicator muscle.
ICV	Ileocaecal valve/Ileo-caecal valve / Ileo-cecal valve.
IM	Indicator Muscle.
IN THE CLEAR	Tested with nothing else in the circuit. E.g. Challenging the ankle joint by jamming the heel would be testing it 'in the clear' i.e. where we are checking the joint itself and not in relationship to anything else. This is opposed to jamming the heel when contacting an old injury site as in Injury Recall Technique.
LESION	A lesion is any damage or abnormal change in the tissue of an organism, usually caused by disease or trauma. Any area of dysfunction that CL's or TLs could be referred to as a lesion.
MANUAL MUSCLE TESTING	The client resists, using the target muscle or muscle group, while the practitioner applies a force.
MRT (MUSCLE RESPONSE TESTING)	Used to detect a wide range of target conditions. Assesses a muscle's response to a neurological command. MRT tests one muscle (an AIM) repeatedly as a binary test.
NL	Neuro-lymphatic point.
NV	Neuro-vascular point.
OVER FACILITATED	The correct term for a hypertonic muscle.
PAUSE LOCK	Information held in the body circuitry by placing the feet apart or stretching the skin receptors.
POSITIVE TEST	Indicating the existence or presence of an imbalance/problem

PRONE	The client lies face down, on their front.
SHOW	Denotes an indicator change, i.e. a positive test.
SIM	Strong Indicator Muscle; the same as an accurate indicator muscle.
SUD	Subjective unit of discomfort. Ask your client to measure their pain/emotion out of a scale of 0 - 10.
SUSTAINED/STATIC CHALLENGE	"A mechanical challenge to a bone or organ using a static pressure *at the same time* as the IM is being tested" (Wolfgang Gerz MD). The direction of correction in response to a positive sustained challenge is opposite to the test.
SUPINE	The client lies on their back.
TL/THERAPY LOCALISE	The point/lesion only shows when the client touches it.
TMJ	Temporomandibular joint.
TWO-POINTING	Touching two-points simultaneously changes the indicator muscle. Used when we are looking for an association between two issues, e.g. if a person has a sore elbow, circuit locating it will unlock the IM. If the same person also has an ICV (ileo-caecal valve) imbalance, circuit locating this point will also change the indicator. If the tester wants to see if there is a relationship between the two, the two points are touched simultaneously. If they are linked, the IM will change.

Start as You Mean to Go On

Welcome to the next stage of your training as a professional kinesiologist. You have already become well versed in the foundations of kinesiology and you will learn some fabulous skills to prepare you to commence your new vocation.

Refer to this section frequently. We all need reminding of where we are, where we've come from and what we have yet to achieve. By considering these issues periodically, you will be able to easily see how far you have already come.

In the words of Goethe – *'begin it now!'*

This section will be identifying some key areas that you need to consider in order to succeed in building a healthy business. Pages have been left at the end of each section for you to write any notes as you go along.

 The Exclamation Icon: denotes Key Points, these need examining closely.

 The Lightbulb Icon: denotes items that you may need to reflect on, or check items that need some further study.

So that you can quickly identify the protocols themselves, look for these icons they will always appear in pink tinted boxes:

 The Magnifier Icon: denotes a Test, these should be explored to denote the relevance of the protocol.

 The Tick Icon: denotes a Correction, If the Test is a positiive one then follow these corrections.

Recommendations

Work on as many people as you can during this time. These will be your future clients and you will have a ready-made practice when you are ready to start charging!

Join your professional kinesiology association and get student insurance cover.

Finding 'Clients'

Start to source people willing to be treated. Be serious about this. People will then look on you as a professional from the start. Ensure that they understand that they have a commitment to you to follow through with treatment and take your advice, especially since you are giving them your time and expertise free of charge.

Put out flyers advertising your services in health shops or at your workplace – even as a student you can treat people for free.

Start as you Mean to go on

Be professional. Make appointments for people and keep to these times.

 The change challenges

1. *Be clear on what kind of change is required e.g. major shake-up vs. moderate progression.*

2. *Plan, Plan, Plan!*

3. *Schedule your time*

4. *Set short-term goals*

5. *The war will only be won by winning the battles along the way. If goals are not met, focus on improvement, not fault – finding.*

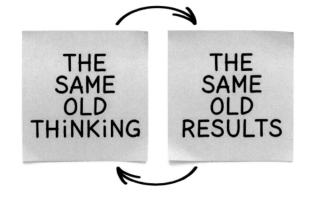

Set Your Sights on the Specific Objective

For example, aim to work on one new person every two weeks or to distribute your leaflets to all the health food shops in town by the end of the month.

Where are you going to see your clients? Can you set aside a room at home? If not, can you investigate where you might be able to hire a room for a few hours a week – maybe sharing a session with another student, if there is anyone who lives nearby. You may ask clients for a donation towards room hire costs or offset your trade discount on supplements that you will now be able to receive. You will then be on the way to being ready to build your practice when you are in a position to start charging. You will already be in 'practice', so the transition will be smooth.

Prime your clients so that they understand that you will eventually be charging a fee. It won't be a shock to them when the time comes, and they will be used to the idea.

Make a point of encouraging those of your non-paying clients, who have felt better as a result of seeing you, to recommend you to others. Give them some of your leaflets to distribute amongst their friends. Begin your business **NOW.**

Begin NOW to grow your business. Make plans and implement them.

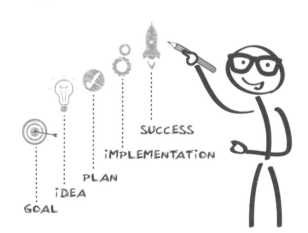

SUCCESS
IMPLEMENTATION
PLAN
IDEA
GOAL

When the time comes, transitioning into a practitioner will be simple.

Your business will already be off the ground.

4 Stages of Learning for a Healthcare Practitioner

It can be quite nerve-wracking to be faced with your first paying client – especially if it's a complete stranger that you have never met before. It can also be stressful to be watched during a practical assessment. We are all aware that when we are under stress, we don't always learn or perform at our best, nor can we concentrate on the matter in hand so easily. Our success can much depend on our ability to keep calm and think clearly – even if things don't go exactly to plan during the session.

Some of the following strategies may help you to consider how you approach learning:

✔ **Gaining experience – work with as many people as you can lay your hands on.**

✔ **Listening and watching demonstrations.**

✔ **Review the protocols. Take time out to read them through again after class then meditate on them (think them through and picture scenarios of how they could be used during a treatment). If you are unsure of the protocol's full implication on the body, research any connected physiology from your A & P book.**

✔ **Learning by practice as soon as possible – within 24 hours after the class if you can.**

When things are new, naturally you will be asking your tutor for a set protocol. We frequently hear in class, 'I see that the protocols have an order, like a recipe book, but when do I use the techniques? Please give me an order of play'. Well you will be shown lots of scenarios on how and when to use them but remember "there are many roads to Rome"! Your course-mate may choose a totally different route from you when addressing a problem that a client has – but remember that neither of these routes are wrong as they all end up in the same place, that is, facilitating the action of change and adjustment in the body itself. The body and mind are the healers and we are only the conduits.

When things don't go to plan in a treatment session, learn from budding pilots who use:

RADAR

It has been found that in over 40% of commercial accidents poor decision-making is a primary factor. Using the wrong mental model of the in-flight situation, or dismissing fresh information, can lead to poor situational awareness. This can happen to a kinesiologist too – not an accident, thankfully, but sometimes, through poor decision making, the treatment can go 'pear shaped' and you, the practitioner feel as though you have achieved nothing at the end of a session. An acute attack of low self-confidence can ensue.

RADAR can help:

R	**Recognise the problem, take in and analyse relevant information.**
A	**Assess alternative solutions to the problem.**
D	**Decide the best option in circumstances – if in doubt go for a safe and simple option.**
A	**Action a plan based on the decision.**
R	**Review the outcome. Has the action taken had the desired effect? If not, start again.**

RADAR can give reassurance that decision-making has been tackled in a systematic way. If new information becomes available, RADAR can be used to check the validity of the original decision and allows you to change it if necessary.

Applying RADAR Principles in Your Kinesiology Session

This can reduce panic when your client is on the couch and things don't go to plan. The simple rule is 'if you are getting confused, don't keep digging in the same hole, go and dig somewhere else'.

Examples of this can be:

- The person is not particularly testable.

- You can't get the body to show anything; therefore, you have nothing to work on. You end up going around in circles and achieve nothing. You start to panic, and things deteriorate because by now you are stressed and can't think clearly; both you and the client finish exasperated. You lose the client.

- Your testing may reveal conflicting results that you can't fathom.

- They may have a catharsis which means that you cannot proceed with the plans you had made for the session.

- You may have planned your session with the client based on their last appointment. However, they present you with another issue, more important to them, that you hadn't bargained for.

Using a tool like RADAR will help you to take stock of the situation, apply a simple option and, if necessary, leads you to start again. You can also use it to check later the validity of the original decision and assess, on reflection, what you might have done differently (recording these situations in a learning journal is really helpful here).

Medicine Act – 1968

These illnesses cannot be treated without a medical licence:

Tuberculosis

Cancer

Diabetes

Epilepsy

Kidney Failure

Paralysis

Cataracts

Locomotor ataxia

Glaucoma

Sexually transmitted diseases

However, helping to strengthen the body so that it can heal itself is perfectly okay.

A model for Mindbody (Psychosomatic) disorders (Sarno, 1999) – Figure 1

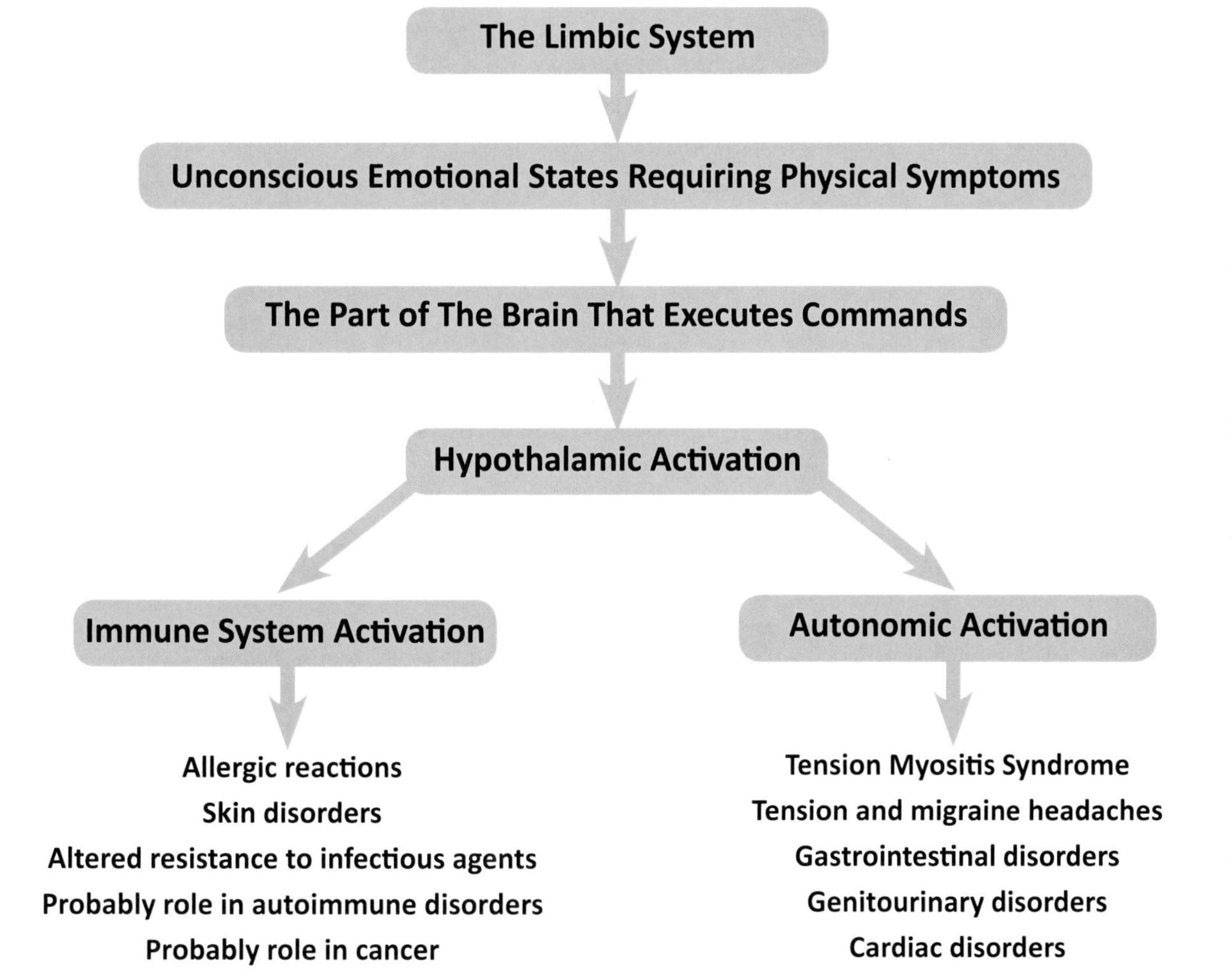

The Limbic System

↓

Unconscious Emotional States Requiring Physical Symptoms

↓

The Part of The Brain That Executes Commands

↓

Hypothalamic Activation

↙ ↘

Immune System Activation | **Autonomic Activation**

Immune System Activation	Autonomic Activation
Allergic reactions	Tension Myositis Syndrome
Skin disorders	Tension and migraine headaches
Altered resistance to infectious agents	Gastrointestinal disorders
Probably role in autoimmune disorders	Genitourinary disorders
Probably role in cancer	Cardiac disorders

Why Muscle Response Testing Works

Centuries of medicine has always addressed the mind completely separately from the body. In fact, it is only fairly recently that treating the mind was in fact deemed as 'real' medicine. However, it really **is** 'all in the mind'. Everything we're doing is in its domain. We need to use our mind to move muscles, talk, eat as well as think.

Let's not be mistaken here. A large majority of illnesses are psychosomatic. What? you say? Terry, are you telling me that what our clients come with is all in their mind? Let's just consider the word psychosomatic. Psycho relates to the mind. Somatic is relating to the body. So, there is another term meaning the same thing – **mind-body** (that sounds more acceptable to most people!).

1. Psychosomatic (mind-body) symptoms encompass many common, harmless physical maladies. These include headaches, stomach ache, allergies and skin conditions.

2. We all experience one or more of these in our lifetime.

3. Mind-body symptoms are responsible for the epidemic of pain syndromes of various kinds that afflict the modern world. These include back, neck shoulder and limb pain (where are all the stomach ulcer sufferers gone? In the 1930s to 1960s stomach ulcer was common and back pain was less so. Have stomach ulcers morphed into skeletal pain? Is the cause the same?).

4. So, we're saying that the body has an innate intelligence which starts in the mind. This is what we harness when carrying out Muscle Response Testing and we address this using techniques that are biochemical, structurally based, emotionally grounded and involve the body's electrical/energy systems.

For model, see **(Fig. 1)** on page ix.

(Sarno, 1999)

When performing a muscle response test, we are monitoring the client's brain replies to the command to activate a group of muscles (we must bear in mind that when a muscle test is performed, we are evaluating the response of the agonist or prime mover, it's antagonist and synergistic muscles).

When we draw the body's attention to a potential problem e.g. a CL point and simultaneously elicit a muscle response generated from the mind, the mind-body has an opportunity to:

> **Reconsider its condition.**
>
> **Reconsider the challenges it faces.**
>
> **Reconsider what resources it has in order to respond.**

❝ We can then enter a dialogue with the body to efficiently and quickly assess the deficiencies in healing and how it can carry that out to its best capacity. We the practitioner are just pointing the way to help the mind-body adjust itself to heal optimally – on its own. ❞

(Feinberg, 2014)

How Does That Work?

The mechanism the body uses for this process is known as the HPA axis **(Fig. 2)** the link between the hypothalamus, the pituitary and its effect on the adrenal glands.

The hypothalamus lies deep within the brain. It's brain tissue, but it is also gland tissue. It influences the endocrine and nervous system and is involved in many important processes. The main job of the hypothalamus is to regulate processes in response to information received from the rest of the body in order to achieve and maintain homeostasis (balance within the body). Information such as sensations of touch, taste and hunger together with changes in body responses to our environment are

HPA Axis – Figure 2

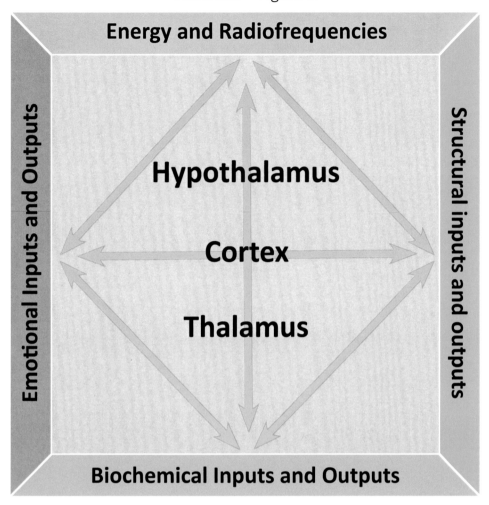

Energy and Radiofrequencies

Emotional Inputs and Outputs

Hypothalamus

Cortex

Thalamus

Structural inputs and outputs

Biochemical Inputs and Outputs

routed back to the hypothalamus. Many experts consider that the feelings of anger, the feeling of falling in love and sadness are sparked by the chemical substances produced by this part of the brain. Therefore, the hypothalamus is like the body's version of a computer's CPU (central processing unit) and is aware of everything that is happening in and around us.

The hypothalamic response is regulated through the autonomic nervous system which includes altering the amount of blood flow through the muscles and tissue depending on whether the body is at rest, exercising, or in repair or renewal mode.

The hypothalamus can switch what it is doing depending on the sensory input it is receiving and will measure the response. The brain knows what to do – assuming it understands the question!

The hypothalamus is the interface between the hormonal system and the nervous system. It sends chemical messengers to the pituitary gland. The information that's sent to the pituitary is based on feedback that the hypothalamus gets from the nervous system. Information from our senses – touch, taste, smell, vision, as well as our thinking centres including emotional and spiritual information – are all processed by the hypothalamus. It then sends information to the pituitary via specific releasing factors. The pituitary then monitors how much work other glands are doing and sends chemical messages to the glands to instruct how much, or how little chemical signalling they should be producing so as to tell cells what to do.

If this process gets out of synchronisation and the tissues, comprised of cells, are receiving faulty signalling, then dysfunction occurs unless it can correct itself. Painful, stressful and emotional experiences all cause changes in hypothalamic activity.

90% of the information that the cortex receives is input that comes from our joints. This stimulates brain function. (therefore, exercise is good for brain function!). This also explains how when we perform a muscle test, the brain receives a barrage of information relating to the joint and muscle that is being tested as well as any sensory input via circuit localization or challenge.

So, what happens when we perform a muscle test? As the hypothalamus is constantly receiving reports from every cell and is 'all seeing', it will be monitoring the moment when muscle testing takes place and subsequently when treatment is offered or administered. It will respond according to the information it receives. This in turn will have a knock-on effect on the responses of the rest of the body.

'There are Many Roads to Rome'

We all know that if we want to visit a location in a large city, there are a number of ways that we can do that. We can either go via the motorway, which may be a longer route in miles, but faster. We can go around the ring road, or we can go straight through the city centre. If we are very familiar with the terrain, we can use back streets and make short cuts and miss all the congested traffic.

For a moment, just transfer that image to kinesiology. When you first learn kinesiology, you will go home from the courses with one technique for one condition. You will memorise and learn it well. Soon you will be accumulating more and more techniques and find that there is more than one way to do something. It does not mean that one way is wrong; it just means that our bodies have biochemical individuality and have idiosyncrasies about their preferences. Don't be alarmed when you learn a different route to the same place. As you become more experienced and knowledgeable, you will be able to use the short cuts more efficiently. This will enable you to get to your 'destination' more quickly. Rome represents our clients' optimum health so that their own bodies can do the healing.

Biochemical Individuality

A simple example of this is when we test many different types of B vitamins. We can stock several brands of similar potency. Yet, when we come to test them for an individual, we may find that MRT will reveal their preferred brand. Does this make all the other brands useless? No, different clients prefer different types of B vitamins depending on their source, manufacturing processes and fillers and binders.

The same is also true when carrying out various procedures. You may have two techniques that may achieve similar ends. One procedure may show as positive the other may not. They may have a similar outcome, and we could be puzzled that both tests did not show. Well, it could be that the individual's body prefers a particular 'route' that the correction will take.

Different Practitioners get Different Results

I'm afraid I can't deny that to some extent, belief in the practitioner is important. Having said that I, like many others, have had astounding results with some professed sceptics who come into my clinic. However, we cannot monitor what is happening in the person's psyche despite what they say. Intention and placebo effect abound.

You will notice that the body never asks for a technique that you do not know. The body will only choose from the practitioner's repertoire that is offered. A good analogy of this is – imagine that you and your client each have a computer for a brain containing all the data of your experience and knowledge. When you are both in physical contact, the information in both computers becomes a shared programme. I believe that if the practitioner is confident, the body will respond to the resource, whatever that might be, that is going to help it reconsider its condition and make the adjustment needed. This could be a different set of imbalances showing if tested by another practitioner.

THIS IS NOT AN EXCUSE FOR SLOPPY PRACTICE!
The body will 'reply' when the practitioner shows integrity and clarity.

A Blueprint for Client Management

Some of these pointers may seem obvious to you and yet, a lot of practitioners fail because they do not consider the importance of these vital principals.

The Appointment

- Who answers your telephone?

- How is your answer phone message designed?

- Do your family members answer your phone? If so, do they know how to answer in a professional manner? A child or a surly greeting can be a major put-off for a potential client.

- Is your appointments book near at hand? Any inefficiency does not build confidence in a new client/practitioner relationship.

- Should you send confirmation and costs by post?

- Should you send your client a questionnaire?

The Client Questionnaire

- Name & address, D.O.B.

- GP's name & address (This is a courtesy you're not necessarily going to contact them)

- Employment (Does their job affect their health?)

- Marital status & children

- History of health

- Operations, accidents, diagnosed diseases

- Current medication, supplements Food, drink, alcohol, cigarettes, recreational drugs etc.

- Current symptoms and their chief complaint

- How did they get to hear of you?

An Example of a Signed Declaration to place at the End of Your Questionnaire:

IMPORTANT NOTE: PLEASE READ AND SIGN THE FOLLOWING

- I understand that all clinic notes are confidential and will be kept for a minimum of 7 years. They will never be shared with any other practitioner / organization without my written consent and that I have the right to see my notes at any time.

- I appreciate that kinesiologists do not give medical diagnoses or treatment. The advice I / my dependent receive/s is not intended to replace or supersede any medical treatment or advice given to me by my doctor or any other medical specialist.

- I recognize and accept that I am responsible for my own/my dependent's health and will consult my G.P about any medical problem that I am aware of or become alerted to.

- I am aware that the Kinesiology Centre needs at least 24 hrs. notice to cancel any appointments. I understand that the appointment fee will still be due if notification has not been received by phone or voicemail in less than 24 hours before the due time and day.

I have read, and understand the information outlined above.

Signature _____Date _____

How to Ensure You're Fit Enough to See Clients

The practitioner needs to be more vibrant than their client, so have regular sessions from another healthcare professional to ensure you're in good health.

Receive supervision and update regularly.

One- to-one with an experienced practitioner or your tutor.

Attend Master Classes or Mentoring Days.

Ongoing post-graduate training is not a waste of time. Plan a percentage of your fees for this tax-deductible training. It's an investment towards making you an even more excellent, up to date practitioner. More people will want to come and see you because you're getting wiser and more knowledgeable. We NEVER stop learning!

Meeting with the Client

- Be there for the client, not for your own healing
- Never make assumptions

Always be:

- Courteous
- Kind
- Benevolently indifferent
- Punctual
- Always maintain confidentiality

Be aware of personal hygiene - for example:

- Clean fingernails
- Smell of lingering food on hands
- No heavy perfumes
- Teeth cleaned and flossed to prevent odour
- Wash hands between clients

The Client's First Visit

- Take a case history
- Listen carefully
- Mirror-back to the client what they have told you
- If appropriate, use a SUDs scale to evaluate the severity of their symptoms. SUDS stands for Subjective Units of Discomfort. 10 being the worst imaginable, zero being no symptom at all
- Write responses in your notes
- Check with client and note down the desired outcome of their visit.

Preconditions for Testing

- Make sure the person being tested is not distracted
- Put aside any items which may cause a negative influence
- Ensure client is properly hydrated
- Maintain a healthy atmosphere for accurate testing.

And then:

- Explain what you do
- Answer their questions
- Demonstrate what you do
- Begin the kinesiology session

The First Session

- Record what you have tested and corrected
- Use shorthand notes
- Record how the person felt afterwards if appropriate
- Record any advice you have given
- Write out for your client the advice, together with prescription if given

The end of the session:

- Briefly summarise what you have done and what you are going to give them
- Set a date for their next visit
- Make a point of touching them on the arm or shaking their hand when you say goodbye. As opposed to a quick dismissal, this helps to build up a rapport and will show your client you're interested in them and care about them.

Follow-up Visits

- Warmly welcome them

- Review what the client told you in their questionnaire

- Give them time to tell you how they have been

- Record their responses

- Check any change in their SUDs scale. Word of advice here – ask the client if they have noticed any change rather than whether they are feeling any better. Some clients will want to please you and tell you they are, if asked that specifically, when perhaps things haven't changed that much

- Occasionally refer to what they had previously told you.

After a Few Visits

- Occasionally check that their expectations are being met - these may have changed so you may need to re-negotiate

- Check with the client that their objectives are being achieved

- Discuss any changes to their original expectations of the outcome of their sessions

- Discuss, if appropriate, whether they are at the level of health that they wish

- If so, discuss frequency of visits from now or a maintenance programme.

Finger Modes

(Also known as Hand Modes or Digital Modes)

Finger modes were introduced by the late Alan Beardall DC. He developed Clinical Kinesiology from Applied Kinesiology in order to solve the dilemma of deciding which technique was the most advantageous approach for each unique client. He realised that many imbalances were actually compensations that the body had made in order to adapt and were not actually a causal factor. Dr Beardall discovered a method of being able to develop a dialogue with the client's subconscious and allow the body to 'unwind' the adaptive patterns and reveal the causal factors that could then be treated. Using finger modes point the practitioner towards the body's preferred protocols and the type of treatment needed to resolve the issue as well as the order in which corrections (or treatments) should be carried out. He found that many of the imbalances he'd previously noted turned out to resolve themselves without further intervention when priorities were addressed.

As is quite common in scientific discoveries, Beardall's development of finger modes was opportune. He was working with a client and noted down a weak muscle. When he returned from writing up his notes to test the muscle again, he found it was strong. He noticed that the patient had several fingers touching together. When the patient opened their hand again, the muscle returned to weak. Beardall was astute enough to realise that this could be 'body language'. He used the computer analogy to describe this 'body language' and called it a Biocomputer Model. He based this on the concept that the body's underlying code operates on the same principles as a computer, which is binary in nature, and operates according to the instructions of the controlling programme (see under section 'Why Muscle Response Testing Works' on page x).

With continuing research, Beardall realised that the Biocomputer Model provided a method to learn the body's language with which the practitioner could then communicate.

Some may ask why I prefer to use modes rather than asking the body verbal questions. My answer reminds me of the phrase 'the body never lies, providing it understands the question'. Using Beardall's Biocomputer Modes takes any emotion or preconceptions the practitioner or client may have, out of the equation. They have been shown to be universal and for reasons not fully understood, have become a common language in kinesiology.

> *For ease of reference, you will find photographs of all the modes illustrated in the protocols on page xxii. There is also a table on page 234 that gives a list of protocols under each 'directory' finger mode. This is useful to refer to when you want to remind yourself of the procedures to test for under that category.*

Beardall went on to develop hundreds of modes and others have added even more. Many of these digital modes can be found on www.knowlative.com. Simply categorised, some modes are equivalent to 'directories' and some are classified as 'sub-directories' or 'folders' within the directory. In order to get to the 'file' with the specific information we need – to identify the body's preferred imbalance and subsequent treatment, we have to search the 'directories'. I would class these as the four basic key finger modes which are Electromagnetic, Emotional/Mental, Biochemical/Personal Ecology and Structural. An example of a sub directory or folder under the Emotional Finger Mode umbrella would be the mode for vibrational essences. Examples under the Biochemical Finger Mode are the modes for Toxicity and Candida. Under the Structural Finger Mode umbrella, we have the mode for Dural Torque.

Modes That Form the Basis of Most Protocols

Priority Mode

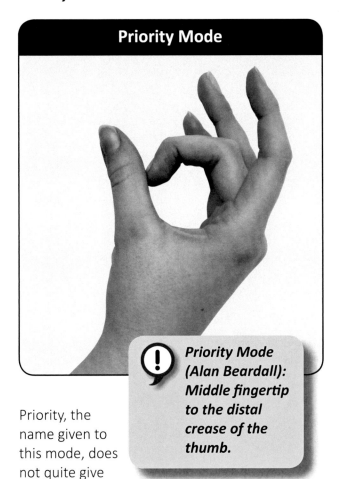

Priority Mode

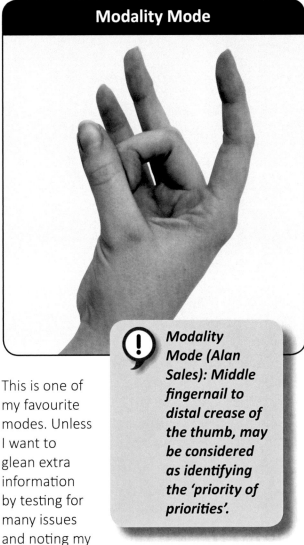

Modality Mode

Modality Mode

> **(!) Priority Mode (Alan Beardall): Middle fingertip to the distal crease of the thumb.**

> **(!) Modality Mode (Alan Sales): Middle fingernail to distal crease of the thumb, may be considered as identifying the 'priority of priorities'.**

Priority, the name given to this mode, does not quite give the right impression as to exactly what it means. The definition of the word priority is 'the most important thing to be dealt with'. The thing with priority mode is that there is often more than one priority; in fact there may be several. Sheldon Deal says that the definition of priority mode is, "it's okay to fix next" – though that would be quite a mouthful to say each time, so the term priority is easier!

We would certainly not recommend addressing an imbalance if it were not a priority or a modality, the reasons being that it may be a compensation that resolves once the priority imbalances have been corrected. Time could be wasted as the correction may not hold because the body's biocomputer needs other imbalances dealing with first.

This is one of my favourite modes. Unless I want to glean extra information by testing for many issues and noting my findings for future use, I will use this as a filter at the beginning of my investigation.

Modality mode, developed by the late Alan Sales, allows the bio-computer to choose a specific state of operation and to make the most appropriate selection from the 'menu' offered. Alan said, "In this way it allows kinesiologists to totally honour the wisdom of the client's body, respecting its knowledge of the true causal factors involved in an imbalance". It also allows the client's body to direct the practitioner to make the most appropriate correction from the 'menu' that the practitioner can offer. ***Occasionally, more than one modality imbalance or correction can show. If this is the case, as long as it is a modality, the order does not matter.***

Raise Vital Force Mode

Raise Vital Force Mode

This is another of my favourite modes. I automatically check this mode against all nutritional supplements and herbs that the body has tested well for. This is because I want to ensure that my client doesn't have a healing crisis or react to the remedy. This mode **greatly** reduces that occurrence and we should be able to help our clients in a gentle way without making them feel worse!

Vital force, vital energy or the concept of ch'i or qi, is a way of describing the body's energy source. Health is maintained by this vital energy (elan vital), and a lack of health is caused by a diminished supply of this vital force.

Vital force is composed of several types. The Chinese medicine concept is that a type of chi (Ku Ch'i) is derived from food that sustains organ

> **!** *Raise Vital Force Mode (Angela Burr-Madsen):*
>
> *Tip of index finger to tip of thumb. Fingers make an 'O'. Remaining 3 fingers remain straight making a fan shape (International Okay sign)*
>
> *Deplete Vital Force Mode:*
> *Activate the Raise Vital Force mode first, then curl the 3 straight fingers into the palm and then test the IM (this is an active finger mode).*

structure and function according to their theory. Another type of ch'i described is from the most fundamental ancestral energy that is stored in the kidney's energy structure (not the organ) and this manifests itself at birth (Hsien T'ien Ch'i)). This type of ancestral ch'i is like a trust fund that you are born with, money can be withdrawn but none can be put back! Another type is the ch'i that we breathe in from the atmosphere. So ch'i comes from different sources. It is by the active flow through the meridian system that this vital force is distributed throughout the physical body. The amount a person has can vary according to their genetic inheritance and the quality of food that they eat, and how they live their lives. (Charles T. Krebs, Tania O'Neill McGowan, 2014) This has an impact as to how much vital force they have available to metabolise nutrients and catabolise waste products.

To make efficient use of the vital force that is in food, herbs, homoeopathic remedies and vibrational essences, the body also expends vital force (energy) to make the changes stimulated by the nutrient/remedy. Unless a person has suffered a sudden catastrophic event, Chi or Qi depletes and regenerates over time. Temporary 'good days' and 'bad days' is not what we're talking about here.

> **!** *Remember that when we see an indicator change from unlock to locked, it tells us that what we are testing for is involved with the problem not necessarily that it's good for the client! For example, a weak tensor fascia lata (large intestine circuit) might strengthen to wheat. Does that mean it's good for the large intestine or does it mean that wheat is involved with the problem? You can check this out with the 'Raise Vital Force' Mode. With the wheat still in circuit, activate the mode. If the indicator changes (unlocks), it does raise vital force. If it stays locked, then it does not. To check if it depletes vital force curl your 3 fingers into the palm. If the indicator changes (unlocks) then the wheat depletes vital force.*

The body uses the nutrition we give it in one of three ways: to build, to support or to detoxify. In doing so, the body can experience a net gain, a net loss or no net change in its vital force level. It is possible for nutrition to create a net loss.

If a person is deficient in energy, the wrong nutrition may actually deplete overall vital force! For example, when working with liver energy in a person who is malnourished, the body may be over-loaded with toxins from junk food or food that is chemically polluted or over-processed or it may be that the person is simply not eating enough of the right nutrients to support the liver. Feeding the body too much of the wrong type of supplement or food could actually deplete vital force if the liver uses more energy to process the nutrition that it gains from the nutritional element you feed it.

The body may actually show a liking for a particular remedy because you see an indicator change (see key point in yellow box). But if the remedy has a higher vital force than the prospective recipient, it may actually cause a reaction because the body is too depleted in energy cope with the intensity of healing stimulus it is supplying.

To use the Raise Vital Force mode:

1. Activate the imbalance (the muscle unlocks)

2. Bring the chosen food supplement into the energy field (the muscle locks)

3. Activate the Vital Force Mode and test the IM again (you are looking for unlock)

If the indicator muscle changes from locked to unlocked, it means that this nutritional supplement increases the vitality of the person. If the indicator muscle does not change and remains in a locked position, it means that this supplement is not increasing the vitality of the person and another supplement should be chosen, even if the remedy tests as a priority.

Circuit Retaining Mode (CRM)

Also known as Pause Lock

The late Dr Alan Beardall introduced the concept of circuit retaining mode. This technique was developed for locking a signal on the body bio-computer by abducting the legs.

Our understanding of why this works is this. As the head of the femur moves in the hip socket the sensors in the joint, called mechanoreceptors (Pacinian corpuscles, Ruffini organs and Golgi tendon apparatus, collectively also known as proprioceptors), activate. These receptors relay information to the brain about the actual position of the legs at any given time. This circuitry enables the brain to know where our limbs are, even if we have our eyes closed. These mechanoreceptors are in all our joints. However, there is a large concentration of them in the acetabulum (hip socket) and this is why we tend to use the legs for recording information.

These mechanoreceptors, when activated, seem to not only record the movement that has taken place, but will also amplify any stress that is being applied to the body at the same time as they are being activated. Although we can then remove the applied stimulus (e.g. circuit locating or testing an unlocked muscle), the information remains in this circuit and is continually fed back into the body's signal handling system/ bio-computer in the brain until the legs are moved together again. We could liken it to a continuous loop of tape playing in an old-fashioned answering machine until the machine is switched off. This is also like a radio receiver receiving a radio transmission on a carrier wave. Although the radio is tuned to the carrier wave, it amplifies the signal transmitted within it, so we hear the sound being broadcast at the time. With CRM, the bio-computer 'plays back' the signals received at the time the mechanoreceptors were activated.

Once CRM is activated, every muscle of the body will then be signalling the stored responses and all correction points that are subsequently found will be related to the information in circuit.

You can use circuit retaining mode (often referred to as 'pause-lock') not only with a specific CL or muscle test, but also with a thought pattern e.g. if someone is having a problem with anger, then thinking about a situation that makes them angry will cause a locked indicator to unlock. To store this thought pattern/emotion 'in circuit', place their feet together (adduct) and then spread the feet apart (abduct the legs) whilst they are thinking of the anger.

How to activate circuit retaining mode (pause lock)

To activate CRM, the feet are moved apart by at least 45cm (18") at the time that we are activating whatever information we want to be held in circuit. That information is then relayed to the brain by the proprioceptors/mechanoreceptors.

Either the tester or the client can hold the circuit. The tester can act as a surrogate retaining the information so long as touch is maintained. In the event that someone has difficulty moving their legs, any joint can be activated; abducting the arms is the next choice, and even the jaw can be opened to retain information.

It is always good practice for the practitioner to first take pause lock into their own hips and then, keeping in contact with the client, transfer the lock by asking them to close and open their legs. Once passed to the client (a bit like handing over a relay baton) the practitioner can remove contact with the client and then close their legs. The practitioner temporarily taking CRM prevents any signal 'leakage' when the client closes their legs for a few seconds before opening them as information is added to the circuit.

Application of Circuit Retaining Mode (CRM)

Circuit Retaining Mode is a way to put information "on hold". Indicator muscle change is always involved in this process. This is extremely useful because:

- It avoids having to hold modes for any length of time.

- It can capture information in the form of a thought, a pain stimulus or an activated meridian whilst the best form of treatment is explored and implemented.

Other CRM Methods

The technique I've described above has been used successfully for many years, however other researchers have found alternative ways of keeping entered information 'playing' in the biocomputer system. The one I describe below was developed by the late Charles Benham. I find it works very well and allows the practitioner to ask the client to turn over or move about, and even get off the couch, because they don't have

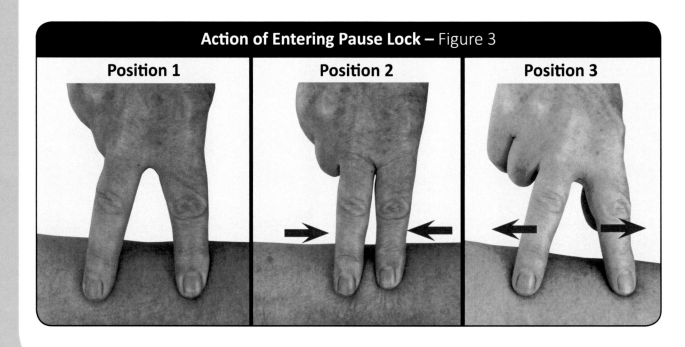

Action of Entering Pause Lock – Figure 3

Position 1   **Position 2**   **Position 3**

to keep their legs apart to hold the circuit. The retained circuit using this method seems to last for about 15-20 minutes.

CRM Using Skin Receptors

Basically, the action of entering pause lock in this manner mimics the same movements as closing and opening the legs, but in the process stimulates skin receptors on any part of the client's visible skin. This is usually done on a bare arm, but the skin receptors on the leg or any other part of the body may be used see **(Fig 3)**.

1. Activate the imbalance (the muscle unlocks) simultaneously open your legs, from being in a closed position, to about 18".

2. Whilst your legs are still apart, place your index and middle finger apart on the skin **(position 1)**

3. Draw your fingers together **(position 2)** then apart again, stretching the skin slightly **(position 3)**.

4. You have now entered the information into CRM which your client now holds, and you can now remove your fingers from the client's skin and close your own legs.

5. All IM will now give you a response according to the information stored in your client's biocomputer.

Hand Modes

Filter Modes

Additional Modes

Key Finger Modes

Structural Mode

Index finger pad to thumb pad.

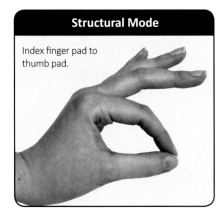

Biochemical/Personal Ecology Mode

Middle finger pad to thumb pad.

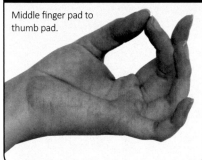

Emotional Mode

Ring finger pad to thumb pad.

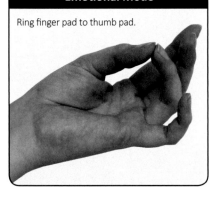

Electromagnetic Mode

Little finger pad to thumb pad.

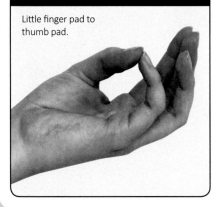

Modality Mode (Alan Sales)

Middle fingernail to distal crease of thumb.

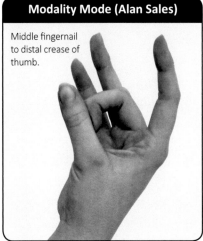

Priority Mode (Alan Beardall)

Middle fingertip to distal crease of thumb.

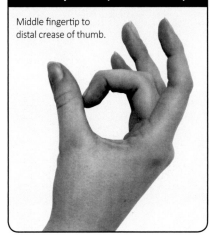

Raise Vital Force Mode (Angela Burr Madsen)

Tip of index finger touches tip of thumb to make an 'O' shape. Middle, ring, and little finger remain straight in a fan shape. Deplete Vital Force Mode, actively curl the 3 straight fingers into the palm of the hand.

Complete Mode

Lateral edge of thumb lies along the lateral edge of the ring finger. If the indicator does not change, there is more work to be done. If the treatment is complete the IM will change.

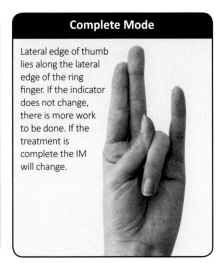

STO Mode

Middle finger contacts the palm of the hand with the rest of the fingers straight.

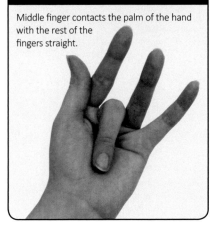

Dural Torque Mode

Thumb pad placed on the on the lateral side of the proximal crease of index finger (structural finger).

Age Recession Mode (Past Trauma Resolution)

Thumb tucked into a closed fist and placed over the client's navel.

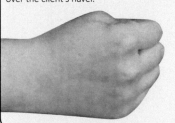

Cloacal Reflex Mode

Tip of little finger to the tip of the thumb. Other three fingers relaxed. When the electrical mode shows, you can narrow down your search by checking this sub-mode.

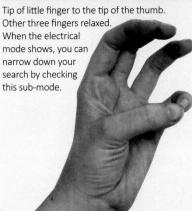

Allergy Mode

With fingers stretched out medial side of middle fingernail touches the medial side of the thumb. This mode includes foods, pollens and contact allergens.

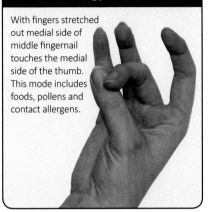

Candida Mode

Middle fingertip touches middle of thumb pad.

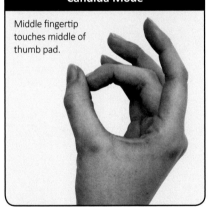

Parasite Mode

With fingers closed into the palm, the thumb tip touches the little fingertip.

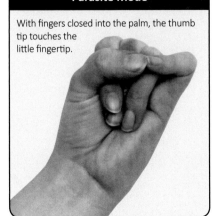

Microbiome Finger Mode
(Andrew Verity)

Middle finger pad to thumb touching the lateral side of the distal crease of the ring finger (biochemical finger mode touching the distal joint of the ring finger).

When this mode two-points to an issue, it indicates that a microbiome imbalance is involved and needs addressing.

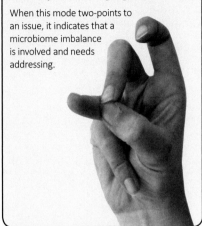

Toxicity Mode

The middle fingernail touches the thumb pad. This may indicate that there is a heavy metal toxicity issue or elimination organ support is needed.

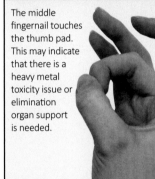

Chakra Mode

The pad of the index finger touches the thumb nail.

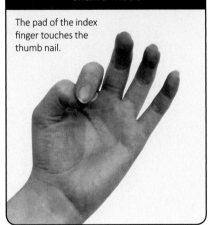

Rules for Therapy Localisation, Circuit Locating and Challenge

There can be an issue when interpreting results of our kinesiology testing. Over the years I have realised that some practitioners are unclear about whether they are looking for a locked muscle or an unlocked indicator muscle, and what that means. Permit me to clarify.

This book is written for Muscle Response Testers who use binary testing. I personally use and teach analogue testing.

What is Binary?

According to Wikipedia a binary code represents text, computer processor instructions, or any other data using a two-symbol system. The two-symbol system used is often "0" and "1" from the binary number system. In kinesiology, we often use computer terminology when tracking down a problem, such as 'opening files', which we do when we activate a finger mode or put a lesion into circuit. We are then clear that we are asking questions that only relate to the open 'file'.

In a binary system there are no in-betweens. The code is either 0 or it is 1. Therefore, when we are testing an accurate indicator muscle (AIM), the impression that a muscle tests as 'spongy' should not exist. Either the muscle response is either a 0 state or a 1 state.

What Does it Mean if an IM Test is Spongy?

This means that your results need checking. It could be that the muscle is tiring through repeated testing, the client has lost their concentration momentarily, they are talking at the time, they are switching …. etc.

The rule is to retest the muscle a few times to clarify your result:

> **If the spongy test is really a locked muscle, then repeated testing will strengthen it.**
>
> **If the spongy test is really an unlocked muscle, then repeated testing will weaken it.**
>
> **If you are still unsure, use a high gain technique which may shed light on it such as Pre-stressing described on page 203. If there is an issue, the results should then be clearer, and the muscle will unlock.**

What do the Results of My Test Look Like in Binary?

The Golden Rule is that **YOU ARE ALWAYS LOOKING FOR A CHANGE**. Practice these examples and see what happens. You'll soon get the hang of it.

Example 1

If you have a chakra imbalance, the IM will unlock when you CL the chakra point. If you want to identify whether it is a priority chakra (the body is saying that it is okay to fix next) activating the priority hand mode will change the muscle to locked. As soon as you remove the mode, the IM will return to unlocked.

Example 2

L = Locked **U/L** = Unlocked. Here is one example of working in pause-lock/circuit retaining mode. Notice that the IM state you are always looking for is a **CHANGE**.

Using an AIM, test the suspected lesion e.g. an area of back pain.

1. CL back Pain and test an AIM **(U/L)**.

2. Add Priority Mode or Modality Mode and enter into Circuit retaining Mode **(L)**.

3. Activate the 4 main finger modes (Structure, Emotional, Biochemical, Electrical) **(U/L)**. Enter this mode into circuit. As you already have priority/

modality mode in circuit, the realm the body chooses will automatically be a priority.

4. Find the correction from one of the techniques in the finger mode category **(L)**. It will automatically be a priority because the priority command is already in circuit.

Example 3

Using finger modes as filters

The rule is that finger modes will never change an indicator muscle in the clear. The reason is that the question we're asking the body is too great i.e. Is there an electrical problem? Is there a structural problem? Well, of course there is – there are lots of them! So, to narrow things down, using kinesiology testing we can ask the following question.

a. "Body, please only tell me about imbalances in the electrical realm/structural realm/ chakra realm" etc.

b. We could also ask, "Body, tell me which mode is a priority/modality for me to work on right now".

To use a Finger Mode as a Filter (a.)

1. Activate the finger mode you want the body to direct its attention to. Let's say you're looking for structural imbalances only see **(Fig. 4 overleaf)**.

2. Place the mode in circuit retaining mode. It will **not** unlock the IM. If you wish you can also add to the circuit the priority mode. This too will **not** unlock the IM. *What you are doing here is entering commands*. The body then will only look for structural imbalances that it gives you permission to address.

3. So now you can search for any of the protocols you know that fall into the structural category. Anything relevant will **unlock** the IM. For example:

   a. you could test any of the 42 muscles. Any that are priority and fall under the structural category will emerge and you can correct them.

b. Other tests such as for fixations, atlas, Ileo-caecal valve (ICV) etc. could be 'online.

4. Once you've found and carried out your correction, close the circuit and retest.

Finding the Priority Mode to Work On (b.)

Another way of using finger modes as a filter. I use this method all the time. as it's a great way of balancing the body and identifying its priorities see **(Fig. 4 overleaf)**.

1. Place priority/modality mode into circuit. The muscle will **not** unlock. You are now filtering information with the question – "Body what would you like me to work on next?"

2. Activate the four key finger modes. You can also use the chakra mode or any other mode you'd like to investigate. The realm that the body would like you to work on will **unlock** the IM. Remember you are looking for change. Place this into circuit.

3. Now, with your unlocked IM, test for the protocols you know within that realm. The body will give you a locked muscle now when you reach the one it needs.

4. Make your correction and cancel the lock. Anchor the correction by retesting the protocol identified in no. 3.

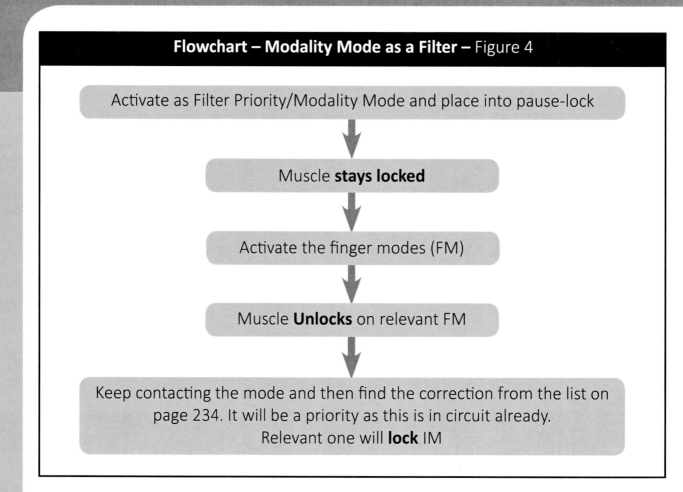

Flowchart – Modality Mode as a Filter – Figure 4

Activate as Filter Priority/Modality Mode and place into pause-lock

Muscle **stays locked**

Activate the finger modes (FM)

Muscle **Unlocks** on relevant FM

Keep contacting the mode and then find the correction from the list on page 234. It will be a priority as this is in circuit already.
Relevant one will **lock** IM

Stacking

Stacking is applying a correction to several connected imbalances in one go.

For the brain to facilitate change, the more information we can give it the better it can expedite neurological adjustments. Any imbalance or lesion very rarely manifests spontaneously or is a result of just one event, unless because of an accident of course. The symptoms are the last thing that appear and the first thing to disappear; in between are a lot of subtle stresses that, if allowed to come to fruition, determine whether the imbalance becomes a problem or whether it naturally resolves itself.

If we stack any stresses that are related to the lesion, the resulting treatment will be more thorough because they too are being addressed when the final correction is administered. We would term stacking as a holographic treatment. Stacking the stresses also enables you to gather information that may be useful in subsequent sessions.

If several circuits are to be stacked, *the binary system will show a change of indicator with each entry which links to everything previously recorded in the biocomputer.*

Process

1. Place the primary imbalance you wish to address into CRM (**Unlock**).

2. If another stress/ imbalance is found while the primary imbalance is in circuit, this will be related to the primary imbalance and will manifest as a locked IM (WE ARE ALWAYS LOOKING FOR CHANGE). To stack this information, we use CRM as usual, adding this to the information already locked into the biocomputer from step 1. (**Lock**).

3. If we wish to find another stress/ imbalance that is involved with those already in circuit (steps 1 and 2), we will now be looking for something that changes the IM once more (**Unlock**).

4. The next stress will manifest itself as **locked** and so on.

5. The last stress/imbalance added to the biocomputer is the one that you make the correction for. This will have a domino effect and automatically correct all the imbalances that were stacked in before it. Afterwards, always recheck the original defective circuit that you were treating, which should now be clear. If it is not, put into pause lock once more for additional work to be done.

Example

When you're new to stacking, it can feel quite complicated. I've found a trick that helps keep me on track, and that is to add each finger mode to the circuit; the example in table 1 below may help you to see why. This isn't strictly necessary, but it does keep the stack 'tidy' because the finger mode entry brings the IM back to 'locked' each time.

	Example of the Stacking Procedure – Table 1	
1.	Enter modality mode into circuit retaining mode as a filter (the IM won't change but every imbalance that shows from now on will automatically be for your client's highest good).	**Lock (no change)**
2.	Ask your client to TL the painful area (e.g. neck) and enter into CRM.	**Unlock**
3.	Activate the 4 key finger modes and enter into CRM the first one that shows, e.g. **Emotional finger mode**.	**Lock**
4.	Test one or more of the following: Did your client express any emotional stress in the consultation? Did the pain start after a stressful event? If they are unsure, CL the alarm points (pp 39 & 40). Enter the result into CRM but do not correct.	**Unlock**
5.	Test the 4 key finger modes again and lock the first one that shows, e.g. **Structural finger mode**.	**Lock**
6.	Test for fixations (P146), test related muscles, find the spinal misalignment (P141), etc., and enter the result into CRM but do not correct.	**Unlock**
7.	Test the 4 key finger modes again, e.g. **Electromagnetic finger mode** shows this time.	**Lock**
8.	As this example is primarily a structural problem with the neck or back, you may want to test cloacals (P4) or perhaps, if you know the problem was caused by an injury, aura leaks (P 24). If the back/neck muscles are tight, you might test for chakras - to quickly find out without testing each one, you could apply the chakra mode first, which if relevant would unlock the IM (Page 21). Let's say the root chakra was positive.	**Unlock**
9.	If the root chakra unlocked the IM, apply the correction, which will also address all the connected imbalances that you previously found.	**Correct**

When do you stop stacking? Sometimes the finger modes will cease to show, therefore make the correction to the last imbalance you entered. Where time is of a premium, stop at any point and correct that last imbalance you arrived at, which will correct everything that was entered in steps 2-8.

Powers of Stress

The late Richard Utt, the developer of Applied Physiology, discovered that when he sedated a hypertonic muscle and entered the over-facilitated response into pause lock several times, the muscle would eventually unlock giving him a normotonic muscle again.

Utt went on to reason that the IM can manifest an over-facilitated response when a large amount of stress suddenly comes online after an issue is entered into pause lock, i.e. the power of the stress may be so great that it causes over-facilitation. We quite often see this phenomenon when a perfectly working AIM suddenly goes hypertonic in response to a stimulus such as sugar, a particular test vial, or something entered into the circuit that causes a sudden energy surge.

Susan Probert observed that whenever an issue was entered into circuit that exceeded the person's conscious or subconscious ability to handle the stress in a homeostatic way, a splitting off, or dissociated response to these types of stresses seemed to occur. "It's as if the personality just cannot deal with the issue and opts to split off leaving the body to cope with the issue. This sudden dissociation causes the over-facilitated muscle state."

How do we Identify this Over-facilitated Response when Stacking?

As described on the previous page there may be a point where the finger modes cease to show. This could be because the IM has shifted into over-facilitation without us realising it. To identify this and add it to the circuit:

1. Check if the IM has become over-facilitated by placing a North Pole magnet on the belly of the muscle. If it no longer unlocks,

2. Keep the magnet in situ and enter the over-facilitated muscle response into circuit retaining mode (1 x power of stress).

3. Again, with the magnet still in situ, test again. If the IM still does not unlock in response to the N. Pole magnet, enter this into CRM as well, making it 2 x powers of stress (the IM will remain locked when entered into CRM).

4. Keep repeating step 3 and eventually the IM will unlock in response to the magnet. Add the unlocked muscle state to CRM.

5. The IM will now be functional, and you can activate the key finger modes to find the body's preferred correction (see steps 7-9 of the example in table 1).

The number of powers of stress is in relation to the type of magnetic stress used to unlock an indicator. Utt found that, as opposed to just pinching the muscle fibres, the more powerful the magnet the fewer powers of stress had to be entered to bring the IM back to a normotonic state.

What is the Significance of Entering the Powers of Stress into the Circuit?

a. You are then balancing a specific, identified amount of stress and not just 'lots of stress'.

b. You have a conscious idea of how much stress is involved in the circuit. Because the powers of stress procedure recognises the degree or extent of the stress caused by an imbalance (the number of powers of stress entered), a deeper balance is achieved as many layers of imbalances can be rectified in one go rather than requiring many circuits to be corrected.

Notes

Notes

Electromagnetic Imbalances and Corrections

Encompasses acupuncture meridians, acupuncture points, centring mechanisms, electromagnetic imbalances, electromagnetic stress, radiofrequency stress, geopathic stress.

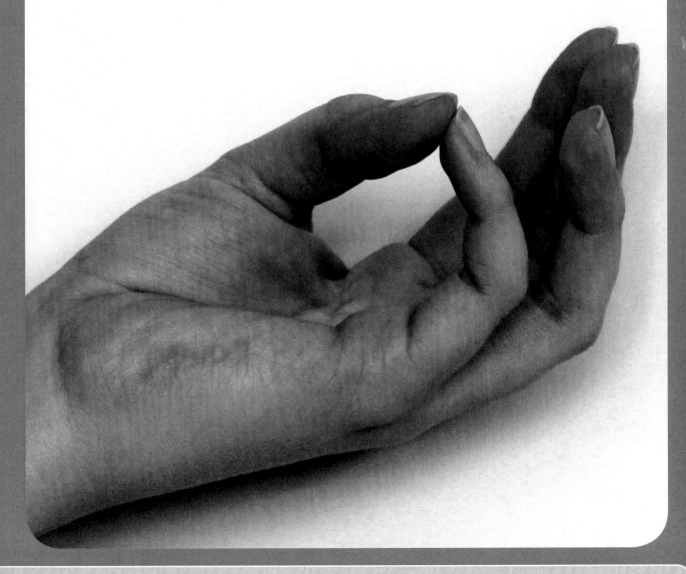

Table of contents

Electromagnetic Imbalances – The Start of Disease?

> **" It could be hypothesized that electromagnetic imbalances may well be involved in the beginnings of all illnesses, therefore, if corrected could be one of the greatest of all preventative treatments. "**

Electromagnetic problems are caused by electrical disturbances in the system – a scrambling of the electrical signals – as contrasted with mechanical problem (bones, joints etc) chemical problems (toxicity, nutritional deficiencies, hormonal imbalances etc.) and emotional disturbances. Tranquillizers and drugs can be a major cause of electromagnetic imbalances as well as constant bombardment from radiofrequencies.

Electromagnetic (EM) testing is important because many of the corrections involved help stabilize the body or help other corrections to hold.

Short cut for Testing if Electromagnetic Imbalances are Online

> If the subject has any EM imbalances disrupting the acupuncture system, there will be an indicator change when 5 or 10 fingertips are placed (like a crab) on the torso (avoid ICV area and surrounding the navel)

CL using 2 hands (i.e. 10 fingertips) if one hand does not show. Either the tester or the client (or a combination of both) can activate this mode. If at any stage the indicator unlocks, there will be a problem with one or more of the following:

Centring (Switching, hyoid, gait, cloacals)	Acupuncture Meridian Imbalances	R/L Brain Dominance
Blood Chemistry	Cross Crawl	Ionisation
Dehydration		

NB Electromagnetic finger mode also indicates that one of the above will be involved.

Cloacal Reflexes

Electromagnetic Finger Mode

Cloacal energy reflexes are to do with centring. Check the cloacals after any work has been done on the spine or gait. These reflexes can be described as an electrical correction for the body. They help to synchronize movement between the cranium and the sacrum. "They are an integral but major part of the neural reflex systems of the body that allow us to accommodate gravity, erect posture and body position. Even though gait implies movement, this system is greatly responsible for the entire gait positions and activity." (Ferreri, 1996)

They can also be involved in persistent switching and may be involved when the electrical finger mode shows in relation to a problem.

The cloacals are four basic but extremely important external energy loops that have an internal effect on the body. They are present as soon as the sperm and ovum become united. They become part of the aura. They were discovered by Alan Beardall DC primarily from clinical evidence. (Beardall, 1988)

> **❝ Treating imbalanced cloacal reflex points can greatly help people with back problems, multiple sclerosis, scoliosis, ME and people with low energy. ❞**

It is a completely safe correction to do at any time even if a test hasn't been carried out. It is also a nice way to end a treatment as it is very relaxing to have done.

Cloaca means sewer and refers to the combined urinary, anal and reproductive organs in, for example birds.

The chicken lays its egg through the cloaca.

There are four bands of energy on the anterior (front) of the body and four on the posterior (back) of the body. Two run ipsilaterally (on the same side of the body); two run contralaterally (diagonally across the body). Each cloacal on the front of the body has a relationship with their opposite numbers. So the ocular righting reflexes on the frontal bone of the skull are energetically connected to the cloacal reflexes on the pubic bone and represent the ends of the four anterior energy bands (Points are shown in **Figures 6 & 7** on page 7 and 8). The neck righting reflex (a.k.a. tonic labyrinthine reflex) are at the back of the skull link to the posterior cloacal reflexes between the sacrum and coccyx and represent the four posterior energy bands. The ends of each energy band are treated simultaneously, there is interdependency between these reflexes. Although they each have independent activity requirements and functions, they must always act or respond in relation to each other. This is part of the very complex neurological activity necessary for gait and posture. Therefore, if there is a deficit in one reflex, there will be a deficit in its partner reflex. Conversely, when testing each reflex point individually, if there is no deficit in one section there will be no deficit in its partner. To save time, it's only necessary to CL one set of points on the back and front of the body. When the cloacal reflexes are out of balance, as has been described, it affects the gait mechanism and is, in fact part of the gait mechanism.

The anterior cloacals tend to indicate an acute problem whilst the posterior indicates a more chronic condition. However, it is noted that because of the fact that in nature, the cloacal reflexes are involved with the male centring onto the female, the male anterior cloacals are more likely to be affected.

 It is important to test the gait and hyoid first. If they are clear, test the cloacals. Once corrected, retest the gait and hyoid - they may have been hidden.

There are two ways of establishing a cloacal imbalance. The first method is the correct way to identify a cloacal problem, the second method is a shortcut. Usually, the short cut test will suffice. However if the client has a problem with dyspraxia or any neurological problems, it is good to use the first method and demonstrate the effectiveness of the correction to both the client and to the brain by performing an anchor test after the correction has been made.

Procedure No. 1

Client is supine. Both limbs should be able to hold against the test described overleaf. If either or both limbs weaken in any of the positions described, there is an imbalance related to the cloacal reflex. For each test, place the body in gait position – the arm level with the shoulder and at right angles to the body. The leg should be raised at about 45 degrees.

See over page for details of positioning for testing (Fig. 5)

Procedure No 2

1. Individually test (or client CL's) each reflex on the head. Test with an AIM. *(See Figs. 6 & 7 on pages 7-8)*

2. If one or more unlocks the AIM, there is a cloacal imbalance. Prioritise if more than one shows.

3. Whilst maintaining contact with reflex, two-point to its two counterparts. The AIM will lock again when two-pointing to the involved cloacal/s. This is the combination that requires treating.

There are two methods that can be employed to correct the cloacals. Method no 2 is preferable, simply because there is an element of correcting the structure. Adjustment of the cranial bones is also being addressed here when the location points are rubbed.

Correction Method No 1

Hold simultaneously the cloacal reflex combination previously found until pulses synchronize. If on the front of the body, the ocular reflexes with the anterior cloacals on the pubic bone. If on the back of the body, the labyrinthine reflex with the cloacal points on the sacro-tuberous ligaments. *(See Figs. 6 & 7 on pages 7-8)*

Correction Method No. 2

On the front, simultaneously rub the ocular reflex that CL'd together with the anterior cloacal that two-pointed to it. On the back, rub the labyrinthine reflex with the cloacal points on the ischial tuberosities instead of the sacro-tuberous ligaments.

Establishing a Cloacal Imbalance – Figure 5

Test the right posterior ipsilateral reflexes

Raise the **right arm** and the **right leg** to gait position.

Place your hands on the outside of the wrist and ankle and **pull inwards towards the centre** of the body to test the left **posterior ipsilateral** reflexes, test as above using **left arm** and **left leg**.

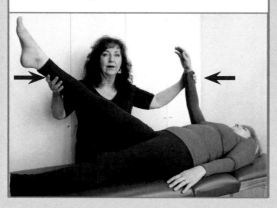

Test the left posterior contralateral reflexes

Raise the client's left arm as previously described and the right leg. Place your hands on the inside of the wrist and ankle and pull in towards the centre of the body. To test the right posterior contralateral reflexes, test as above using **right arm** and **left leg**.

Test the right anterior ipsilateral reflexes

Raise the client's right arm and leg into position. Place your hands on the inside wrist and ankle and push out away from the body – arm towards head and leg towards couch (superior and inferior) To test the left **anterior ipsilateral** reflexes, test as above using the **left arm** and **left leg**.

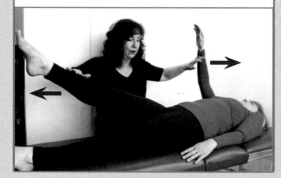

Test the right anterior contralateral reflexes

Ask client to raise their right arm and left leg. Place your hands on the inside of the wrist and opposite ankle and push out away from the body, arm towards the head, leg towards the couch (superior and inferior). Test as above using **left arm** and **right leg**.

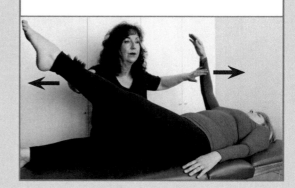

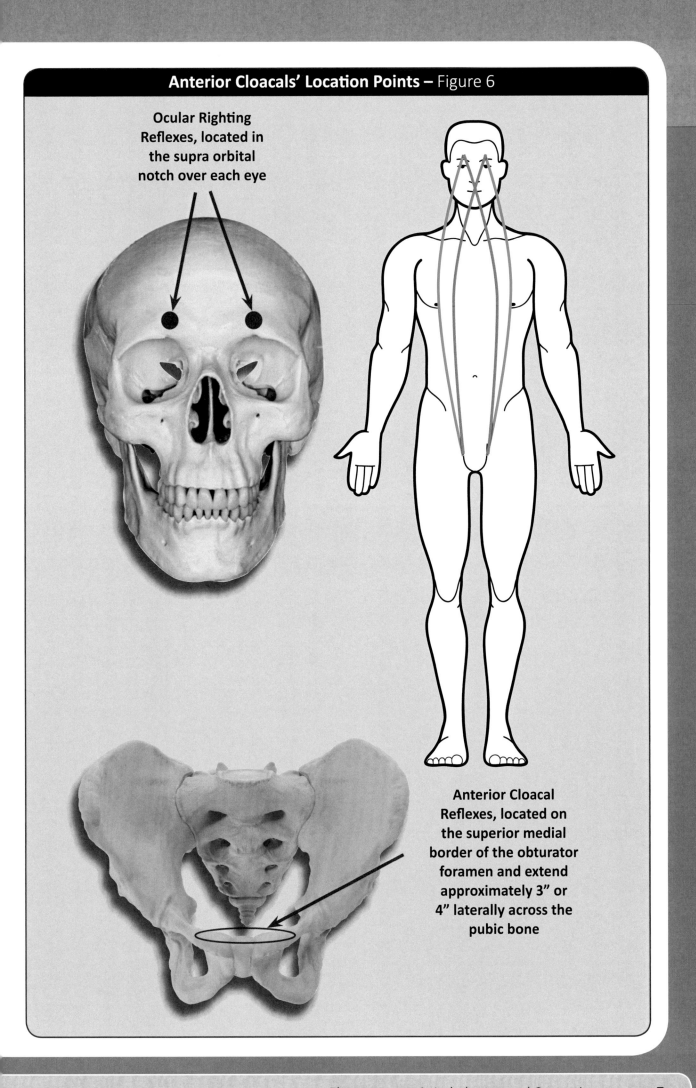

Anterior Cloacals' Location Points – Figure 6

Ocular Righting Reflexes, located in the supra orbital notch over each eye

Anterior Cloacal Reflexes, located on the superior medial border of the obturator foramen and extend approximately 3" or 4" laterally across the pubic bone

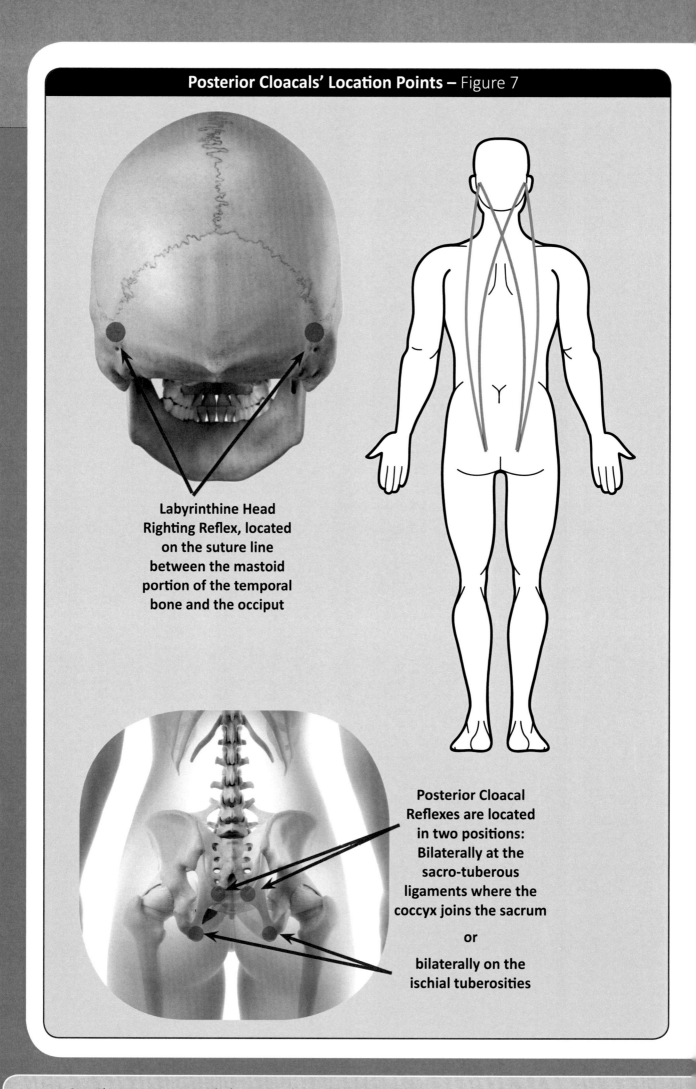

Labyrinthine Head Righting Reflex, located on the suture line between the mastoid portion of the temporal bone and the occiput

Posterior Cloacal Reflexes are located in two positions: Bilaterally at the sacro-tuberous ligaments where the coccyx joins the sacrum

or

bilaterally on the ischial tuberosities

Hyoid

Electromagnetic Finger Mode/Structural Finger Mode

The hyoid bone is a free-floating bone suspended in the front of the throat by several different muscles See **Figures 8 & 9**. Part of the centring mechanism, it is involved in cerebral hemisphere dominance problems and TMJ dysfunction. It may also be involved when it is noticed that the client speaking, changing the position of the head or moving the tongue causes a positive test in a remote area that was previously negative.

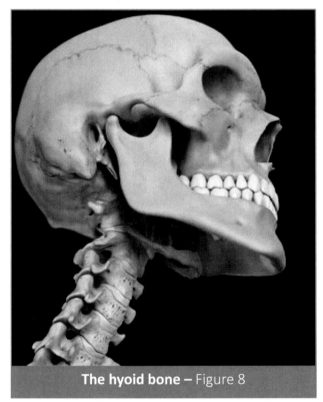

The hyoid bone – Figure 8

Goodheart has compared hyoid suspension with a gyroscope in an aircraft guidance system. "A gyroscope is flexibly mounted in an object such as a ship or an aeroplane so that it can maintain its equilibrium. Sensors relay information about any change in position between the vehicle and the gyroscope providing a kind of feedback. This information is used by, for example an automatic guidance system such as an autopilot. It also allows a pilot to know the aeroplane's orientation in space. If the plane and the gyroscope are not level with each other, the instrument will show the disparity.

Testing the hyoid bone – Figure 9

The proprioceptors of the hyoid muscles appear to provide afferent (messages sent to the brain) information that is compared with total body position for orientation in space. Because of the widespread positions of the muscles that are attached to the hyoid bone (origins in the skull and mandible, the sternum, clavicle, scapula and thyroid cartilage), there would be lots of information about the orientation of these structures in relation to one another. The hyoid bone alters position every time we alter the position of our head." (Walther D. , Hyoid Muscles and Function, 1988).

See **Fig. 10** for some of the individual muscles attached to the hyoid bone.

Rationale

If any of the muscles attached to the hyoid are hypertonic, they will pull the hyoid out of its correct positioning in relation to the head and torso causing imbalance in part of the centring mechanism. Carrying out neuromuscular spindle cell technique on these tight muscles will allow the hyoid to return to its correct position.

Individual Muscle Groups Attached to the Hyoid – Figure 10

Digastric Muscle

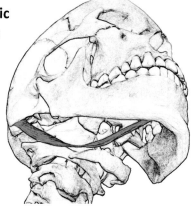

Lateral challenge stretches the posterior belly of the digastric, stylohyoid, omohyoid and possibly other hyoid muscles on that side.

Digastric Muscle

Inferior challenge stretches the mylohyoid, geniohyoid and bellies of digastric and stylohyoid muscles.

Geniohyoid Muscle

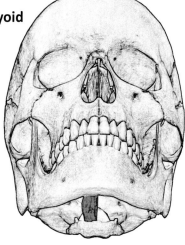

By torqueing the hyoid, this can help to isolate various muscles involved.

Thyrohyoid Muscle

Inserts into the thyroid cartilage and depresses or raises the thyroid.

Mylohyoid Muscle

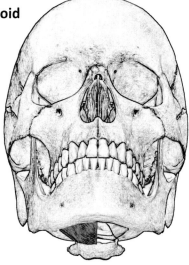

Push hyoid posteriorly to stretch the anterior belly of the digastric, geniohyoid and mylohyoid.

Sternohyoid muscles

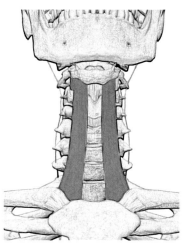

Superior hyoid challenge stretches these muscles.

Wiggle the hyoid bone back and forth whilst testing an AIM. **(See Fig. 9)** for location of the hyoid bone. If the indicator unlocks move the bone in each of these following directions, again testing the indicator muscle, and note the results.

Left to right	Right to left
Clockwise	Anticlockwise
Inferior*	Superior*
Posterior*	Anterior*

Can only be one side, never both.

Figure 10:

- **A right and left challenge stretches the posterior belly of the digastric, stylohyoid, omohyoid and possibly other hyoid muscles on that side**

- **By torqueing the hyoid, this can help to isolate the various muscles involved**

- **Push hyoid posteriorly to stretch the anterior belly of the digastric, geniohyoid and mylohyoid**

- **Inferior challenge stretches the mylohyoid, geniohyoid and bellies of digastric and stylohyoid muscles**

In the specific direction challenge, the muscle that needs correction is the one that caused the indicator weakness when it was being stretched. This can be verified by having the client TL that particular muscle. Pinch belly of this hypertonic muscle to tone down the spindle cells.

OR

1. Put two fingers under the jaw and, with firm pressure work to the middle and stretch the neck muscles downward with your fingers.

2. Place thumbs on each clavicle and firmly press the muscle insertions.

3. Then using spindle cell technique, treat all of the muscles attached to the hyoid as per diagrams. Pinch together the bellies of the muscles in the direction of the fibres.

4. Re-challenge hyoid. The IM should now lock.

Nutritional – Right/Left Brain Dominance
Wiggle the hyoid bone after all 8 directions have been cleared. If IM muscle still unlocks, have the client chew on their own fingernail clipping. If the indicator locks, the person needs trace minerals to balance the brain (e.g. spirulina).

NB If there is a left/right brain dominance problem, then an AIM will unlock when the person either hums or counts. This could be due to a hyoid imbalance. If this is the cause then the IM will lock when the person hums or counts after the hyoid has been corrected.

Centring

Electromagnetic Finger Mode

Centring involves three of the electromagnetic energy control systems of movement.

1. Hyoid, which is thought to be related to our relative position in space.

2. Gait reflexes that determine the muscle rhythms/ patterns for walking.

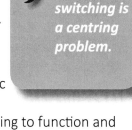

The root cause of switching is a centring problem.

3. Cloacals - external bands of energy, which form a specific energy field that assists our whole being to function and controls coordination between the pelvis and cranium.

Method of Checking

Hit the body to shock it and test an AIM. Rocking the couch may have a similar effect if you prefer. This test can disorientate someone who has a centring problem. If the IM remains locked, the above three are in balance. If the indicator unlocks, check the hyoid, gait reflexes, and cloacals (always check and correct cloacals last).

To Test if the Person's Environment is Causing Them Stress

Electromagnetic Finger Mode

Ask your client to put a bowl of water in the room they are often in, or a room they suspect causes them a problem, for 24 hours. The water will absorb the frequency of the environment. On their next appointment, get them to bring some of this water, in a clean glass jar, to test against an AIM. It's a good idea to ask them to bring a control sample of some water from the same source in case they're reacting to the water itself and not the frequency.

There are numerous devices available on the market claiming to enhance the body's ability to protect itself from environmental stresses. To check if the device has a positive effect, place it on the body together with the affected water. It should negate the unlocked IM, test as a priority or highly effective remedy and also raise vital force. (Some devices can have adverse effects on some people).

Blood Chemistry

Electromagnetic Finger Mode

Look for this imbalance in cases of allergies, ICV, malaise, post viral fatigue syndromes, onset of cold or infection.

The checks and balances of the body require that many systems operate with only a small amount of tolerance. For instance, if the body temperature varies by more than a few decimal increments from 37°C, we immediately know something is wrong. Blood sugar is to be maintained within margins, since too low or too high levels give rise to impairment of function. Checking the levels of various components of the blood may assess many other aspects of health.

This test checks whether the blood chemistry is appropriate for this person now or if it needs to be balanced. It is particularly useful in cases of chronic ill health, tiredness, use of powerful drugs, post-operative recovery, and low immune systems. This is an electromagnetic check and correction, so the results of using this technique are immediate.

Test AIM – the quadriceps are good to use for this so that the hands are kept free.

1. Client TL's spleen 21 with a light touch. Sp21 **(Fig. 11 overleaf)** is located at the 6th intercostal space at the midline of the body on the coronal plane, that divides the body into front and back and approximately parallel with the nipple. Test both right and left sides separately. If the AIM unlocks on one or both of these, there is an imbalance.

2. Whilst the client maintains contact with Sp21, they simultaneously contact K27 **(Fig. 11 overleaf)** on the right, then the left side. One side will two point with Sp21 i.e. will change the indicator muscle to locked*. It may be either or both K27s. If both Sp21s are active, then only one K27 should two-point to both Sp21s.

3. Once you have found which combination gets a change of muscle response, firmly tap these two points together, quickly in about ten groups of three, or long enough to make the indicator lock when retested.

4. Retest SP21 both sides remembering that the client TL's the points.

NOTE: if spleen 21 is challenged, it is a test for cross crawl on the right side and chakra imbalances on the left.

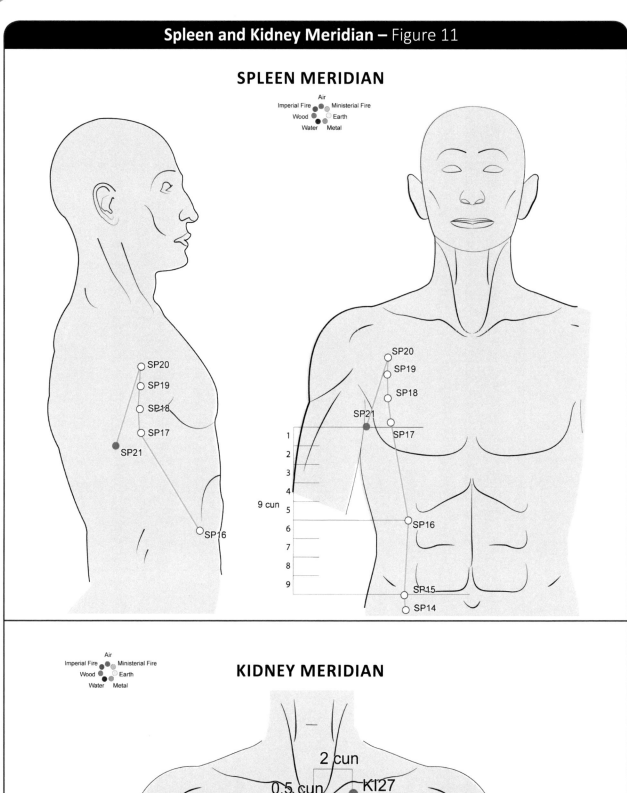

SPLEEN MERIDIAN

KIDNEY MERIDIAN

Ionisation

Electrical Finger Mode

Ionisation or ionization, is the process by which an atom or a molecule acquires a negative or positive charge by gaining or losing electrons, often in conjunction with other chemical changes. The resulting electrically charged atom or molecule is called an ion. (Ionisation, n.d.)

Oriental and Hindu physiologists state that with every inhalation through the right nostril, positive electrical current flows down the right side of the spine, and with every inhalation through the left nostril, a negative electrical current goes down the left side of the spine. The right nostril is a chamber for positive ions, and the left is on for negative ions.

 What do you know about positive & negative ions and how the nervous system works?

Breathing pattern dominance changes from one nostril to the other about every 20 minutes.

Ion imbalances are primarily corrected by nutrition. This is due to a ration imbalance between calcium and potassium, not a deficiency. This test is very important to do on stormy days. There is an increase of positive ions before a storm and negative ions when it rains, which will disturb many people's ionisation balance. The problem is that lots of things can affect the dominant ions in the atmosphere, for example being near a waterfall, in the woods or the phases of the moon.

The main reason for including this technique is that if none of the other electromagnetic imbalances show, there could be an ionisation problem.

The following health problems may indicate that there is an ionisation problem involved and correcting it would be of benefit:

If this imbalance is present, the client will be unable to TL satisfactorily. Under normal circumstances a positive TL should show whether a lesion is touched with the fingertips, elbow, wrist etc. If ionisation is out of balance and a client is low on negative ions, they will only TL with backs of hands in contact with the body (palms up); if they are short of positive ions, they will only TL with palms down.

Ionisation and Torticollis

Dr Goodheart was working with a patient who had chronic unremitting tonic-clonic torticollis. This is an excruciating condition where the person experiences muscle spasms in the neck and has to use their hands to hold their head straight. This is such a debilitating condition that there is a high suicide rate in sufferers. Dr Goodheart found that if the patient was to breathe through one nostril only for roughly one hundred times, they could hold their head straight for 10 minutes. It was later discovered (originator unknown) that if one of two minerals were given, then clients could hold their heads straight for 24 hours – for left nostril breathing it was calcium and right nostril breathing potassium. (Deal)

Ionisation and Serotonin Levels

Ionisation affects the level of serotonin in the blood (Tal E., 1976). According to research, positive ions increased, and negative ions decreased levels of serotonin in blood cells. In other research projects levels of either negative or positive ions in the atmosphere were shown to affect mood and depression. Therefore, the balance of ions that the body is taking in can cause the body to produce more serotonin.

Respiratory problems or sinus problems	**Migraines**
People who have suffered severe burns	**Insomnia**
People sensitive to changes in weather	**Irritability**
People who work surrounded by electrical equipment	**Anxiety**
Clients with torticollis (excruciating wry neck)	**Hot flushes**

The Test

The Client should ideally not take any supplements on the day of the test.

1. Instruct the client to keep their mouth closed. Ask the them to breathe in through the left nostril and out through the right, holding the inoperative nostril shut. Follow quickly by testing an AIM.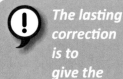

    An unlocked muscle indicates the need for calcium and positive ions are needed.

    When testing with therapy localisation, this client's palms must be against the body (Palms down).

2. The client breathes through the right nostril and out through the left as described in step 1.

    A positive test (unlocked muscle) indicates a need for potassium and negative ions.

    When testing with therapy localization, the client's palms face away from the body (Palms up).

    A positive test on both breathing sequences indicates that both calcium and potassium are needed. Your client will not be able to use TL until this problem is corrected. Also check for cranial faults (Structural section on page 170).

> **!** *The lasting correction is to give the nutrient*

If both sequences show a negative test (IM remains locked), then a client may TL with palms up or down in subsequent therapy localization.

> **✔** Test for the type of calcium or potassium needed and give for one month. However, a temporary change can be brought about for convenience of testing. Also, if this is an imbalance that frequently shows in testing, the client can do the following at home.
>
> ***Breathe in several times through the appropriate nostril and out through the mouth.***
>
> ***If in left and out right weakens (too many negative ions)– client breathes in through the RIGHT nostril and out through the mouth several times to increase breathing in positive ions.***
>
> ***If in right and out left weakens (too many positive ions) – Client breathes in through the LEFT nostril and out through the mouth several times.***

MEMORY KEY	
● Breathing in on LEFT weakens,	● Breathing in on RIGHT weakens
● Needs Ca (CALCIUM)	● Needs K (POTASSIUM)
● CL Palms DOWN	● CL Palms UP
● + POSITIVE ions	● - NEGATIVE ions
● LCD+	● RKU-

Alarm Points

Electrical Finger Mode, but can also be used with other key finger modes.

Alarm points are a set of 14 special points that give a read-out of stress involved in the associated acupuncture meridian.

(See Figures 12 & 13 overleaf)

 Contacting the alarm point with a light touch shows associated hypertonic muscles (over-energy), touching with a heavy pressure indicates hypotonic muscles (under-energy).

Tradition Chinese Medicine (TCM) describes only 12 alarm points. They are also called anterior mu points and they are used to assess and balance the energy of the organs. "The Chinese translation of mu is 'recruit, collect, enlist' i.e. the point is where the energy of the relevant organ gathers. These points are also called 'Front Collecting Points'. They are used both for diagnosis and treatment. They are used for diagnosis because they become tender on pressure, or spontaneously, if the organ becomes diseased. In treatment they are used to regulate the internal organs by tonification or sedation" (Macoicia, 1989).

In Specialized/Applied Kinesiology we also use GV26 as the alarm point for the governing vessel and CV24 as the alarm point for the conception vessel. These extra alarm points are not included in Touch for Health but are used in many areas of kinesiology.

"The diagnostic aspect is very important in kinesiology. When a meridian and its associated organ is out of balance, the alarm point is tender, and it will respond to CL or TL." (Knowlative).

Depending on how they are used, these points can determine if a meridian has a deficiency of energy or an excess of energy that has 'blown the circuit'.

 Kinesiologists usually use the alarm points to identify over-energy in the corresponding meridian.

The practitioner touches lightly the alarm points while testing an AIM. Any points that unlock indicate an over-energy.

Gordon Stokes, formerly a training director for Touch For Health and one of the developers of One Brain and Three-in-One, has shown that **if the practitioner applies a heavy pressure, any changes in the IM indicate an under-energy in the associated meridian.**

Using the Alarm Points to Narrow Down Your Search

As we've discussed, these points are used by kinesiologists for investigative purposes. After carrying out a 14/42 muscle assessment, the practitioner can contact the alarm points in order to identify which associated meridian the over-energy lies in. Then, using the Theory of the Law of the 5 Elements, the priority meridian that is under-energised can be found by testing the associated muscles. These muscles can then be balanced to correct the energy flow.

Alarm points are valuable tools that can be used to identify and narrow down additional searches. Here are a few examples and these will be further discussed under each section category.

- If the *emotional mode* is in circuit, touching each of the alarm points will give you information as to which meridian is out of balance for an emotional reason. **(page 40)**

- Contacting the alarm points when the *biochemical mode* is in circuit will tell you which organ needs nutritional support. **(page 78)**

- When the muscle response tells us that the client needs a correction from our structural 'database', the *structural mode* can be put into circuit. The active alarm point/s will narrow your search down to the group of muscles that need attention thus saving a lot of time trying to locate the muscles involved with the pain. When the *reactive muscle mode* is applied, alarm points can be used to identify reactor muscles. **(page 164)**

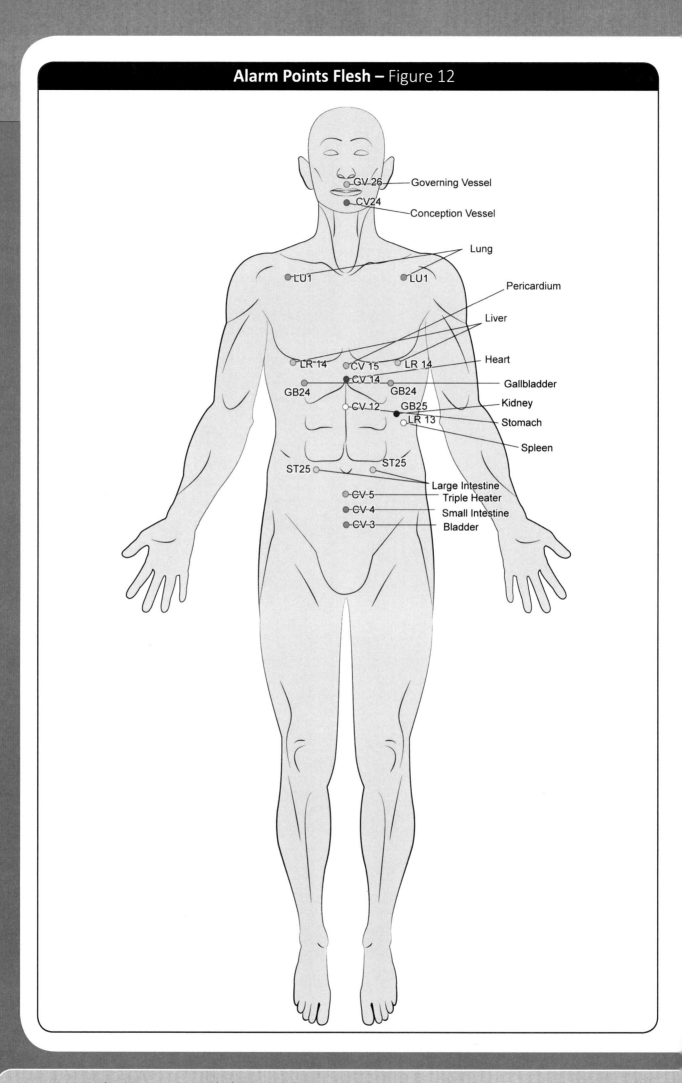

GV 26 — Governing Vessel
CV24 — Conception Vessel
Lung
LU1   LU1
Pericardium
Liver
LR 14   CV 15   LR 14 — Heart
CV 14
GB24   CV 14   GB24 — Gallbladder
CV 12   GB25 — Kidney
LR 13 — Stomach
Spleen
ST25   ST25
Large Intestine
CV-5 — Triple Heater
CV-4 — Small Intestine
CV-3 — Bladder

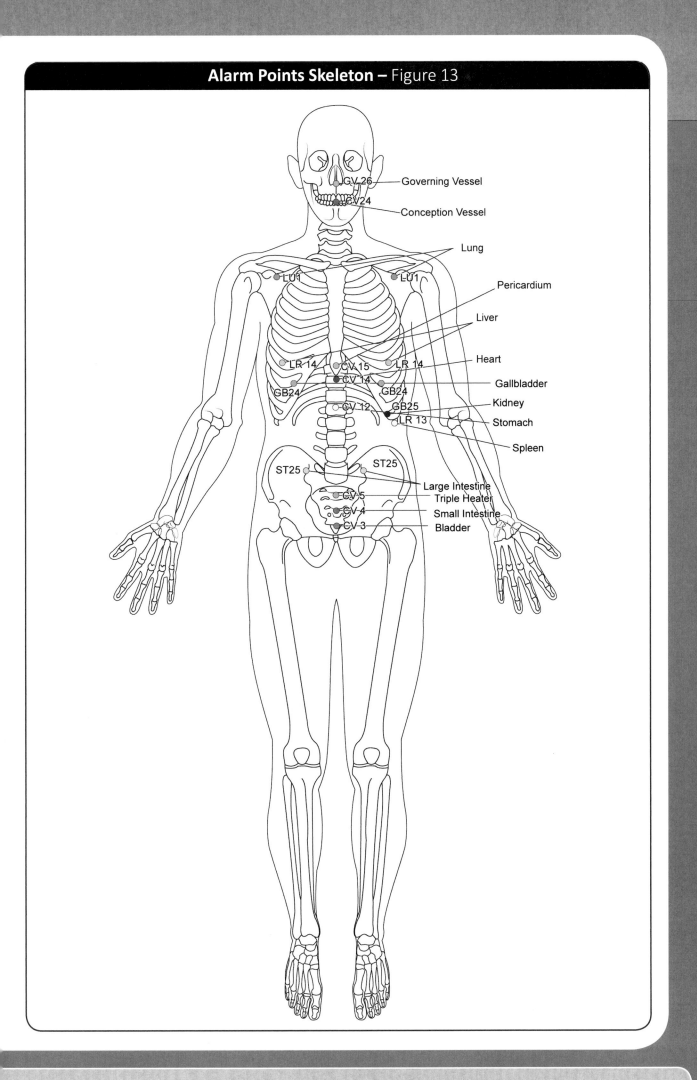

Governing Vessel
Conception Vessel
Lung
Pericardium
Liver
Heart
Gallbladder
Kidney
Stomach
Spleen
Large Intestine
Triple Heater
Small Intestine
Bladder

GV 26
CV 24
LU1
LU1
LR 14
CV 15
LR 14
CV 14
GB24
GB24
CV 12
GB25
LR 13
ST25
ST25
CV 5
CV 4
CV 3

Scars

Electrical Finger Mode

 Scar tissue impairment can affect many health issues. You could check for this at the same time as checking all old injuries for injury recall (see page 205)

Scars should not CL or TL. However, if they do it means that the incision has cut across an electrical conductor. The scar is interfering with electrical communication occurring via the skin. Sometimes scars may dissect an acupuncture meridian causing an impaired flow of acupuncture energy (chi) and this is when this technique is particularly applicable. (Deal)

Dr Goodheart had heard about a group of German doctors, living in Colombia after WW2, who were treating scars by injecting them with novocaine, which was producing profound therapeutic effects. A woman came to him complaining of an extremely painful wrist after breaking her radius after slipping on the ice. The X-ray showed that the bone had healed normally yet she was still in excruciating pain. Dr Goodheart noticed that she had a very small scar on her wrist. She explained that the scar was twenty years old when she cut herself with a kitchen knife. Rather than injecting novocaine into the scar he froze the area. The pain went away completely. The scar was interfering with the healing process despite the fact that her bone had healed.

 Ask your client to TL the scar. If it is a large scar, ask them to TL, with two fingers, a section of the scar at a time. If the scar TL's along any section, this protocol is appropriate.

 There are a few ways to bring about an improved electrical flow through scar tissue:

a. Ice spray. Use ice spray that does not contain menthol. (The best ice spray for this technique is ethyl chloride, which puts a frost on the skin, but it is not easily available due to its highly flammable and anaesthetic properties).

b. Placing a magnet over the scar. This does seem to work.

c. Running a laser pointer over the area.

Using Ice Spray

DO NOT DO THIS ON NEW INJURIES/ OPERATION SCARS. THE SCAR SHOULD HAVE HEALED PROPERLY FIRST.

1. Spray the scar area until it gets very cold, then stretch the scar as if trying to pull it apart. It's okay if it becomes a bit red as the blood goes to the site.

Using a Magnet

1. Place a magnet over the area of the scar that TL's. The pole that locks the IM is the correct one to use for the correction.

2. Leave the magnet in situ over the scar for a few minutes.

3. On retesting, the scar should now no longer TL.

Using a Laser Pointer

1. Direct the laser beam, at a 45° angle, over the scar sweeping over the area a few times.

2. The scar should no longer TL after this procedure.

In my experience pulling apart the scar tissue, when really cold, seems to have the greatest impact. However, some of the chemicals used for the ice spray aren't pleasant and ice spray without menthol isn't always available.

Chakras – Pre and Post Ganglionic Technique

Electrical Finger Mode

I.C.A.K. prefer to call chakras the above as it sounds more scientific. There are many in the scientific world who are not ready to accept the Eastern philosophy of chakras. A physiological term suffices much better for some.

This technique refers to the nerve plexuses that are stemming from the spinal cord in the chakra vicinity. **(See Fig. 14)** Think of the chakras as transformers, which act as a link or a step down from our subtle bodies to our physical body. They are vortices of energy.

> *If you, the reader, have an interest in the chakras, there are many books and theories on this subject that you can explore in more detail. You may find that some information conflicts, but don't be put off by this. The positive effects of addressing this important energy conduit system can be astonishing.*

Each chakra has a specific association with it i.e. organs, glands, acupuncture meridians, times in our lives when they are more prominent, particular emotions or reactions to our external environment. However, they all interact with each other too. If one chakra is out of balance, it will affect all of them, hence they need to be addressed piecemeal. It's possible that by correcting one chakra, it can affect another that tested negative initially, so keep re-testing them all until they are completely clear.

Because the chakras affect our whole being, the corrections that you can use are many. The most popular options are vibrational essences, colour, crystals, and sound. This can be incorporated into your protocol below.

***N.B.** Blockages to the heart chakra are fear and understanding. If the person has external manifestations of the heart through the chakras, they could benefit from chelation therapy.*

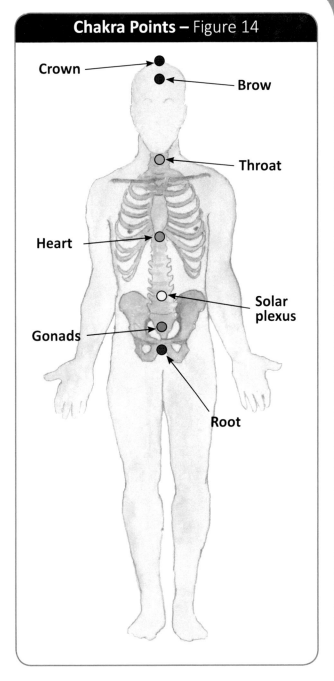

Chakra Points – Figure 14

Crown · Brow · Throat · Heart · Solar plexus · Gonads · Root

A blanket test that will indicate that the chakras are out of balance is challenging i.e. **the tester touches** Sp21 **on the left (Fig 11. on page 14).** If the IM unlocks there is a chakra imbalance online.

The chakra mode is another way of accessing the chakra 'programme'. However, it will not unlock an IM in the clear. When activated it acts as a filter, allowing the tester to identify which chakra is out of balance and whether chakras are involved in a particular problem. See examples below:

1. You or the client holds the chakra mode (using the mode in conjunction contacting the chakra adds clarity to the test). Using an AIM, place hand about 5cm or 2 inches away from the body over each chakra. The indicator will unlock on any that are out of balance. *If more than one shows, check and correct in order of priority.*

2. For chakras on the body, place hands over them, front and back simultaneously until pulse synchronization is felt. For the crown chakra, place on hand on crown, and other over left eye. For the brow chakra, place one hand on brow, and other over right eye.

3. Using an AIM, place your hand over the chakra that you have just treated. The IM should now lock.

4. Re-check all the other chakras again. Sometimes correcting one will send another out of balance, or it may have automatically corrected any that were previously showing out of balance.

Place pad of index finger on to thumb nail

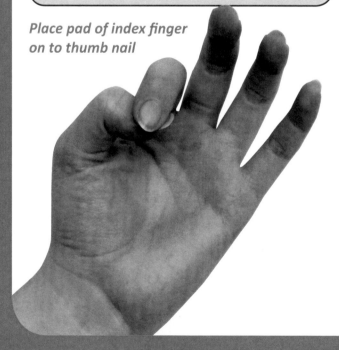

More Examples of Balancing Chakras

1. Activate the chakra finger mode. The tester or the client can hold this, or the command can be activated and then placed into pause lock. It will not change the indicator muscle because the mode is acting as a filter. The body now understands the question clearly and will only give you imbalances that are chakra related. You could add modality mode or priority mode to the filter by entering it into the circuit. Again, it won't change the IM, but it means that you will only see chakras that are a modality/priority.

2. CL the chakras as above. Any that show as being out of balance – muscle changes to unlocked place into pause lock/circuit retaining mode.

3. Find the kind of treatment that the body requires. Try testing:
   a. Vibrational essences
   b. The client looking at the colour associated with the chakra
   c. The client saying an affirmation relating to the chakra **See Table 2**

The IM will lock when you find the right remedy. The type of correction will automatically be a modality/priority because you already have this entered into the circuit in stage 1.

4. You can now hold the chakra while the person either:
   a. Takes the vibrational remedy
   b. Looks at the colour
   c. Says the appropriate affirmation

5. Cancel the lock and using an AIM, reactivate the chakra mode and check the chakra again (anchoring).

6. Repeat from stage 1 until all the chakras are balanced.

This is an example of a holographic treatment because there is more than one type of treatment being administered at the same time.

CHAKRA COLOUR, ORGAN AND EMOTIONAL CONNECTION – Table 2

CROWN – Pineal, Upper brain, Right eye – Violet

I am at one with universal energy	I am open to all knowledge
I am enlightened	I enlighten others

BROW – Pituitary, Lower brain, left eye, Ears, Nose, Central nervous system – Indigo

I can see clearly	I am focused	I am alert
I am at ease in the 'now'	I comprehend what is happening	

THROAT – Thyroid, Parathyroid, Throat, Mouth, Bronchioles, Lungs - Turquoise

I can speak freely	What I say has value	I have the right to be heard
I am secure in what I say	I speak the truth with comfort	I can express myself

HEART – Thymus, Heart, Circulatory system, Blood, Arms, Hands – Green

I know and understand love	I accept love from others
I am connected to myself	I give of myself freely

SOLAR PLEXUS – Pancreas, Stomach, Gall bladder, Liver, Sympathetic nervous system – Yellow

I acknowledge my gut feeling	I do not absorb negative energies
I am in touch with my universe	

GONADS/SACRAL – Gonads, Reproductive organs, Spleen – Orange

My sexual expression is fulfilled	I am comfortable with who I am sexually
I enjoy being male / female I am fruitful	I reproduce with ease

ROOT/BASE – Adrenals, Kidneys, Bladder, Colon, Legs, Spinal column – Red

I am grounded in my being	I am secure in who I am
I am comfortable with my heritage	

Aura Leaks

Electrical Finger Mode

Every living thing is surrounded by an aura – an electromagnetic field that is measurable by Kirlian photography. Someone with high vitality will have a thicker aura than someone with low vitality. Anyone can have a lesion or a leaking aura as a result of illness, injury or drugs. People with chronic health problems frequently have aura leaks. Leaks can occur anywhere around the body, but they often occur around the head area.

The innermost part of the aura, consisting of four superimposed ethers, extends approximately one and a half inches from the body's surface. Etheric currents flow generally in a clockwise direction, moving up the left side from the foot to the head and then down the right side of the body. These can be manipulated by hand so that lesions can be filled in and leaks stopped up.

> 1. Whilst testing an AIM, pass your hand over the body at about 1 ½ inches away. The indicator will unlock when a leak is passed over.

> 2. Circle both hands, one over the other in a clockwise direction (as if polishing a car with two cloths) at not more than 1½ inches from the body. Begin at a point relatively distance from the lesion and smooth and spread the aura, as you would icing on a cake, until you reach the site of the leakage. Fill the lesion in well and smooth it out so that it matches the rest of the aura in thickness.
>
> 3. Retest the area of leakage. An AIM should now lock.
>
>   You may be able to feel the aura as you work – it can feel like a layer of slightly denser than usual air. Visualise it spreading and equalising as you work. The exact route of your hands is not significant if you finish where the leak is and fill it in well. If the treatment does not hold, test for priority.

> **Think of aura leaks in the case of people with ME, MS, auto- immune diseases, tiredness or old injuries. When the electrical finger mode shows, this may be indicated.**
>
> **People who are regularly exposed to electrical smog may particularly suffer if they have aura leaks.**

For Pain

Physical sensation including phantom pain is felt in the etheric body. To diminish pain of any kind, brush the ether away from the pain toward the centre of the body. If necessary, continue for 10 minutes. For phantom pain, if etheric brushing does not eliminate it, acupuncture sedation points may help. Wherever the amputations, the stub will contain all of the acupuncture points contains in the amputated limb. Treat the sedating points in the stub.

Case History

This young woman, now in her early twenties, had been a client since her parents brought her as a small girl. On this occasion she came to see me after experiencing an odd sensation after hitting her head. She explained the feeling as 'if someone was behind her all the time'. She described the sensation as being just over her right shoulder and was quite disturbed by it.

After carrying out Injury Recall (General Technique Section see page 205), a test for Aura Leaks was carried out. There appeared to be a large gap in the aura around the right side of her head where she had been hurt. After the session, she immediately felt that the feeling had lifted and reported later that the sensation never returned.

Walking Gait

Electromagnetic and Structural Finger Mode

This technique is helpful in chronic conditions or resistant neck problems. It will improve many conditions involving the head and neck, or eye and hand coordination. Walking gait will almost always be involved with chronic temporomandibular joint (TMJ) problems and if left uncorrected it can inhibit improvement. The muscles being tested in a walking gait position are the sternocleidomastoid (SCM) and the upper trapezius. This is a type of centring mechanism and the correction involves stimulating stress receptors situated on the cranium.

The sternocleidomastoid (SCM) **(Fig. 15)** and the upper trapezius muscles **(Fig. 16)** have an unusual relationship to the gait mechanism. Each of these muscles have a dual nerve supply (1) from the cranium (cranial XI) as well as (2) the brachial plexus. They enable these muscles to turn off and on as the body swings with the forward gait. (Deal)

A correct gait pattern involves muscles turning on and off in a sequence at exactly the right moment, in other words synchronised.

Sternocleidomastoid – Fig 15

For example, in stepping forwards the quadriceps turn on and the hamstrings on the same leg has to turn off. Otherwise the limb would not be able to move if both muscles were contracting (or relaxing) at the same time.

When the weight is on the left foot the left upper trapezius should turn off and the left sternocleidomastoid muscle (part of the anterior neck flexors) should be turned on. The same principle applies to the right side. If this configuration does not take place there is an imbalance in the walking gait.

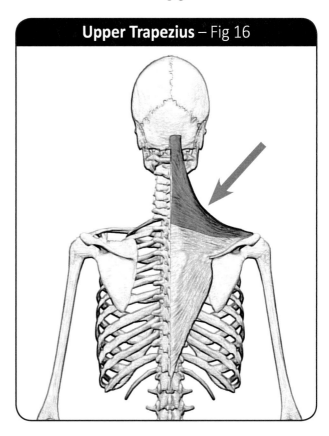

Upper Trapezius – Fig 16

Stress Receptors

The correction for this technique to stimulate upper trapezius **(Fig.18 overleaf)** or the SCM's **(Fig. 17 overleaf)** stress receptors. Stress receptors are skin reflexes that are located in various places on the cranium and each receptor is associated with a muscle.

Stress receptors respond to both weak and hypertonic muscles. In fact, these were the first reflexes used in applied kinesiology that dealt with hypertonic muscles. They respond to linear digital stimulation whilst the client takes a specific phase of respiration. Stress receptors will TL.

To find the direction of correction they are challenged by applying digital pressure, either in *each direction of the arrows* indicated in the linear receptors, or in *any direction if it is represented by a circle* on the chart.

SCM's Stress Receptor – Fig 17

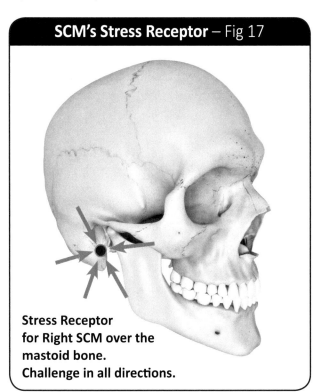

Stress Receptor for Right SCM over the mastoid bone. Challenge in all directions.

Testing the Right SCM – Fig 19

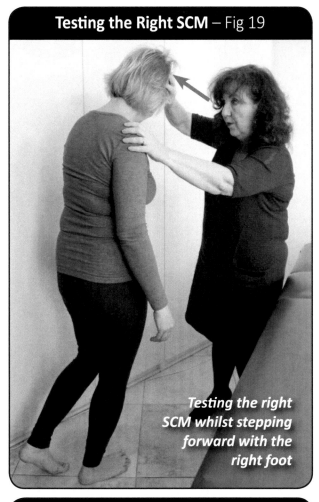

Testing the right SCM whilst stepping forward with the right foot

Upper Trapezius Stress Receptor – Fig 18

Stress Receptors for left and right upper trapezius muscles. Runs from the glabella and over the frontal bone. Challenge in both a superior and inferior direction.

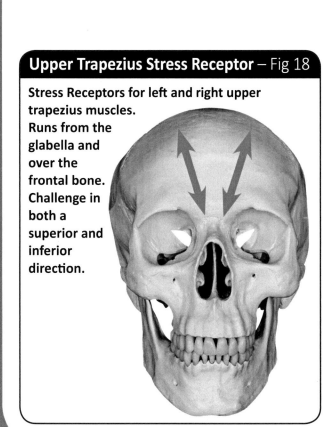

Testing Right Upper Trapezius – Fig 20

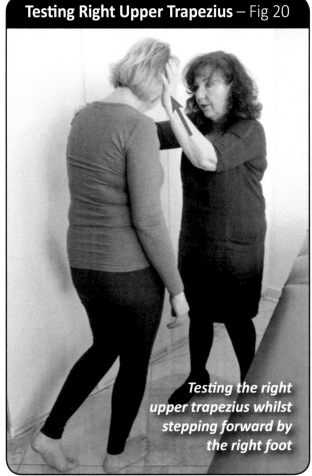

Testing the right upper trapezius whilst stepping forward by the right foot

Make any necessary corrections that may be applicable to the presenting problem, for example the TMJ.

1. Check that both the SCM and the upper trapezius are strong in the clear when your client is standing.

2. Your client then stands in a simulated walking position. The leading foot should carry the most weight and the trailing leg with the weight just on the ball of one foot:

RIGHT leg forwards   The right SCM should be switched on **(Fig. 19)**

                               The right upper trapezius should be turned off **(Fig. 20)**

LEFT leg forwards   The left SCM should be switched on

                               The left upper trapezius should be turned off

If either the SCM or upper trapezius tests differently from the above, the walking gait mechanism is out of balance.

Have your client TL each stress receptor associated with the SCM and the upper trapezius **(Figs. 17 & 18)** whilst they are in a normal standing position. The stress receptor that is in dysfunction will unlock an AIM.

3. Whilst they continue to touch the stress receptor, check with an indicator muscle whether breathing in or out changes the indicator to locked. Your client should carry out this phase of respiration whilst the correction is employed.

4. Then establish the direction that the correction needs to be made in. Dynamically challenge the stress receptor, in each of the directions shown by the arrows on **(Figs. 17 & 18)**. An IM will unlock on the correct one.

5. Digitally stimulate the active receptor in the appropriate direction with a firm pressure, 5 or 6 times during the appropriate phase of the client's respiration.

6. Repeat step 2

Other considerations; check for a hyoid imbalance and TMJ dysfunction.

In applied kinesiology the rule is that corrections requiring inspiration assist are a priority. If the correction requires and expiration assist, then the lesion is not a priority.

How to Reset the Biological Clock

Electrical Finger Mode

The body has a circadian rhythm, in other words we have our own internal body clock. It should be set according to the position of the sun and not set by a physical clock. We know that the 12 meridians are more active or less active at certain times of the day. These times are based on the position of the Sun and when we are working on this premise we need to correct for any time adjustments. Some people's biological clocks have difficulty adapting when they enter another time zone or when daylight saving time is altered and this method will reset it. Sometimes over-energy, which is identified by testing an alarm point, can be due to a biological clock inconsistency. This technique, devised by Christopher Smith DO, has shown to be extremely helpful in the situation. (Deal)

1. Check the time of day and adjust this for daylight saving time if operational. Identify which meridian is currently active in the corrected time; we call this the 'now point'.

2. If the person's biological clock is correctly set, the 'now point' should two-point when TL'ing closed eyelids (unlock). If the alarm point does **not** two-point, go to step 3.*

3. Using the Law of the 5 Elements, identify the active meridian's pair e.g. If the 'now' time is 12pm which is in Heart time its paired meridian is Small Intestine.

4. To correct the biological clock, ask your client to TL the paired meridian's alarm point **(Figs. 12 & 13 on pages 18-19)** (e.g. CV4 for small intestine) as you tap GV20 **(Fig 21)** thirty times.

5. Retest step 2.

*Some kinesiologists find that an AIM unlocks when the 'now' alarm point is contacted. Personally, I do not find that. However, if this works for you, then in step 2, if the alarm point does not unlock an IM, continue with the correction.

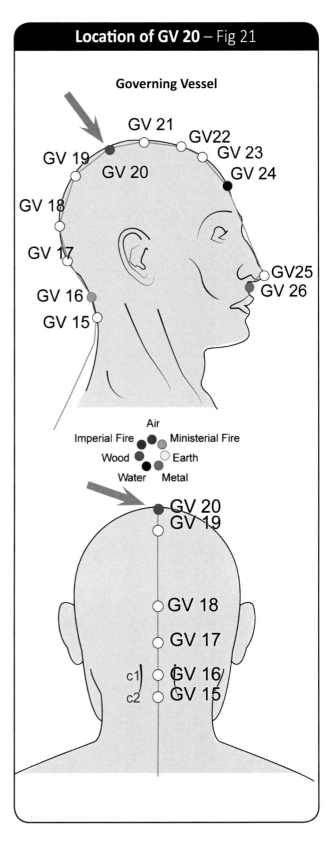

Location of GV 20 – Fig 21

Governing Vessel

Pitch, Roll Yaw and Tilt (PRYT) Technique

Electromagnetic Finger Mode

These are names given to coordinated imbalances of attitude between the neck/head & pelvis. The terms pitch, roll and yaw are analogies used as aeronautical terms for aeroplane rotations around the three spatial axes. The concept is that the body is made up of segments: arms, legs, head, and trunk. This technique, which is very thorough, is used to ensure that the body segments are coordinated with each other by correcting the neck muscles in relationship to the sacrum. I have categorised this as an electromagnetic imbalance and correction because it is involved in centring.

If a client feels as if there is something giving out on them when they walk or if you watch them walk, and something is not right with their gait, yet the gait pattern tests are negative, it is likely to be their PRYT. Gait is specifically involved with walking whereas PRYT is involved with any coordination activity. Check this regularly with anyone who has a neurological disease such as MS, where coordination is a particular issue. Look for in cases of dyspraxia. If you are working with sports people, this can refine their sports technique and may improve their game. PRYT is a helpful for someone with chronic neck problems.

> **(!)** *Check this out with sports people and clients who have dyspraxia, a neurological disease, chronic neck problems, or coordination problems.*

Symptoms

Pitch:

Pitch pertains to an aeroplane ascending and descending. In the human body, it relates to the body when it tilts forward and back. It is a common problem with people who walk with their head down or they tilt forward. The buttocks

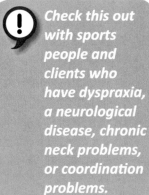

and back of head will both be tilted either superiorly or anteriorly. Reaching towards the toes when sitting with the legs straight in front will be difficult. Pitch is related to up/down switching and CV24 and GV26 when touched simultaneously will TL.

Roll:

When the attitude of an aeroplane is that one wing is higher than the other, the plane is starting to roll. People who walk with their shoulders down, arms still, their head tilted, and shuffle their feet will likely have this imbalance. In the case of the body, the pelvis and head will again have a coordinated tilt but this time one hip will be raised and the head will tilt over towards the same side. When standing and leaning over to one side with the legs straight, one hand will reach further down the leg than the other. It is related to left and right switching and the client may confuse right and left or complain of walking into doors. K27 will bilaterally CL.

Yaw:

Yaw is when an aeroplane is pointing in one direction, but the wind is causing the plane to travel in another. In terms of the body, looking down onto the top of the head, the shoulders will appear to be rotating in one direction, whilst the hips will be rotating in the opposite direction. The reach measured with the hand towards the opposite toe will be unequal when sitting with the legs straight out in front. The client may complain of bumping their hips into furniture.

Tilt

Tilt is when the body is leaning to one side. Look for this in people who play racquet sports or handball games as it particularly pertains to hand and eye coordination. You could improve an athlete's game by correcting this imbalance for them.

Pre-tests

In the case of P.R.Y.T, the issue is that a person cannot coordinate two actions at once, but they can do each component singularly. To make sure that none of the positions that you place the body in are going to cause a weak indicator muscle to begin with, check the following:

i. Check and correct if necessary, gait, hyoid and cloacals (centring).

ii. Ask your client to bend and raise their knees leaving their feet on the surface and test an AIM. If it unlocks there could be a problem with the knees. Correct knee related muscles or enter the unlocked muscle into pause lock and find appropriate correction. Rubbing both the PSIS may also help. If not, there could be a shock absorber problem with the knees (see page 163 Structural Corrections and Imbalances).

iii. With the legs now straight on the couch, ask person to raise their head and test an AIM. If it unlocks, check and correct the neck muscles, atlas (See page 137), or pause lock the problem and find a correction using finger modes.

iv. If turning the head to one side changes an AIM, auricular lock (kinesiology at Foundation Level) needs to be corrected first.

v. Since eye coordination in relationship to hip position is involved, check for Ocular Lock (Visual Inhibition).

The following corrections are in the preferred order of sequence. However, you can prioritise between them.

In order to incorporate whole body actions, the IM to be used in this procedure is a bilateral PMC, both tested together. They should both test strong in the clear. If any of the following body attitudes cause the bilateral IMs to unlock, carry out the appropriate correction procedure. **The arrows show the direction in which the client needs to push** if the IMs unlock in the illustrated position.

The correction for all imbalances is to correct the neck muscles using resistance whilst the body is in the position (attitude). Ask your client to raise their head, do not do this for them. The pressure applied should provide resistance without overcoming their ability to push and carried out with inspiration assist (the client breathes in during the resistance phase). Each movement should last about 3 seconds. To anchor the correction and check that it has been successful, repeat the test and recheck the posture. For the individual tests and corrections **(See Figures 22-27).**

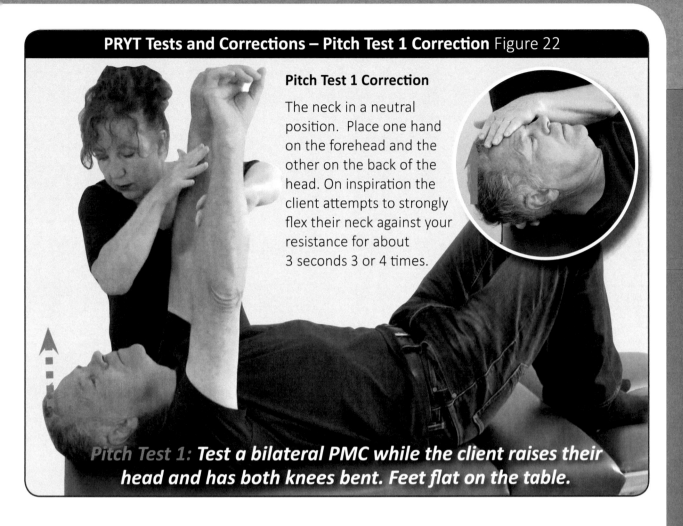

Pitch Test 1 Correction

The neck in a neutral position. Place one hand on the forehead and the other on the back of the head. On inspiration the client attempts to strongly flex their neck against your resistance for about 3 seconds 3 or 4 times.

Pitch Test 1: **Test a bilateral PMC while the client raises their head and has both knees bent. Feet flat on the table.**

Pitch Test 2 Correction

Whichever side unlocked the PMC's, client raises head against your resistance whilst taking an in breath. Repeat 3 or 4 times.

Pitch Test 2 Rotation: **test with knees bent and head flexed, and test with the client rotating their head to the left as they breathe in. Repeat with their head rotated to the right.**

Pitch Test 3 Correction

Client resists with an upward pressure on inspiration 3 or 4 times.

Pitch Test 3 Extension: **Test a bilateral PMC while client lies supine with head dropping off the table and the legs straddling the couch.**

Roll Test and Correction – Figure 25

Roll Correction: In the position of the positive test, with the neck relaxed and in a neutral position, turn the client's head in the same direction as their legs. Push the side of the head towards the couch as they resist on the in breath. Repeat 3 or 4 times.

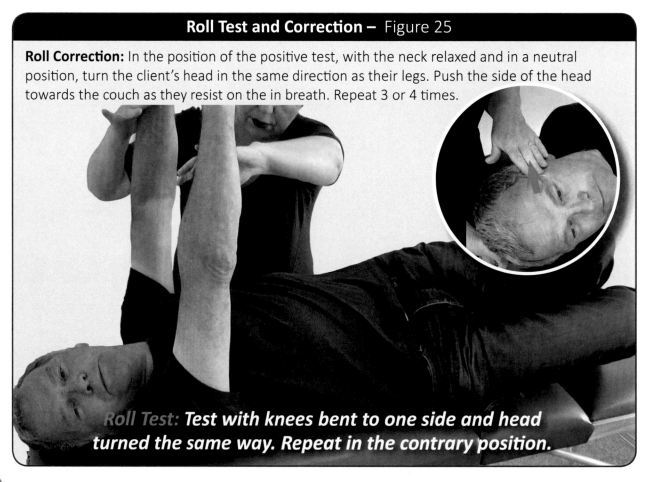

Roll Test: **Test with knees bent to one side and head turned the same way. Repeat in the contrary position.**

Yaw Test and Correction – Figure 26

Yaw Correction:

In the same configuration that showed and with the head in a neutral position. Place your hand on the client's forehead while they press their forehead into your hand on inspiration. Repeat 3 or 4 times.

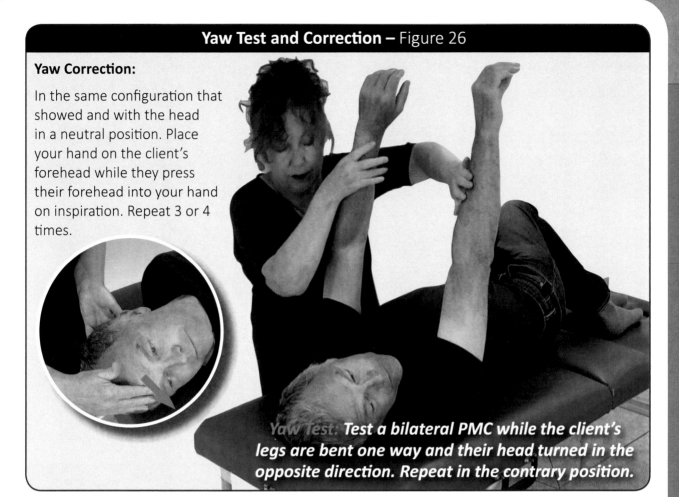

Yaw Test: **Test a bilateral PMC while the client's legs are bent one way and their head turned in the opposite direction. Repeat in the contrary position.**

Tilt Test and Correction – Figure 27

Tilt Correction:

Start with the client's head positioned midline. With resistance on inspiration, **(1)** let them push their head into your hand for 3-4 seconds. Repeat, as you gradually reposition their head towards their shoulder. **(2)** Take their head back to the midline by reversing the procedure

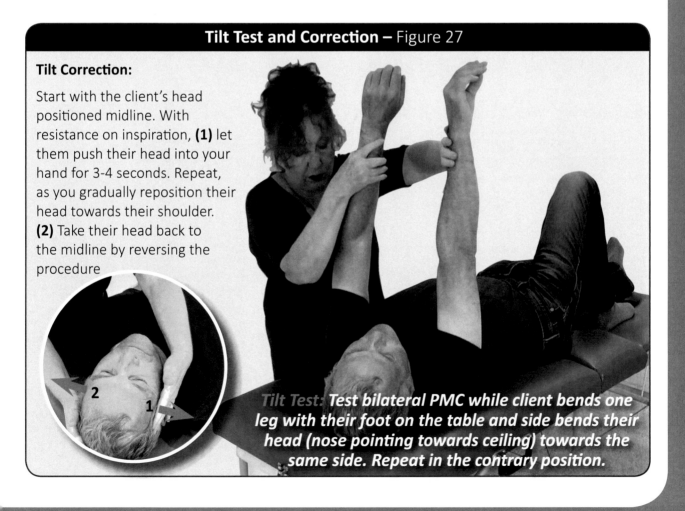

Tilt Test: **Test bilateral PMC while client bends one leg with their foot on the table and side bends their head (nose pointing towards ceiling) towards the same side. Repeat in the contrary position.**

Emotional Imbalances and Corrections

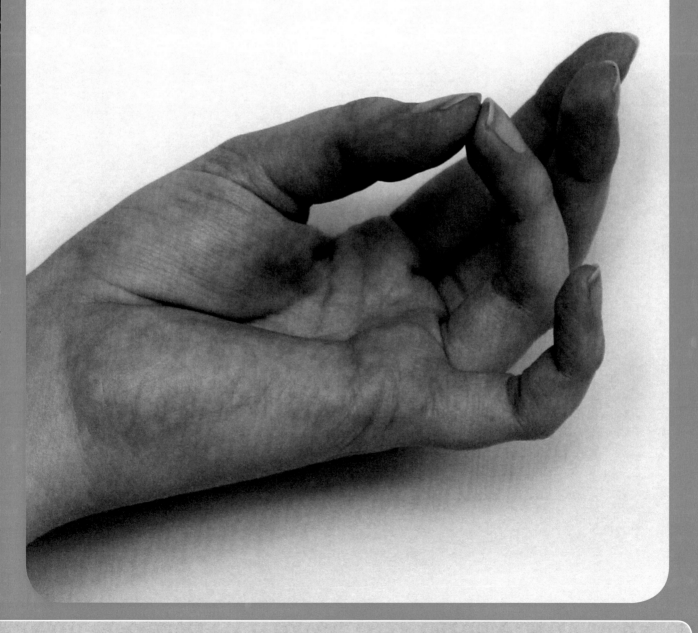

Encompasses techniques that help to resolve negative thought patterns, mental conflicts and the effects of past trauma.

Table of contents

Addressing Matters of the Mind

Emotional Finger Mode

We deliberated in the introduction the interweaving connections in mind-body disorders and the part that the hypothalamus has to play in interpreting the message it gets from stress responses both environmentally and via the rest of the limbic system. We discussed how it relays messages to our hormonal system which then responds by issuing commands to the body's cells.

The work of Dr Candace Pert and her colleagues is probably the best 'hard science' that has been done in this area. Dr Pert was probably the first to speak of the biochemistry of emotions. Receptors exist for feelings of rage, joy, hunger, pain, pleasure, grief, and for all of the emotions as well as for body reactions like appetite, sexual behaviour and water balance. Emotions might include an assortment of intangible, subjective experiences that are probably unique to humans such as spiritual inspiration, awe, bliss and other conscious states. (Pert, 1997)

The question we now ask is, what can we do about faulty messaging and stuck patterns of emotional behaviour which can subsequently translate into unhappiness or disease?

Don't Try to Solve Clients' Problems

It's tempting for a practitioner to try to offer solutions when a client tells them their stories. Being a good impartial listener is mostly what a person needs. So, resist the temptation to 'wade in'! What we, the practitioner can offer is TLC and techniques that help to reset old thinking patterns and make room for new ones. Using open-ended questions can help your client think about what they want to impart.

First Things First

There is something that I have observed over the years of working with clients.

It is pointless working on emotional issues if the person is tired all the time, has poor eating habits, has food intolerances etc. etc. This can make anyone depressed! People can think and reason more clearly if they are feeling well. Many of their stresses will disappear leaving the fundamental emotional issues ready to be addressed.

Many clients come to my clinic who have already tried talking therapies and they just haven't worked. I believe, and have seen to be true, that their fundamental problem is their physical health affecting their mental health. Neuropeptide production is greatly affected by food intolerances and autotoxicity. The psychotherapist the late Roger Callahan, the founder of the original Thought Field Therapy Meridian Tapping Techniques, knew that food intolerances would make his treatments assuaging emotional problems totally useless. My experience has been that once a client feels physically better, a lot of their fears and anxieties melt away.

> **❝ As kinesiology practitioners we have an amazing skill set that can address the physical, emotional, biochemical and electromagnetic imbalances to help us get to the root of the problem. Keep an open mind and deal with the body's priorities ❞**

Verbal Challenges

When the finger mode for the emotional realm of stress shows, sometimes it's difficult to identify what the emotional issue 'online' is related to:

 The first port of call is to think about what your client talked about at the beginning of their session before they got onto your couch. The chances are that because that discussion is 'online' for the person, it's probably going to be to do with something they've said.

If that's not the case, verbal challenging is a good way to identify the relevant area of stress. The practitioner verbalises the headings below and relevant areas of stress will cause and AIM to unlock. If there are more than one, prioritise. Here are some suggestions. (Prestwich)

- Birth trauma
- Childhood traumas/bullying
- Brothers and /or sisters
- Mother and/or Father
- Relationships, partner, friends
- Guilt (define areas)
- Lack of confidence
- Lack of money
- Lack of self-esteem
- Loneliness and /or separation
- My worst destructive habits
- What I would most like to become
- Work related problems /goals
- Fear (*see opposite list to help define areas)

*FEAR OF:

- Authority
- Being a parent
- Being in a relationship
- Being abandoned or alone
- Being powerless
- Being right/wrong
- Being taken advantage of
- Rejection/not being liked
- What others think/criticism
- Cancer/disease
- Dying/others dying
- Public speaking
- Success
- Crowds/small spaces/dark/hospitals/dentist
- Lack of money/debt
- Failure
- Being inadequate
- Change
- The future
- Dependency
- Starting own business
- Working for others
- Letting go of past hurts (define)
- Letting go of a grudge
- Letting go of guilt/fear
- Letting go of resentment/jealousy

Alarm Points and the Emotional Finger Mode

For the Alarms point charts see section on Electrical imbalances on pages 18 & 19.

In TCM, each meridian has associated emotions. If a meridian is out of balance, it can be responsible for a person being overly affected by the emotion associated with the meridian. For example, if there is a chronic over energy in the liver meridian, the person may experience unreasonable and inappropriate anger (Law of the 5 Elements emotional connection). Conversely, if a person is very angry about a situation, this in turn could cause the liver meridian to be over energised and eventually affect the liver itself. In TCM, acupuncture is used to sedate or tonify the meridian system to bring about balanced emotions once more.

John Diamond M.D. in his book *Life Energy & the Emotions* employs the concept of over energy causing negative emotions. He says, "each acupuncture meridian is associated with specific muscles of facial expression, gesture and vocalisation. Most importantly for our present purposes, each meridian is also associated with a specific negative and a specific positive emotional state. Thus, through implementing [MRT] it is possible to determine which emotional states are most affecting each of us, both mentally and physically at any given time. We have found that by bringing this to the person's attention and by using imagery techniques, the changes that can be produced are immediately apparent." (Diamond, 1997)

Dr Diamond's technique uses MRT to find the alarm points that show over energy in the associated meridian. This helps the practitioner find the associated emotion that is out of balance. The practitioner then taps the alarm point to disperse the over energy whilst the client says affirmations or focuses on the imagery that balances the meridian and thus the emotion.

For a chart of the alarm points see section on Electrical Imbalances and Corrections on pages 18 & 19

When the Emotional Finger Mode Shows but the Client Can't Identify the Emotion

Here is a scenario that all kinesiologists have experienced.

Problem: You've identified a lesion and have it in circuit. You're looking for a solution and activate the 4 key finger modes in order to find which realm the body prefers as a correction. The emotional finger mode changes the indicator muscle. However, neither you nor the client have any idea what the emotion is.

Solution: With the emotional finger mode in circuit, touch each of the alarm points (see chart in Electromagnetic Section on pages 18 &19). Any that change the IM will show you the emotion that is associated with the lesion. Check the chart in **Table 3** overleaf to find out which ones. You can then share what you have found with your client and see if it reveals anything that they had previously forgotten about. You can then proceed to carry out any emotional balancing work or administer flower/gems/homoeopathic remedies. If you have found an affirmation connected with the alarm point, you can ask your client to repeat it while you disperse the over energy by tapping the involved alarm point.

 Could you check for any other emotional treatment procedures here?

A Procedure for Identifying and Balancing an Emotion

Use this method when you specifically want to concentrate on the emotional realm. It's useful when you are aware that the client has certain issues but is not able to voice them.

1. Hold the emotional finger mode or ask your client to do so.
    You can, of course, place this mode together with modality mode into circuit (pause lock) if you choose. The IM will not change. Putting these modes into circuit first will act as a filter. You will only pick up imbalances that are associated with this realm of stress. Any alarm points that are active will be connected to an emotional state only and any solutions you find will also be for the person's highest good (a modality).

2. With this mode activated, touch each alarm point and test an AIM.

3. Note any alarm point that unlocks your IM and place it into pause lock. The muscle will remain unlocked.

4. Identify which remedy will enable the IM to lock by placing the Bach remedy in **(Table 3)**. The chart identifies the Bach remedy, but any type of flower or gem essence can be used.

Meridians and Emotions – Table 3			
Meridian	**Positive Emotion**	**Negative Emotion**	**Bach Flower Remedy**
STOMACH	Contentment	Disgust, disappointment, bitterness, greed, emptiness, deprivation, nausea, hunger	**WILLOW**
SPLEEN	Security	Anxiety	**MIMULUS**
HEART	Love	Anger	**HORNBEAM**
SMALL INTESTINE	Joy	Sadness, sorrow	**STAR OF BETHLEHEM**
BLADDER	Peace	Frustration, restlessness, impatience	**IMPATIENS**
KIDNEY	Sexually Security	Sexual Indecision	**SCLERANTHUS**
CIRCULATION-SEX	Generosity	Regret, remorse, jealousy, sexual tension, stubbornness	**HOLLY**
TRIPLE WARMER	Buoyancy	Depression, despair, hopelessness, grief, despondency, loneliness, solitude	**MUSTARD**
GALL BLADDER	Forgiveness	Rage, fury, wrath	**CHERRY PLUM**
LIVER	Happiness	Unhappiness	**AGRIMONY**
LUNG	Humility	Disdain, scorn, contempt, prejudice, false pride, haughtiness	**WATER VIOLET**
LARGE INTESTINE	Cleanliness	Guilt	**PINE**

For more details on how to use this chart, see John Diamond's book - Life Energy & The Emotions. You can use this chart to identify any major stressors your client has. You can then address using the techniques to diffuse stresses taught in this course.

Techniques to Diffuse Negative Thoughts

Emotional Finger Mode

Researchers in Muscle Response Testing (kinesiologists) are like magpies looking for shiny objects. Their research very often involves picking out protocols used in other modalities and adapting them for use with muscle testing. Most of the techniques described here have a foundation in Roger Callahan's work – Thought Field Therapy (TFT). From there, others have developed and adapted his work calling it Emotional Freedom Technique (EFT), a simplified form of Callahan's work. Further sources used in these techniques originate from Neuro-linguistic Programming (NLP). For example, eye positions are regularly used in NLP to access, or focus on specific areas of the brain.

Fundamental Conflict/ Psychological Reversal

This technique deals with the thought processes that play a major role in a person's health.

Check for This First!

It is common knowledge that repeating positive thoughts out loud can reprogram the brain into thinking in a more positive way. However, sometimes affirmations will weaken a muscle if the brain doesn't really believe the statement being made. The person is sometimes not even aware of this. They may even PERCIEVE the statement to be true E.g. in statements such as "I want/deserve to be well", "I want/deserve to be happy", "I want/deserve to be slim", "I deeply and profoundly love and respect myself" or "I want to give up smoking", the person can be psychologically reversed. This means that no matter how many times they repeat the positive statement, it will not make any difference to them. Also, as in the case of "I want to be well", consider that the reason why treatments do not work with some people could be because they are psychologically programmed to wanting to be sick! We can often say to ourselves "I wish

I was happy/well". The question is, which "I" is stopping us from achieving our heart's desire, causing a fundamental conflict. There may be a part of us that is stopping us from doing that and we don't even know it. Resolving these conflicts allows healing to take place and self-esteem increases.

There could be psychological conflict/reversal in relationship to our nearest and dearest. For example, we can fundamentally love our partner, but there may be areas where we don't get along with them. Our mind is in conflict, but we're not even aware of it! This can drain our energy without us knowing it. It's worth exploring this conflict if our client's problems involve others.

When we say, "I deserve to be happy", "I let go of my guilt", or "I deserve to enjoy life", and part of us resists this to the extent that an indicator muscle will then test weak – we have a problem! When a positive statement is made which makes the muscle unlock, but the IM stays strong with a negative statement, this is a reversal of the way things should be.

Dr Callahan found a "key" to deal with this problem. He found that activating the acupuncture point small intestine 3 **(See Fig. 28 on page 43)** resolved this energy conflict. What an inspiration! If an AIM unlocks when a positive life – goal statement is made, the client is "reversed" and tapping SI 3 will resolve this.

Check that the client isn't psychologically reversed before giving them affirmations, visualisation techniques or addressing

How to Determine if the Statement is a Psychological Conflict/Reversal.

A psychological conflict is not just an affirmation. Be warned, saying these statements can make people cry, and sometimes they find them hard, if not impossible to say. If the latter is the case, find another statement they can say and then go back to the difficult one later when they can usually then address it.

Here are some tips on how to recognize statements likely to be psychologically reversed:

1. **These are beliefs that we all fundamentally have.**

2. **An area of conflict with our nearest and dearest ones.**

3. **A key word to include in the statement is "I deserve...", "I let go of......"**

4. **Small Intestine 3 is CL'd whilst the person says the statement will remove the reversal.**

It is wise to check for psychological reversal from time to time if one is dealing with a person in depth. In the same way that some will "switch" during a session, others will "reverse". So, check occasionally that the individual has not suddenly "reversed" or suddenly "switched". If either has occurred, you need to correct it.

Because a different part of the brain is activated when the eyes are closed, and in the dark, compared to having the eyes open in the light, it is very well worth checking both of these aspects when dealing with a psychological conflict. The results of your testing may well be different, and the problem will not have been thoroughly addressed if these are not checked and corrected in the mode.

Key Point: If your client is not responding to treatment, they may have psychological conflict. They will not improve until this is dealt with. I.e. "I want to be well"

Look out for this imbalance interfering with your allergy testing and weight loss. There is often a feeling of guilt that causes psychological conflict. For example, smokers will often test weak on "I love to smoke" when they should enjoy smoking if they are a smoker! Also, for slimmers, try testing "I enjoy eating". We should all enjoy eating. Guilt causes a psychological reversal that could block treatments from working.

The person may express a desire to be slim, for example, but every type of treatment or diet fails to achieve this aim. There may be a psychological need to be overweight and the person may be unaware of this. In this case, the person's subconscious mind may differ from the conscious mind and they may feel frustrated that they never succeed.

When testing this type of individual, an AIM will unlock when they say, "I (Name) want/deserve to be slim". The reverse is also true i.e. the indicator muscle remains strong when they say, "I (Jane) want/deserve to be overweight".

> **❝ All chronic problems that are slow to recover or change, no matter what the nature of them is, will have a root somewhere in psychological reversal. Anything slow to heal will have a psychological component to it – after all, any condition of long standing will take its toll on anyone. ❞**

This can also apply to any aspect of life e.g. job, relationships, health, ambitions, passing an exam etc. They usually tend to see the negative aspects of the situation and to have low self-esteem. The statement "I (Jane) deeply and profoundly love and accept myself with all my faults and failings" may show psychological reversal.

When conflict is present, the indicator muscle stays locked on the negative thoughts and unlocks on the positive ones. They should stay locked on *"I want to be healthy/happy"* and unlock on *"I want to be ill/miserable".*

1. Ensure that the person is not switched.

2. Ask your client to verbalise aloud the appropriate positive statement. If an IM unlocks on the positive statement but stays locked when the opposite negative statement is verbalised, there is a conflict.

> *What might happen to your results if the client WAS switched?*

3. To ascertain if psychological conflict is the problem, CL'ing Small intestine 3 will reverse the muscle response in step 2. SI 3 is on the edge of the hand in the depression just below the knuckle of the little finger. **(Fig. 28)**

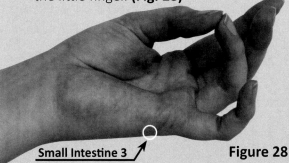

Small Intestine 3   Figure 28

4. Before the correction is made, an optional extra would be to find which Bach Flower Essences also reverse the response in step 2. These could then be administered as part of the treatment.

5. When a conflict is found, have the person repeat the sentence that unlocked the muscle whilst you tap SI3 20-30 times bilaterally.

6. When the eyes are closed, or the eyes are exposed to darkness rather than light (at night) brain patterns alter. This is seen when measuring brain waves on an EEG. To ensure a thorough treatment, in these modes test the statement with eyes closed as well as in a darkened room with the eyes open.

7. Repeat the procedure again, using the same statement, and with them in the mode of eyes closed and then in the dark. To simulate darkness, you can close the blinds, your client keeps their eyes open.

> **!** *To reinforce the treatment, identify which flower remedy may help **before** making the correction. Enter the statement into pause lock and find the remedy that locks the IM. The chosen remedy/ies can then be given whilst tapping SI3. The person can subsequently take the remedy for a time at home.*

8. Ask your client to repeat the phrase again, but instead of saying their name, change the phrase to 'my inner being'.

9. Before moving on, after making any corrections in steps 5-9, ask the person to repeat the statement again. The IM should now remain locked and should unlock when they now say the negative statement. You can then proceed to check for any other psychologically reversed statements.

Statements may not show with eyes open, but conflict could be present when the eyes are closed, or the person is in the dark. Quite interestingly, statements may only test positive when, instead of saying *"I"* or their name, they say *"my inner being"*. To ensure the most thorough treatment has been carried out, check all of these permutations.

Statements That Address Fundamental Conflicts

It is always a good idea to ask the person to **say their name in the statement** e.g. I, Jane deserve to be well. The brain is really good at filtering out information that seems irrelevant. However, the brain is alert to our own name. You'll have experienced this yourself in a crowded room where everyone is talking at once. Our brain is able to filter out the noise and concentrate on the conversation we're engaged in. However, if someone across the room happens to say our name, we immediately focus on where in the room it came from because our brain identifies it as important.

 Think about the circumstances that you might use these techniques in your own practice

All statements should be made in the present tense.

Examples

- **I deserve to be well**
- **I deserve to enjoy life**
- **I deserve to let go of my guilt**
- **I consciously/truly want to let go of all past hurts**
- **I truly want to totally resolve my ………….**
- **I truly believe that it is possible to totally resolve my ……………**
- **I truly love my partner/mother/father/best friend etc.**

Some More Suggested Statements to Check For:

- **I accept myself completely even if I never get over my health problems/have pain in……**
- **I deeply and profoundly love and respect myself**
- **I have deep and profound confidence in myself**
- **I enjoy smoking (if a smoker)**
- **I enjoy food/eating (important to get relationship with food right)**
- **I want/deserve to lose weight**
- **I want/deserve to be slimmer**
- **I want to be well**
- **I deserve to be well**

Eye Rotations

Emotional Finger Mode

Eye rotations are used to eradicate **old** patterns of thinking or behaviour. It's useful in situations where people have a compulsion to do or think in a certain way. The key phrase here is "I release….."

This is a left/right brain hemisphere balance. Whenever we are retrieving memories or information from our brain's memory banks, we will turn our eyes in certain directions to help us to recall something. Eye positions are used extensively in NLP, TFT, EFT and PTSD treatments to access and recover information from different parts of the brain. This gives the brain the opportunity to erase old patterns of thinking and imprint new ones with positive statements.

 This technique helps to forge new neural pathways by releasing old ones

Neural pathways make me think of paths in a wood. In order to find our way, we will automatically use the well-trodden pathways – because it feels safer and easier! It doesn't mean that it will take us out of the wood though; we might be going around in circles all of the time. In order to get out, we might need a machete to forge new pathways that do lead us to the outside. If we use the new paths we've made for long enough, **they** will be the ones that are easy to walk along and the old pathways, that lead nowhere, will grow over because of infrequent use. This technique helps us to release old pathways.

1. Have the person make a statement that indicates he/she is willing to let go of the pattern – e.g. "I release the need to be a victim". If this unlocks a strong indicator muscle bilaterally when tested both together, use eye rotations whilst the client repeats the statement.

2. Use either the tips of two of your fingers, a pen, or a large X cut out in cardboard for them to follow with their eyes. Make circles in one direction a few times, then the opposite way. Watch for glitches in the smoothness of eye movement or blinking. This indicates that they are avoiding the issue at some level or are finding it difficult to deal with. Go over that sector of the circular path several times to 'polish out' the glitches. Get the person to track with their eyes whilst you draw with your fingers a figure of eight, on its side, tracking upwards in the middle

Continue with the eye rotations until the eyes follow the path smoothly.

3. Retest an AIM whilst the person is saying the statement. The muscle should now remain strong.

If the Statement Only Unlocks an IM Unilaterally:

- Have the client extend their arms out to the side, then repeat the statement whist looking straight ahead in soft focus and drawing their extended arms together in front of their body until they can clasp their hands.

Temporal Tap

Emotional Finger Mode

 This technique may be particularly useful before exams, dental work when prone to gagging, athletes before an important event or before public speaking.

The temporal tap technique bypasses the brain's conscious sensory system to 'write new messages' into the subconscious to aid the resolution of a given condition. It is extremely useful, when used in conjunction with psychological conflict and eye rotations, to 're-programme' the subconscious with new statements. Tapping sharply around the temporal sphenoidal (TS) line **(See Fig. 29)** appears to penetrate the sensory nervous system that is usually blocked. It also is involved with bilateral brain function. Dr Goodheart found that as long as the statement made whilst tapping the TS line was acceptable to the individual, it made positive affirmations more effective. He learned about this technique from a Czechoslovakian chiropractor who had good results asking his clients to say affirmations to reduce smoking, whilst he manipulated the temporal bone. (Walther D. S., 1988)

The brain hemispheres are dedicated to different functions, i.e. simplistically, the left side of the brain receives information and the right side processes the information and deals with the effects of previous life experiences. ***Temporal tapping should be performed with the correct hand, as the polarity of each hand is slightly different.***

1. The client says the statement whilst testing an AIM.

    If the indicator unlocks but relocks when the temporo-sphenoid line is CL'd, temporal tapping is appropriate.

2. Temporal tapping is done with quick sharp taps around the temporo-sphenoid line (TS line) – **(See Fig. 29)**, tracing an elliptical path

just above and behind the ear. Start the tapping just at the front of the ear. Whilst tapping, the person can repeat the statement, or the practitioner can input the statement – e.g. "You no longer need to smoke" whilst tapping around the right ear.

Temporal tapping – Figure 29

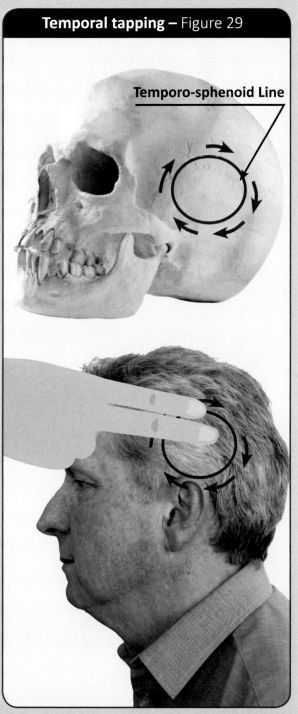

Temporo-sphenoid Line

Tap the left TS line if the statement is a positive one, e.g. "I can always think clearly when I'm speaking in public". This is inputting a new idea whilst stimulating the left brain.

Tap the right TS line if the statement contains the word 'never, no, not', e.g. "I no longer feel fear when I speak in public". This is bypassing the right brain's previously formed beliefs. ✓

To tap in positive statements, the practitioner uses their right hand to tap the left TS line and their left hand to tap the right TS line. If the client is given homework to for himself or herself, they use their right hand to the right side of the head and left hand to left side.

3. The indicator muscle should now lock when the positive statement is verbalised.

 All affirmations should be made in the present tense, e.g. I am, NOT I will, because the future may never come!

To check how the person will respond to temporal tapping, tap a non-contentious positive statement into the left side – e.g. If the person has dark hair, tap in the statement "You have fair hair", an AIM will unlock because it is a false statement. Similarly, tapping in "You do not have dark hair" to the right TS line should also cause an indicator muscle to unlock.

Those who react abnormally may benefit from cross crawl.

❝ Sometimes the mind goes blank when trying to think up meaningful, succinct affirmations. If it does, there is no shame in asking your client to formulate one – after all they know how they feel! I sometimes use Louise Hay's book, You Can Heal Your Life (1984) to prompt me. The book has affirmations for specific health issues, but any of them can be used with ANY problem. Whenever you're looking for affirmations, it doesn't matter if they seem 'over the top'. The more positive the better! ❞

Dispelling Fears and Phobias

Acknowledgement:
Roger Callahan – Thought Field Therapy

Emotional Finger Mode

Together with the tools that you already have for getting to the root of a fear or phobia, this technique is a powerful way of resolving real issues like fear of snakes, fear of flying etc.

> **❝ It is important to tread carefully and not force the person to confront something that they do not want to do. The person must feel safe, even though they may feel uncomfortable. ❞**

As in all kinesiology techniques, it is ideal to treat people 'in the mode'. Therefore, in the case of flying for example, to treat them prior to embarking at the airport is preferable if possible. In the case of spiders or other creepy crawlies, showing them a picture, or even having one available may prove to be advantageous.

Rationale

If a person is in a situation that causes fear or panic – or any kind of emotional overload – it will case an excessive amount of energy in the stomach meridian. By tapping Stomach 1 whilst the person is in the mode, this will dispel excess energy, causing a return of equilibrium within the energy system. Stomach 1 is situated on the notch felt on the bony orbit beneath the eye, in line with the pupil when the eyes look straight ahead. **(Fig. 30)**

For this example, we will consider a person who is afraid of going in a lift.

Test an AIM whilst the person says a statement such as:

"I ....(person's name) feel perfectly comfortable about going in a lift"

"I ………. am free from the fear of the lift breaking down when I am in it."

"I ………… no longer have a phobia about travelling in a lift"

Notice the statements are all in the present tense, in other words we want the brain to acknowledge that the fear/phobia is dispelled NOW, NOT in the future.

Another example might be a morbid fear of spiders or snakes. Perhaps you could get them 'in the mode' by showing the person a picture of the insect/reptile first as a drawing, then a photo and if appropriate eventually the real thing! Ensure that you don't move on to the next stage until the person is perfectly happy looking at the image. In this instance, the person can look at the object and tap their own ST 1 without saying an affirmation. They can also think about the problem whilst tapping ST 1.

> Use a SUD scale (Subjective Units of Discomfort) by asking the person to rate on a scale of 1-10 how severe their fear is. This is useful because you can then check the SUD scale again at different stages of the session. It's a good guide to how well the treatment is working. Be thorough in listening to the client and questioning them to establish the fundamental issues that make them phobic. Ensure that you address those. If you can break down the issue into small bite-size pieces, this is more effective than trying to address the problem as a whole. Once you have

established the thoughts/events that unlock an AIM, you could then find out which one of these is the modality. If modalities are dealt with first, this is not only more effective, but you'll usually find that a lot of the individual issues then resolve themselves.

> **!** *It really anchors the treatment if you can give a vibrational essence along with this technique.*

1. Ask the person to think about an aspect of the fear/phobia or find a way of getting them into the mode. Test an AIM.

2. If the IM unlocks, tap simultaneously and bilaterally St1 **(See Fig. 30)** whilst they repeat the phrase*.
    To anchor, check the phrase again using an AIM. If this does not work, try tapping spleen 1 at the medial edge of the root of the nail of the big toe (hallux). **(See Fig. 31)**

    Retest the IM as they think of the fear/phobia again. The indicator should now lock.

    *Adding a flower essence can really enhance your treatment. Find the essence first **before** tapping St 1. To do this, put the feeling/ phrase that unlocked the IM into pause lock then find the remedy that locks the IM.

Stomach 1 – Figure 30

Stomach 1 centrally just below the eyes

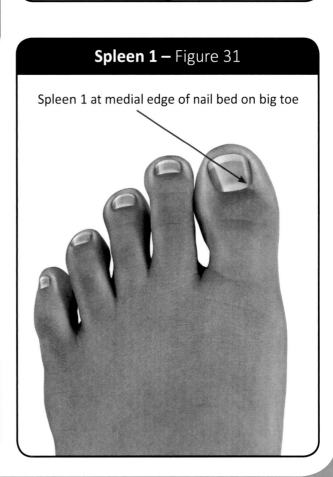

Spleen 1 – Figure 31

Spleen 1 at medial edge of nail bed on big toe

A Great Anchoring Technique

In TFT, Roger Callahan uses this protocol after tapping the acupuncture point.

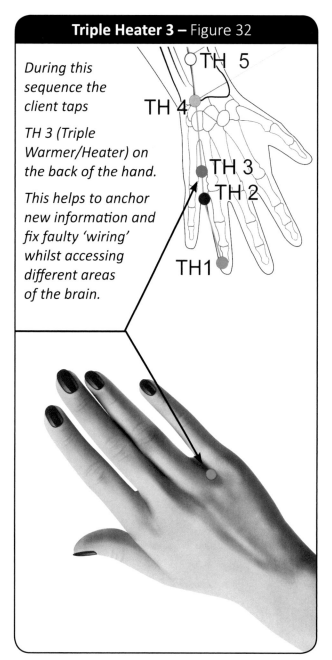

Triple Heater 3 – Figure 32

During this sequence the client taps

TH 3 (Triple Warmer/Heater) on the back of the hand.

This helps to anchor new information and fix faulty 'wiring' whilst accessing different areas of the brain.

TH 5
TH 4
TH 3
TH 2
TH1

Whilst the client is tapping TH 3 throughout **(See Fig. 32)**, ask them to carry out the following:

1. Close Eyes

2. Open Eyes

3. With head straight look down to the left

4. With head straight look down to the right

5. Help the client to rotate their eyes clockwise
    (e.g. hold a pen for them to follow)

6. Client now rotates their eyes anti-clockwise

7. Client hums –so as to focus on the right side of the brain, not a tune, just random notes

8. Client counts – ask them to count quickly or in multiples. This is to focus on the left side of the brain

9. Client hums again

10. Finally, client taps again a few times the meridian previously related to the issue, e.g. St 1.

Emotional Bruising Technique

Emotional Finger Mode

This technique may be indicated when the emotional finger mode shows in relation to an injury or operation site, or when someone has residual pain from an old injury. It signals the brain to diffuse any lingering emotional 'fingerprint' that is still associated with the lesion. Note, this correction is different from Injury Recall Technique (See General Section page 205) which encompasses the effects of physical trauma.

> The injury/lesion will two-point to one, or both of the ESR points on the frontal eminences. ❓
>
> 1. Using an AIM, CL the point of pain (unlock).
>
> 2. With two fingers or a thumb, (neutral touch) contact one ESR point at a time＊. Either one or both of these two neurovascular points will two-point (lock) if this technique is applicable.

> 3. Place your hand about ½"/1cm over the point of pain. With the other hand, very lightly contact the active ESR neurovascular point/s. **(See Fig.33)** ✔
>
> 4. As these points are held, ask your client to recall the event/s where the injury took place and visualise the actual accident, if possible. They can verbalise these events or think of them silently.
>
> 5. Repeat step 1.

Other Considerations

If practical, it can be extremely beneficial for clients to go physically through the motion of how they received the injury whilst the ESR point/s are held. For example, someone who slipped on the ice and hurt their shoulder could literally gently and gradually go through the motion of falling on it. It may be necessary to have another person available to aid the client to 'fall' without hurting themselves while one person holds the point/s.

＊ Previously we have been taught to contact the ESR points together bilaterally. In fact, one NV for the PMC could be in over-energy and the other in under-energy which, if the two points were contacted together would add up to a neutral contact. This means a positive CL would be missed. Therefore, **any time** the ESR protocol is indicated testing the ESR NL points separately would be more accurate. (Deal)

Emotional Bruising Technique Step 3 – Figure 33

With two fingers or a thumb, (neutral touch) contact the ESR point that shows

Place hand 1cm above point of pain

S.T.O. Technique

Emotional Finger Mode

S.T.O stands for Sternocleidomastoid (SCM)/ Trapezius/Occiput. It refers to an area that is bordered by these three anatomy areas the centre of which is the lamina of the 3rd cervical vertebra **(See Fig. 34)**. If this specific area two-points to an area of injury it means that there is an emotional component that may be impeding recovery.

 If the Emotional Finger Mode shows when TLing and injury area, try contacting the ESR points for Emotional Bruising Technique and then the STO mode to see which method is the most beneficial.

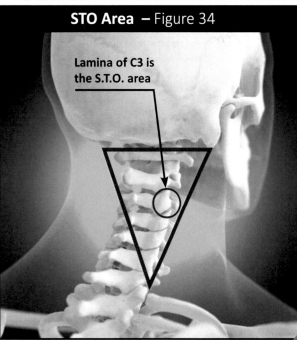

STO Area – Figure 34

Lamina of C3 is the S.T.O. area

When It's Useful

- When your client has had an injury that is not responding to treatment as it should (for example, falling on the ice and hurting a shoulder) yet testing the involved muscles and surrounding tissue does not show any weakness or hypertonicity and the area does not TL even though they are suffering pain. If you ask your client to TL the STO and retest the muscles/point of pain, any hidden lesions related to an emotion connected to that injury will then be revealed.

- It is a powerful technique. Sometimes, when the client has had many procedures and there is still pain, their pain can melt away once this mental connection is made.

- The finger mode can be used to identify if any injury would benefit from carrying out the S.T.O. procedure. The middle finger to the palm.

- When the emotional finger shows in relation to an injury you can then activate the S.T.O mode to identify if this technique is needed.

The client must be able to remember how the injury occurred for this technique to be used.

1. Using an AIM check if the S.T.O. area two-points to the injury site/area of pain as the result of an injury. The S.T.O. area usually relates to the same side as the injury but if it doesn't two point, try the opposite side.

2. Ask your client to touch both the injury area and the S.T.O. area on the same side. They can do this by placing the heel of their hand on the SCM, their palm on the upper trapezius and their little finger and ring finger over the mastoid. If this isn't physically possible it then you can hold the STO area for them. If there is an STO component to the injury – even if the injury doesn't TL – the IM will change.

3. Ask your client to visualise and relate the circumstances of how the injury occurred. If there is a particular part of the event that they can't recall, ask them to describe what they imagine. It is important that they do this in the present tense as if they were actually there. It's quite easy for them to slip back into the past tense, so you may need to assist them with that. An emotional connection is being made with the S.T.O. point when this is happening. Sometimes people can become upset, so be prepared for this.

4. The client finishes by saying, "My........ is fully functional".

5. After you have carried out the protocol there are two possible outcomes:

   a. The lesion no longer TL's.

   OR

   b. Further work on the issue can now be done as the lesion will now TL and related muscle imbalances will now show.

Summary of Addressing Matters of the Mind

- Listen carefully to your client and refrain from making assumptions.

- Ask the client for a SUD scale, 10 being the worst imaginable, 0 being no problem at all. Note it down.

- Check for psychological reversal/conflict first. A good indication that this might be needed is this blanket test. TL'ing the neurolymphatic points for the quadriceps (just below the edge of the ribcage from the xyphoid process to the midline) will unlock an AIM if psychological reversal/conflict is present, even if the quadriceps muscles are strong in the clear.

- Use eye rotations to release old unwanted thought patterns.

- Use temporal tap to anchor positive affirmations.

- Use Emotional Stress Release (Foundation Courses) to diffuse stress around situations/thoughts etc.

- Use 'Dispelling fears and phobias' technique for a wide variety of fears from fear of flying to fear of having no money. If this technique is appropriate, contacting St1 will negate the positive test.

- Flower/gems/homoeopathic remedies can be very effectively used in conjunction with the above techniques. In relation to the problem, remember first to find the remedy that locks the IM again before applying the correction. You can give the remedy simultaneously and/or ask the client to take the remedy for a period of time as a daily treatment to anchor the adjustment.

- After applying the correction, remember to recheck your IM whilst the client says the statement/thinks about the issue. The IM should now remain locked.

- Ask the person for a SUD scale periodically throughout the session to check their progress and write it in your notes.

Spondylogenic Reflex to the Diaphragm

Emotional Finger Mode

This imbalance is caused by emotional trauma, but there are other structural imbalances that might occur simultaneously too.

'Spondylo' means 'vertebra' or 'vertebrae'. Spondylogenic means produced by or caused by vertebrae. The spondylogenic reflex is therefore a neural reflex that stems from the spine.

The stomach, sitting just below the diaphragm, and the diaphragm itself are both seats of emotion. Any emotional trauma takes its toll on this area of the body. Whenever we have felt a 'knot' in the stomach, this neurological response could affect the rest of the body, possibly leaving a 'footprint' that can last for a whole lifetime.

Check for this imbalance in cases of:

Shortness of breath, asthma, fatigue, indigestion, panic attacks, bloating, weak arms, sciatica, loss of flexibility and even pain in the big toe!

Even at birth the spondylogenic reflex can have a lifelong effect on the body. Babies have to rapidly make a transition from getting nutrients and oxygen from the umbilical cord to breathing air into their lungs. The diaphragm suddenly has to rise and fall to pump the lungs and the trauma of this huge shift at birth can sometimes leave a neurological footprint on the body.

The test and correction for this very common reflex problem was discovered by Dr George Goodheart. This technique directs the nervous system to 'let go of', 'dissolve', or wipe away this footprint.

Yardstick Measurements

You might consider taking a few of these 'before and after' yardstick measurements. This will identify whether you have achieved anything after making the correction. You don't have to carry out all of these tests unless you choose to.

a) Measure with a tape how much the rib cage expands when your client inhales.

b) Measure the client's peak expiratory flow rate using a peak flow meter.

c) Look at your client's feet position when they are lying supine. Do the feet invert evenly?

d) Compare the client's leg length whilst they are supine.

e) Check both quadratus lumborum muscles.

f) With client's arms bent at the elbows, abduct their upper arms towards their head. Note and compare sides.

g) Note any restrictions in trunk rotation when they are sitting. Hold your client's shoulders still whilst they move both their legs to either side.

Procedure

1. Test an AIM (a quadriceps or gluteus medius works well here) whilst your client TL's their navel. **(See Fig. 35)** This should not unlock the IM. If it does, a correction is needed before continuing with the test.

2. Test an AIM whilst the client TL's just below the xiphoid process (the pointed end (inferior) of the sternum [breast bone]). This test also should not unlock an IM.

3. Test an AIM whilst the client holds points 1 and 2 simultaneously (two-pointing) – you can see why you need to use a leg or hip muscle as an AIM! If the IM unlocks there is a spondylogenic reflex dysfunction and the correction is called for.

Spondylogenic Reflex Treatment Points
Figure 35

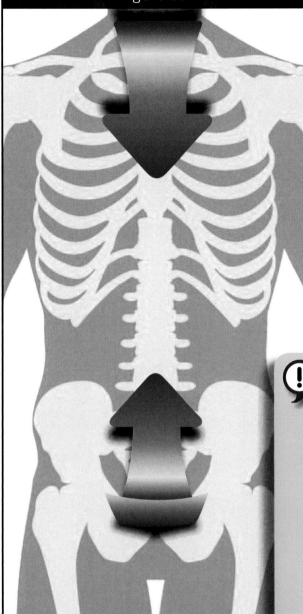

6. Hold these two positions until the tissues soften or you have the sensation of them melting. This may take several minutes. ✓

7. Repeat step 3. The indicator muscle should now be locked in the clear.

8. There may be more work to do, however. To check if the procedure needs repeating, CL the bladder alarm point (CV3). If the IM unlocks, repeat steps 5-7 until CV3 no longer unlocks an IM. This procedure could need repeating a number of times before the reflex is stable.

Imbalances That May Occur Simultaneously

These are separate unrelated findings, but if your client has a positive spondylogenic reflex of the diaphragm, they also may have these problems. (Deal)

Weak Abdominals

The oblique abdominal muscles may be weak. Instead of actually testing the muscle itself you can two-point to the following areas: ?

a. T12 (thoracic vertebra)

and

b. The top (superior) surface of the pubic bone, which is the insertion of the rectus oblique muscles.

! Tip: If you are testing the abdominal muscles and they remain strong in the clear, CL'ing the O & I at the same time may cause them to weaken.

If so, the correction is to tap T7 (thoracic vertebra)

4. If the client is female, stand on her left. If the client is male, stand on his right. ✓

5. Using the fingertips, the practitioner pushes one hand straight down, posteriorly (towards the spine) just below the tip of the xyphoid process. The other hand is pushed down posteriorly into the navel and then vectored up towards the diaphragm. **(See Fig. 35)**

The correction is to firmly rub the adductor muscles from the inferior pubic bone, along the inside of the legs to the knee. These are the neuro-lymphatic points for the abdominal muscles. ✓

Foot Pronation

Take a look at the way your client stands. If the ankle turns inwards but the outside of the heel is worn, go to their big toe (hallux). This tests the big toe's supinator muscle.

1. Ask the client to pull their toe up towards their head whilst you pull downwards (inferiorly). 95% of the time the weakness will be their right foot.

2. To correct this, at the side of the ribcage near the midline, locate the 4th and 6th rib so that rib 5 is in the centre. Place one hand above rib 5 and the other below. Whilst your client inhales, pull the 4th & 6th ribs apart for about 25 seconds.

3. Retest step 1.

Notes

Notes

Biochemical Imbalances and Corrections

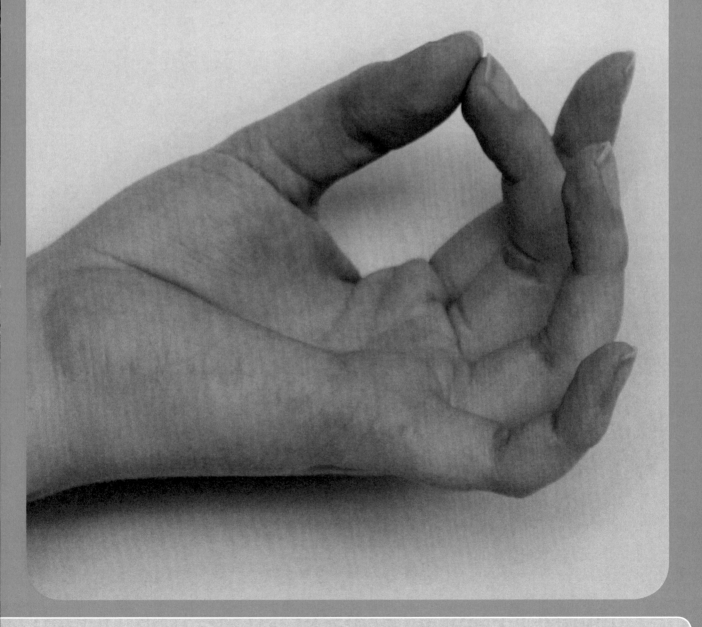

Encompasses allergy or food intolerance, toxicity, microbiome imbalances, body chemical imbalances, nutritional supplementation, homoeopathy, allopathy, nutrition and herbs.

Table of contents

What Does it Mean
When the Biochemical Finger Mode Shows?

Deficiency or Therapeutic Dose?

We tend to think of the biochemical chemical finger mode (thumb pad to pad of middle finger) as pertaining to a vitamin or mineral deficiency. However, the mode has a broader scope. Using MRT, we can discover **deficiencies** via the Ridler's Reflexes or in some cases via weak muscles associated with organs and meridians. **A therapeutic dose** is different. A person may not necessarily be deficient in a nutrient, but the body would really like to utilise more of it to bolster the healing process. For example, it's possible that a person may require quite large doses of B Complex but on checking the Ridler points B deficiency doesn't show. The body will often enjoy the benefits of herbal combinations, but we could hardly say that it is suffering from a deficiency of that herb.

We can use the Biochemical Finger mode to:

1. Identify a biochemical imbalance that the body needs addressing.

2. Identify that the body prefers a biochemical correction.

Some of the areas that are covered under this mode are:

Key Points:

Toxicity – This could include candidiasis, parasite infestation, a toxic bowel, liver overload, or heavy metal toxicity. It may show if the ICV or Houston rings are dysfunctional causing toxicity. (See Toxicity sub-mode)

Allergy – Encompassing a reaction to food or a chemical or airborne substance. (See Allergy sub-mode)

Food intolerance

Nutritional deficiencies or excesses that can then be addressed using food as medicine or taking supplements, therapeutic remedies such as herbs, vitamins, minerals, amino acids, complex homoeopathy

If the biochemical finger mode shows, then employ these additional modes to help you to narrow down your search.

If neither of these modes show in relation to the chemical mode, you may assume that the body is telling you that it needs nutritional supplementation.

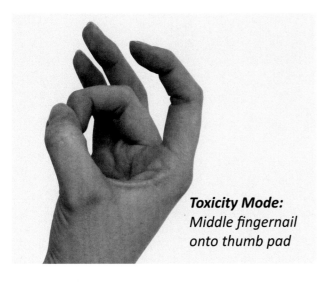

Toxicity Mode:
Middle fingernail onto thumb pad

Allergy Mode:
Lateral edge of finger onto lateral edge of thumb at base of nail.

Why Give Nutrition?

"Why do I have to take nutritional supplements? I have a very good diet", is a frequently asked question.

Answer

Life has become increasingly stressful due to life expectations. This increases the body's need for nutrition to keep up the pace that is expected of the body. It is known that when a person is under stress, they rapidly use up Vitamin C and B vitamins, for example.

Modern food production has depleted food of usable nutrients that they used to contain as well as introducing a wide variety of toxic substances into the food chain.

The body responds to outside factors such as gravity, the electromagnetic force of the earth, electromagnetic smog. The body is itself driven by electricity. Its delicate balance is compensating constantly for external influences. These influences have changed over the last few decades. It has far more to cope with because of man-made alterations to the environment. This takes energy and the body needs raw materials, in the form of nutrients to produce energy. Unfortunately, we often can't eat enough food of good quality to do this effectively.

The body requires more nutrients when it is ill. When using other therapies, e.g. acupuncture or homoeopathy, it still needs raw materials to make new cells and produce energy needed to bring about changes. The body still needs fuel for energy adjustments to cascade down into altering physical function. For a list of nutrients in food **see tables 4 and 5 on pages 64-65**.

Some people cannot get the nutrients out of their food through poor digestion.

> **❝ I believe that nutrition facilitates quicker recovery in most cases. People feel better quickly and stay better. Supporting the body through nutrition, whatever their problem, will help the treatment to hold. ❞**

Nutritional Rewarding

You will notice that in other sections, such as the Endocrine System (See page 216), that often, nutritional assist is listed. Whatever procedures you may carry out, support it with nutritional assist wherever possible even if the biochemical finger mode does not show. Your results will be far quicker, superior and longer lasting.

Reflect on how you feel about giving clients supplements. It's easy to make assumptions about your client and decide for them whether they will want to afford it. Your client has come to you because they want to get well. Trust that they want you to do the best for them. Your results will be spectacular, and people will recommend you because you got them well so quickly, so they can be very cost effective!! (A nutrition course will offer you detailed guidance). If you're a little shy about asking for money, make it clear, in the information pack that you give to new client, that supplements may be involved. Then there are nasty surprises and the client knows what to expect. I give my clients a rough guide of what to expect e.g. supplements may cost around the price of a cup of coffee a day.

The key to being confident in using nutrition

Learn about products available on the market. Read the catalogues of the companies that you have chosen to deal with. Many companies provide informative days from which you can learn a lot very cheaply.

If you haven't already undertaken a nutrition course, I strongly advise it as an important addition to your skills. This will give you confidence in safely prescribing vitamins, minerals and essential fatty acids. It will also give you a good background in giving dietary advice.

Before giving supplements/herbs check for any contraindications with any medication that your client is taking. For example, some vitamins and herbs are very good at making the blood less sticky. These might be a problem if the client is taking anticoagulant drugs. See Alan Gaby's A-Z Guide to Drug-Herb-Vitamin Interactions (2006).

Pregnant and breastfeeding women need nutritional support. However again use caution, particularly with herbs.

There are other kinesiology courses that will help you to become confident in using nutrition and herbs and give you additional skills that once acquired, you will wonder how you managed without them!

Some examples of these courses are:

- Polarity Reflex Analysis Nutritional Assessment (PRANA)
- Everything You Ever Wanted to Know About Test Vials
- Lyme Protocols for the Kinesiologist

www.postgraduatekinesiology.com

Using Test Vials

I'm a big test vial user and this is something to explore in addition to the skills you'll learn from this book. Not only do they give the practitioner a wealth of information that would otherwise be difficult to find out, they are a great way of double-checking your results. Test vials can be used to identify the best kind of nutrition to give a client, but they can also be placed on the body and, if there is an imbalance, one can go through the key finger modes and carry out any appropriate kinesiology treatment.

There is a tendency to get lazy though and the balance of your sessions could be skewed towards test vials and nutrition. Remember that the beauty of the techniques discussed in this book is that you can provide a truly naturopathic approach, addressing all aspects of health!

Vitamins in Foods – Table 4

A	-Milk, eggs, butter, yellow fruits & vegetables, dark green fruits & vegetables, liver
C	-Citrus, cabbage family, chilli peppers, berries, melons, asparagus, rosehips
D	-Salmon, sardines, herring, milk, egg yolk, organ meats, sprouted seeds, sunflower seeds
E	-Cold-pressed oils, eggs, wheatgerm, organ meats, molasses, sweet potatoes, nuts
F	-Vegetable oils, butter, sunflower seeds
K	-Green leafy vegetables, egg yolks, safflower oil, blackstrap molasses, cauliflower
Q	-Pinto beans, legumes, soybeans
T	-Sesame seeds, raw seeds, butter, egg yolk
U	-Raw cabbage, sauerkraut, leafy vegetables
B-1	Thiamine - Brewer's yeast, whole grains, blackstrap molasses, brown rice, organ meats, egg yolk
B-2	Riboflavin - Brewer's yeast, whole grains, legumes, nuts, organ meats, blackstrap molasses
B-3	Niacin - Lean meats, poultry & fish, brewer's yeast, peanuts, milk, rice, potatoes
B-4	Choline - Egg yolks, organ meats, brewer's yeast, wheatgerm, soybeans, fish, legumes
B-5	Pantothenic Acid - Organ meats, egg yolks, legumes, whole grains, wheatgerm, salmon, brewer's yeast
B-6	Pyridoxine - Meats, whole grains, organ meats, brewer's yeast, molasses, wheatgerm
B-7	Biotin - Egg yolks, liver, unpolished rice, brewer's yeast, sardines, legumes, wholegrains
B-8	Inositol - wholegrains, citrus fruits, molasses, meat, milk, nuts, vegetables, brewer's yeast
B-9	Folic Acid - Dark green leafy vegetables, organ meats, root vegetables, oysters, salmon, milk
B-12	-Organ meats, fish, pork, eggs, cheese, milk, lamb, bananas, kelp, peanuts
B-13	Orotic acid - Liquid whey, beets, carrots, celery root, garlic, horseradish, onion, potatoes, radish, sweet potato, turnip, yam, parsnips
B-15	Pangamic Acid - Brewer's yeast, rare steaks, brown rice, sunflower, pumpkin & sesame seeds
B-17	Laetrile - Apple seeds, grape seeds, beans, lentils, legumes, nuts, seeds
PABA	Para-amino butyric acid - Organ meats, wheatgerm, yoghurt, molasses, green leafy vegetables
P	Bioflavonoids - Citrus fruits, blackcurrants, buckwheat

Minerals in Foods – Table 5

Arsenic	- Asparagus, celery, quail, salmon
Bromine	- Melons, cucumber, alfalfa, turnips, seafoods
Calcium	- Raw egg yolk, shellfish, milk, cheese, greens, apricots, figs, cabbage, bran
Chlorine	- Goat & cow milk, salt, fish, cheese, coconut, beets, radishes, avocado, kelp
Chromium	- Corn oil, clams, wholegrain cereals, brewer's yeast
Cobalt	- Organ meats, oysters, clams, poultry, milk, green leafy veg, fruit
Copper	- Organ meats, seafood, nuts, legumes, molasses, raisins, wholegrain cereals
Fluorine	- Cauliflower, cabbage, cheese, raw goats' milk, raw egg yolk, Brussels sprouts
Fluoride	- Tea, seafood, fluoridated water
Iodine	- Sea lettuce, kelp, seafood, carrots, pears, onions, tomatoes, pineapple
Iron	- Organ meats, eggs, fish, poultry, molasses, apricots, potato peelings
Magnesium	- Nuts, figs, green vegetables, seafood, molasses, yellow corn, coconut, apples
Manganese	- Beets, peas, citrus, bran, green vegetables, kelp, egg yolk, nuts, pineapple
Molybdenum	- Legumes, wholegrain cereals, milk, liver, dark green vegetables
Nickel	- All vegetables
Phosphorus	- Milk, cheese, meat, fish, fowl, grains, nuts, egg yolk, beans,　lentil　peas
Potassium	- Lean meats, dried fruits, legumes, vegetables, cereals, nuts, seeds
Selenium	- Tuna, herring, brewer's yeast, wheatgerm & bran, broccoli, wholegrains
Silicon	- Apples, kelp, grapes, beets, onions, almonds, seeds, parsnips, grains, tomatoes
Sodium	- Watermelon, romaine, celery, kelp, asparagus, okra, carrots, coconut
Sulphur	- Eggs, meat, fish, cabbage, Brussels sprouts, horseradish, shrimp, chestnuts
Tin	- Plants & animals
Zinc	- Sunflower seeds, seafood, organ meats, mushrooms, Soybeans, brewer's yeast

Ridler's Reflexes

Biochemical Finger Mode
(See Figures 36 & 37 and Table 6)

These reflexes show the deficiency or excess of vitamins and minerals in the **tissues**. (Testing an individual muscle for a nutritional deficiency e.g. Psoas for Vit A, indicates a **blood** deficit) (Deal)).

> ***To test for deficiencies:*** The **tester** uses an AIM and tests each point individually with two fingers (neutral), looking for a change in the indicator muscle.
>
> ***To test for excesses:*** The **client** double TLs the point i.e. touches the point with 2 fingers of both hands. Use a quadriceps or leg muscle for this, again you're looking for a change, indicating an excess of that substance in the tissues.

Find appropriate supplement

> 1. Either continue to hold the Ridler's point or enter into pause lock.
>
> 2. Place the appropriate supplement on the body will change the IM. (remember different brands may yield different results)
>
> 3. Check that it is a priority or modality. This will change the IM again.
>
> 4. After removing priority or modality mode, check that the supplement will raise vital force (the ubiquitous 'OK' sign – the tip of thumb and tip of index finger placed like a ring with the other straight 3 fingers placed in a fan shape, **See page xviii on Fundementals**). If it does, it will change the IM. This means that the supplement is unlikely to cause an intolerance.

To find dosage: When the appropriate nutrition is placed on the body. The muscle will usually show as **locked** (assuming you are not stacking). Place the tablets on the navel one at a time. The optimum dose is reached when the muscle **unlocks** again. Before cancelling pause lock, tap the glabella (just between the eyebrows) 3-4 times to 'key in' the supplement into the circuit. When recommending supplements always check that they are a priority and raise vital force.

Alternatively, a verbal challenge may be used. With the nutrition on the body, count the number of capsules/drops to be taken in 24 hours. The muscle will **unlock** when you arrive at the correct dose.

Additional Ridler's Reflexes That do not Appear on the Chart

- *Rancid Fats -* Place the back of your hand under the chin. If there is a change of indicator, there is a need for antioxidant vitamins and minerals (Vit A, E, C, selenium, and possibly digestive enzymes). (Deal)

- *Folic acid deficiency -* Use a quadriceps or hip/leg muscle as an AIM. Client places either right hand on right side of the torso or left hand on left side of torso with the other hand placed on top of it. Avoid the ICV and navel area. If indicator changes, there is a need for folic acid. (Deal)

> ❝ *A note to those of you who are not yet trained in nutrition; even if the dose tests out as being higher, please do not give your client any more than the maximum amount indicated by the supplement manufacturer.* ❞

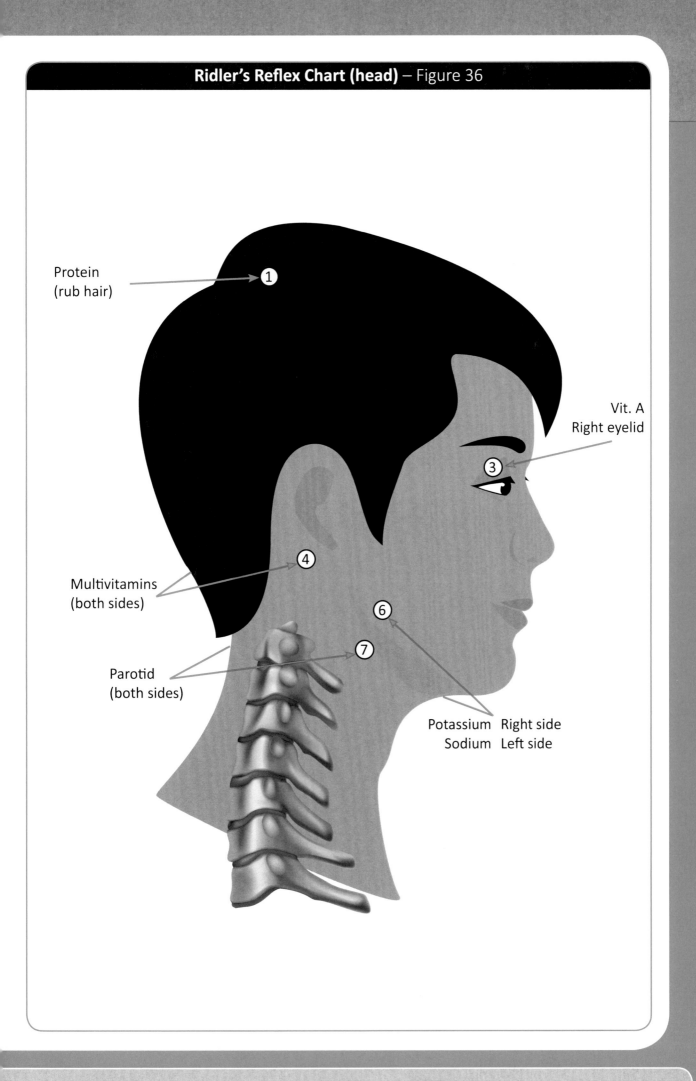

Ridler's Reflex Chart (head) – Figure 36

Protein
(rub hair)

①

Vit. A
Right eyelid

③

Multivitamins
(both sides)

④

⑥

Parotid
(both sides)

⑦

Potassium   Right side
Sodium   Left side

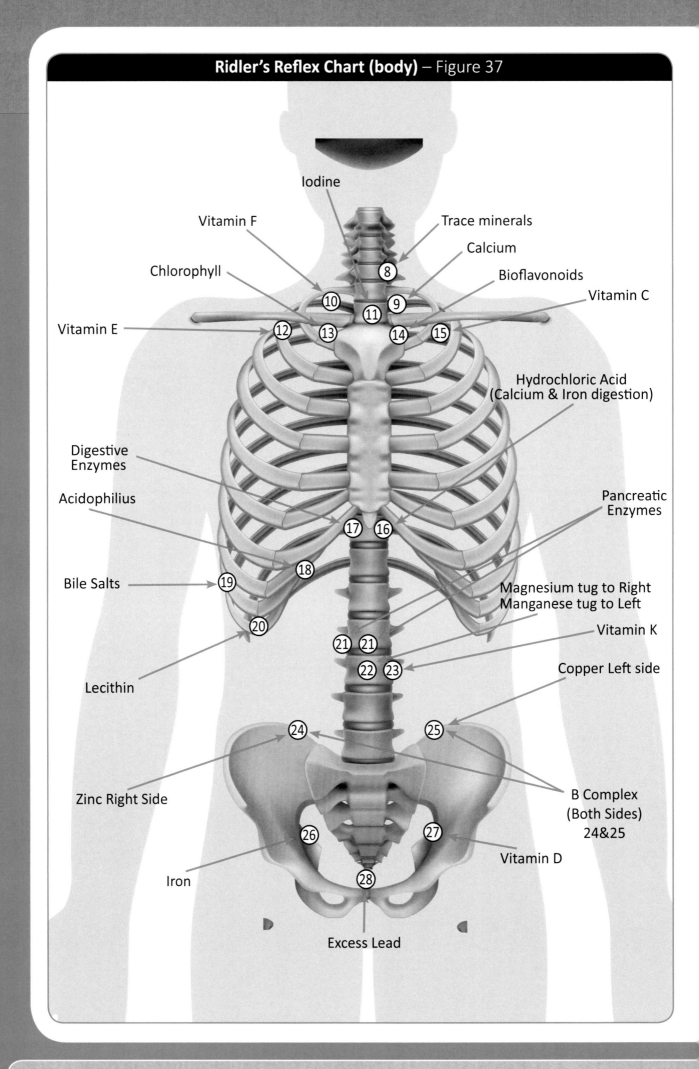

Ridler's Reflex Chart (body) – Figure 37

Iodine

Vitamin F

Chlorophyll

Vitamin E

Trace minerals

Calcium

Bioflavonoids

Vitamin C

Hydrochloric Acid
(Calcium & Iron digestion)

Digestive
Enzymes

Acidophilius

Pancreatic
Enzymes

Bile Salts

Magnesium tug to Right
Manganese tug to Left

Vitamin K

Lecithin

Copper Left side

Zinc Right Side

B Complex
(Both Sides)
24&25

Iron

Vitamin D

Excess Lead

8 10 9 11 12 13 14 15 17 16 18 19 20 21 21 22 23 24 25 26 27 28

Tester challenges with **ONE HAND to find deficiencies** Client TL's with **BOTH HANDS to find excesses**

Substance	Point	Location
Vitamin A	3	Right eye only - light pressure on lid
B Complex	24/25	½ way between navel & iliac crest Hold both sides at same time
Individual B's	5	Client holds one finger on end of tongue
B6	5/6	One finger on tongue & one on jaw
Vitamin C	15	Below left clavicle - 1½" from sternum
Vitamin D	27	Left side - ½ way between pubes & iliac Crest
Vitamin E	12	Below right clavicle - 1½" from sternum
Vitamin F	10	Above right clavicle - ½" from sternal notch
Vitamin K	23	½" to left of navel
Multi - Vitamins	4	Under each ear at the same time
Bioflavonoids	14	Below left clavicle - ½" from sternum (e.g. Rutin,& Hesperidin)
Calcium	9	Above left clavicle - ½" from sternum
Chlorophyll	13	Below right clavicle - ½" lateral of sternum
Copper	25	Left side - ½ way between hip and navel
Iodine	11	Sternal notch
Iron	26	Right side - ½ way between pubis & iliac crest
Lead	28	Centre of pubis – Double TL
Lecithin	20	2-2½" right of midline at level of lowest rib
Magnesium	22	Navel - tug to the right
Manganese	22	Navel - tug to the left
Potassium	6	Right side of jaw - masseter muscle
Protein	1	Hair - protein assimilation. See also HCl
Sodium	6	Left side of jaw on masseter muscle
Trace Minerals	8	Left side of neck 1" above sternum
Zinc	24	Right side - ½ way between hip & navel
Acidophilus Bacillus	18	Right side - between base of sternum & outer. Tip of rib cage
Bile Salts	19	Right side - outer tip at bottom of rib cage
Enzymatic	17	Right side at base of sternum (Veg protein digestion)
HCL	16	Left side at base of sternum (Protein, Calcium & Iron digestion)
Pancreatic Digestion (lipase)	21	1" above navel & 1" right of that
Parotid	7	Right & Left sub maxillary gland under jaw

Location Chart of Ridler's Reflexes – Table 6

Digestive Insufficiency

Biochemical Finger Mode

 For an in-depth presentation on how to use test vials for this problem, learn more in the course 'Everything You Ever Wanted to Know about Test Vials'. www.postgraduatekinesiology.com.

Insufficient hydrochloric acid (HCl) is common in modern cultures with the advent of ubiquitous preservatives in food, making the body have to work harder to digest them; use of antacids, and higher stress levels impair digestion.

If the pH is incorrect in the stomach, it affects the pH throughout the digestive tract, giving rise to ideal conditions for candida and parasites to flourish in the gut. The outcome of hypochlorhydria (lack of stomach acid) is early-stage malfunction in protein breakdown and insufficient acid to trigger the production of the more alkaline pancreatic enzymes to continue the digestive process.

> **❛❛ Pancreatic enzyme insufficiency prevents adequate breakdown of proteins, fats and carbohydrates into amino acids, essential fatty acids and simple sugars respectively. When the stomach and pancreatic enzymes are insufficient, nutritional insufficiency is very common. ❜❜**

Why is Low HCL so Common?

HCl and digestive enzymes reduce as a consequence of getting older, so, supplementing these for the elderly will help digestion and food assimilation.

Constant stress will also reduce digestive performance. After all, it makes sense that if we are in the unfortunate position of being chased by a lion after we've just had our breakfast, getting away from the lion is going to take priority over our body excreting enzymes to digest our egg and bacon! The increased blood flow around the digestive system will be diverted to our muscles and brain so we can get away. That's why when under constant low-level stress our whole digestive system can be impaired, from our stomach to our bowels, because the body thinks the blood and nerve signalling is better utilized elsewhere.

I remember a case of mine some years ago. A woman came to me with severe problems digesting food. She would vomit after every meal. She was emaciated, very tired and very sick. She had, of course, previously visited her GP and had numerous tests which all proved negative. Her friends thought that she was bulimic. This lady had 6 children with ages ranging from teenager to baby. Can you imagine what mealtimes were like for her? Pandemonium I expect! She came to me to check for any food intolerances. There were one or two, however it was apparent to me that she needed to eat in peace at mealtimes, out of the constant stress, so that the blood and nervous system could 'concentrate' on the job in hand. To allow digestion to take place she was advised to take her meal into another room and do some deep breathing, then eat slowly, chewing her food well. She followed that advice and made a full recovery. Clearly her poor body was so busy adapting to the stress of bickering family at the table, plus seeing to everyone else's needs before her own, digestion was taking second, or even third place. She was also given some digestive enzymes to help along the way.

Some Symptoms of Hypochlorhydria

Food Intolerances	Protein deficiency
Discomfort after eating	Possibly candida/or parasites
Small Intestine Bacterial Overgrowth	Beneficial Bacteria Deficiency

Tests for Digestive Insufficiency

1. Test Ridler's Reflexes for HCL deficiency and digestive enzyme deficiency **(see Ridler's chart, Figure 37 on page 68)***

2. If IM unlocks check for priority/modality. The muscle will lock.

3. For low HCL, use Betaine HCL, available from some suppliers. For digestive enzyme deficiency, test brands of digestive enzymes available to you.

   Note: A bilaterally weak pectoralis major clavicular, tested at the same time, indicates low stomach HCl. Correcting this with spinal reflexes and neurolymphatics will help HCl production. (Thie)

   *To check for excess, the IM will unlock when the client double TLs the Ridler's point for HCl

Dose test, but bear in mind the following principles:

Important – if the client has allergies and food intolerances, ask them to gradually increase the dose during each meal until they experience mild indigestion. The dose per meal is one less than the dose causing indigestion.

If they have indigestion after food, ask them to increase the dosage with food, until indigestion stops. As time goes by, the need for HCl should decrease as the stomach learns the new 'regime'.

Digestive enzymes are not acid forming and can usually be used to address the Ridler's reflex. If unsure, check with your supplier.

Important Note

Even if people need HCl, do not give it if they have:

- Intestinal bleeding
- Ulcerative Colitis
- Oesophageal reflux
- Chrohn's Disease
- Stomach ulcers
- If someone feels "better for eating"

Other supplements that may assist production of HCL at the right time, and you can use them safely with the above conditions, are:

Slippery Elm	Zinc 20-30mg daily
Aloe Vera juice	Vitamin C 500mg 3 x daily
Vitamin A	Fresh Cabbage Juice
Flavonoids	Digestive herbal combinations
Papaya	B Complex

Supplements that help with HCl production will negate the positive reflex for low HCl. To anchor the connection, you can rub the NL and NVs for the pectoralis major clavicular whilst the supplement is still on the body so that the brain makes the connection between the stomach and the supplements.

See **Table 7 overleaf** for the list of consequences of impaired digestion.

Some Consequences of Impaired Digestion – Table 7	
Malabsorption of Nutrients	Intestinal Permeability
Weak and cracked fingernails	Inflammatory Bowel Disease
Food Intolerances	Chronic Nutritional Deficiencies
Immune Deficiencies	Candida & Parasites
Auto-Immune Disease	Arthritis
Acne	Acne Rosacea
Anal itching	Halitosis (bad breath)
Osteoporosis	Indigestion

For Most Health Complaints, Start with Digestive Impairment

Correct digestive function, hypochlorhydria, digestive enzyme deficiency:

- Hiatal hernia
- Digestive Enzymes
- Determine food sensitivities
- Reverse nutritional deficiencies
- Support liver function
- Cleanse colon
- Supplement with probiotics and Aloe Vera
- Support immune system
- Correct electrical & structural problems:
- Dural Torque
- Atlas
- Blood Chemistry
- Retrograde Lymphatics

Correct endocrine imbalances:

- Endocrine glands (See page 214)
- Adrenal stress syndrome (See page 215)
- Hypoglycaemia (See page 111)
- Digestive valve dysfunction (See pages 118-134)
- Support integrity of intestinal mucosa (See page 101)
- Deal specifically with Candida Albicans, parasites etc. where present (See pages 97 & 106)
- Address any emotional problems and stresses in lifestyle
- Recommend a healthy eating plan, high in alkaline - forming foods (vegetables, fruit)

> **If the client reports blood in the stool, or abnormal colour of stool, refer them immediately to their doctor.**

Allergies

Biochemical Finger Mode, Allergy Mode

"Over a lifetime a person can consume over 25 tons of food. The body has a protective mechanism as part of our defence system to prevent external organisms and toxins that accompany it" (Institute of Functional Medicine, 2005) We are exposed to myriads of substances, both beneficial and detrimental when we breathe air, lie in our beds, come into contact with carpets and chemicals, eat a meal, take a shower, clean our teeth, etc.... If our body is to function well from our environment it must determine what is good and what isn't. So, it's essential that the body can correctly identify and process substances that enter the body. Allergy can be described as an adverse hypersensitivity response to a substance.

There are many food reactions that are not directly linked with the immune system, such as lactose intolerance, gluten intolerance, sulphite sensitivity etc. As MRT testers we find these intolerances all the time. Here we're discussing allergies that are immunoglobulin E (IgE) dependant. Immunoglobulins are antibodies produced by the immune system. Their purpose is to protect the body from invading organisms, which they do by binding to specific molecule(antigen) on each 'invader' and then binding to specific cells in the body to trigger the appropriate immune response to remove the invader from the body. In the case of IgE, the immunoglobulin binds to mast cells, triggering the release of chemicals that create inflammation. IgE is mainly produced in the lungs, skin and mucous membranes. The action of IgE causes an acute onset of symptoms. Examples of these are urticaria, asthma, hay fever, rhinitis (inflamed lining in the nose) and in severe cases anaphylaxis, palpitations or severe headache. Each type of IgE has specific affinity for each type of allergen (substance that produces the allergic response). That's why some people are only allergic to cat dander (they only have the IgE antibodies specific to cat dander) while others have allergic reactions to multiple allergens because they have many more types of IgE antibodies.

Let's just keep in mind that an appropriate immune response can be a good thing, which in the short term may save us from death!

Histamine is secreted from specific white blood cells (basophils) and mast cells near a site that has been irritated. Histamine is the culprit that aggravates the nerve endings and causes itching at the site. Histamine increases the permeability of the cell walls of blood capillaries so that it makes it easier for the white blood cells to move into the affected tissue and deal with the perceived invader but also allows fluid to escape which in turn gives us the classic symptoms of runny nose and watery eyes. Antihistamines are given to prevent the histamine reacting in this way thereby giving the person relief.

I don't want to give you the impression that histamine is a bad thing! It has numerous other positive functions in the body. That's why taking antihistamines have side effects!

In summary, allergies are inappropriate responses to substances that should be harmless, due to the action of IgE antibodies against those substances.

What Causes This Inappropriate Response?

 We have a hollow tube inside us, right from mouth to anus. This tube has an 'inside skin' – a barrier in our intestinal wall that is designed to not only allow beneficial substances through it but keep detrimental ones out. A major portion of our immune system surrounds our gut in the form of gut associated lymphoid tissue (GALT). This makes sense because if the intestines were ever penetrated, or compromised, the body would be flooded with all sorts of nasty toxins and we wouldn't last long! In this internal skin, there is an army of white blood corpuscles. This is worth researching further. If the gut wall is compromised and becomes leaky, as well as allowing beneficial substances in, it will also allow undigested food, chemicals, parasites, fungi etc to get through this barrier.

The 'army' reacts to these foreign substances and produce antibodies to try to protect the body against what it perceives to be bad. Sometimes it can become so over-sensitive, because it's on red alert, that it reacts to substances that are harmless to the body and an IgE response ensues. From this understanding it makes sense that the first line of defence against allergies – of any kind- is to heal a leaky gut and identify what's making it leaky in the first place. See also page 101.

Is that IT Then?

Sometimes people grow out of allergies that occur in childhood, but then they reappear in later life. Clients who present with severe hay fever have reported that the symptoms have diminished altogether over a couple of years. One could argue that some seasons are worse than others but there does seem to be a definite trend of improvement. The key is not only getting the brain to be less reactive to the substance (using the 30 second allergy balance), but also:

a. Removing food intolerances from the diet at least 6 weeks before the hay fever season.

b. Addressing low blood sugar which is a major causal factor in allergies. (See page 111)

c. Ensuring that the client's bowels are working well. Check for and deal with gut issues such as candida and parasites, beneficial bacteria deficiency and leaky gut (test vials work best for this).

d. Carrying out any balances that the body requires.

e. Using the 30 second allergy balance, is best carried out after a., b. and c. are in place.

Case Study

A few years ago, a young client presented with a severe egg allergy. Her mother was concerned that she might be inadvertently exposed to egg despite measures to eliminate it from school meals etc. Her diet was very limited because she was a fussy eater. The way forward was not to step in and carry out anti-allergy balances; the first thing to sort out was her eating and improve her gut health. She tested as having a candida and gut parasite issue. After these were addressed and her general health and diet had improved, we finally did some work on her allergy. It was decided that it would be unwise to place even a test vial containing the frequency of egg into her mouth so the vial was placed on the body and using finger modes, the realms of stress were stacked **(see page xxvi)** and the appropriate protocols administered.

To find the right treatment for the allergy, you can place the vial/substance on the body and using finger modes, stack the stresses and find and administer the correction.

After a few sessions the mother wanted to try her with egg, Epi-Pen at the ready. As a practitioner I could not take responsibility for this, however the mother was willing to be accountable. She first tried egg white and there was no reaction. After a few weeks they tried the whole egg and still no reaction. The little girl's mother was advised to still be cautious, and if her daughter became 'under the weather' or ill, eggs should be avoided during this time.

30 Second Allergy Balance

Biochemical Finger Mode

This test applies to food allergies, airborne allergens such as pollens and moulds, dust mite allergies, metal allergies and chemical allergies.

This balance works by resetting the neurological 'switches' that alert the body to react to a potential allergy. It's done, through emphasising eye movements, by drawing the brain's attention to the allergen whilst simultaneously placing a neutralising substance in the mouth – one of the body's special senses. This signals the hypothalamus that it is genuinely a safe substance.

If the allergen you're testing is severe, it will unlock an AIM without the mode described below. The mode will identify more subtle allergies.

1. Test the atlas **(page 137)** and if out of balance, correct it first.

2. Whilst the client touches one side of the transverse process of the atlas, place the substance on the navel. If the AIM unlocks, the substance is an allergen, **not** an intolerance, and this procedure is appropriate.

3. Client contacts one side of the atlas with two fingers whilst the substance is on navel. The indicator muscle should be **unlocked**. At this point, supporting nutrition can be checked and dose tested. E.g. homoeopathic allersodes, zinc, quercetin, vitamin C, nettle leaf tincture, butterbur tincture, fenugreek, proprietary brand supplements. These should negate the unlocked IM. You can check if highly effective etc. These are ongoing support after the treatment has been done.

4. Remove the helpful nutrition from the body.

5. With client still contacting atlas and the substance on the navel, determine which eye position negates the unlocked indicator muscle. Putting the eyes into distortion accesses different areas of the brain (NLP). Ask them to look up to the left (this is the most common position to correct), up to the right, down to the left and down to the right. If none of these change the indicator to locked, ask them to look straight to the left, right, up and down. At least one of these positions should lock the indicator muscle. If there is more than one, prioritise.

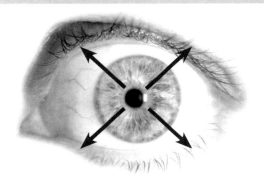

6. Place the allergen or test vial of allergen into a small sealed plastic bag together with a natural antihistamine supplement such as Quercetin Plus from Biocare. You can also use an over-the-counter synthetic antihistamine for this purpose. Place the substances in the bag between the lips.* The client does not swallow the antihistamine, it is just for brain signalling purposes.

7. Ask your client to close their eyes but look straight ahead. Do check that they do not have any eye problems or that they are not wearing contact lenses.

8. With your thumbs, gently but firmly push both eyeballs in the direction of correction as found in step **5**. Do this at the rate of about twice per second. Continue for 30 seconds.

9. Remove the plastic bag and its contents from between the lips.

10. Retest substance as described in step. **2.**

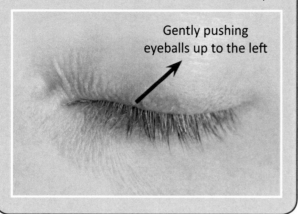

Gently pushing eyeballs up to the left

If the substance/test vial is likely to cause an anaphylactic reaction, do not place in the mouth.

Ask the person to avoid the allergen as much as possible over the following few days. Give them the nutritional support that you determined during the test.

Memory Aid

1. **Test for allergen**

2. **Find nutrition and remove from body**

3. **Find eye position that negates test**

4. **With allergen and capsule between the lips, exaggerate eye position determined in step 5.**

5. **Remove substances from between the lips**

6. **Retest as in step 2.**

Cross Crawling with the Offending Food in the Mouth

> This works well if a food cannot be avoided or has been eaten inadvertently. This protocol may not be as thorough as some other techniques but can be done without equipment and in an emergency. ✔

1. Place the allergic substance in the mouth.

2. Place both hands over the navel and cross crawl. ✔

Spinning Down an Allergic Substance Using a Laser Pointer

This technique is quick to do and works very well for both foods or other substances that a client might be allergic to such as metals, nylon in clothes, metal or plastics in spectacles etc. If it is food, this technique will only work for the food that is treated. Dr Deal talks about clients bringing their food shopping into the clinic every week to be treated with the laser. However, if it is an item such as spectacles, the battery in a watch, a piece of jewellery or an item of clothing (a client of mine would bring in her tights to be treated and this stopped an allergic reaction occurring), the treatment of the substance lasts for the life of the item that has been treated.

Fritz Albert Popp, a scientific researcher into biophotons, was able to measure the very weak frequency emitting from the body. This can vary from 380-780 nanometres depending on the part of the body being measured. The skin emits a general frequency that is similar to a red/orange laser (a red/orange laser measuring 635nm is used for treating acupuncture points). The laser light bombards the substance with photons that resonate at the frequency of the skin, 'tuning' the substance to the individual's body. A red laser pointer, found in many outlets, emits a frequency of 650-660 nm and this seems to still be effective.

1. Place the allergen on your client's navel. It is important that the substance is in contact with the client, but it can be placed over clothes. ✔

2. Shine the laser over the allergen, circling it in an anticlockwise direction.

Psychological Reversal and Food Intolerances

There may be times when a client knows that they have an intolerance, but it does not show up in your testing. Roger Callahan was aware of this and realised that foods could cause a psychological reversal to occur (see page 41).

Callahan had a client who was always very sick when she ate cherries. It puzzled him that whenever he tested her with cherries, her IM always remained locked. He then found that the client became psychologically reversed when she had the cherries in her mouth and this masked the test.

This technique will reveal hidden allergies.

1. Test for psychological reversal in the clear first. A quick way is to ask the client to say, 'I love myself'. If the IM unlocks when this statement is made, correct the psychological reversal by tapping SI3 whilst the client says the phrase. (**See Page 41**)

2. Once the baseline psychological reversal is cleared, place the allergen on the client's navel and repeat step 1. If psychological reversal now shows when the food is placed on the navel, then not only is the hidden food discovered, but eating the food can actually induce psychological reversal. (Callahan)

3. With the food still placed on the navel, repeat step 1. The food should now show as an allergy in the clear.

High Gain Technique to Reveal Allergies and Food Intolerances

Putting the neck into extension simulates the activation of a primitive reflex (Landau), which, coupled with a stressor, will create more strain on the system. This can be useful to a kinesiologist when tests don't show in the clear. When your client adopts this position, it should not cause an AIM to unlock. If it does, check and correct their atlas and neck muscles.

This high gain technique can be used to reveal any hidden imbalances

1. Ask the client to tilt their head backwards and test an AIM. The IM should not unlock.

2. Place the suspected substance on the body. If the IM does not unlock, ask your client to tilt back their head and retest. If the substance is an allergen or intolerance, the muscle test will reveal any hidden issues.

❝ To save time you can put the head placed back in extension into circuit retaining mode before testing foods! ❞

Use the Alarm Points to Identify Organs/Systems that Need Nutritional Support

We have discussed how the alarm points tell us about organ dysfunction. If the ***nutritional finger mode*** is employed whilst testing the alarm points, the body will only show which organs/systems need nutritional support.

For alarm points chart see section on Electromagnetic Corrections on pages 18-19 Figs 12 & 13.

Using an AIM, find the lesion and enter into pause lock. The IM will now be unlocked.

1. Activate each of the 4 finger modes. The nutritional finger mode shows (locks the IM).

2. Add the nutritional finger mode to the circuit (lock)

3. Touch each of the alarm points. The alarm point e.g. for circulation sex / pericardium meridian unlocks the IM.

4. Add the active alarm point in the circuit (unlock).

Try this as an experiment – test all the alarm points in the clear. This will give you a 'readout' of the energetic (electrical) state of the meridians.

Now enter into the circuit, or hold, the ***nutritional finger mode*** and test the alarm points again.

Now do the same thing but instead enter the ***emotional mode*** or the ***structural mode***

What did you note?

5. Find the nutrition that is associated with the meridian. In this example it could be vitamin E, vitamin B complex, herbs or nutritional support designed for hormonal issues (your client's case history will probably give you a clue) for either females or males. For some ideas, see charts **Table 8**. A suitable nutritional remedy will lock the IM.

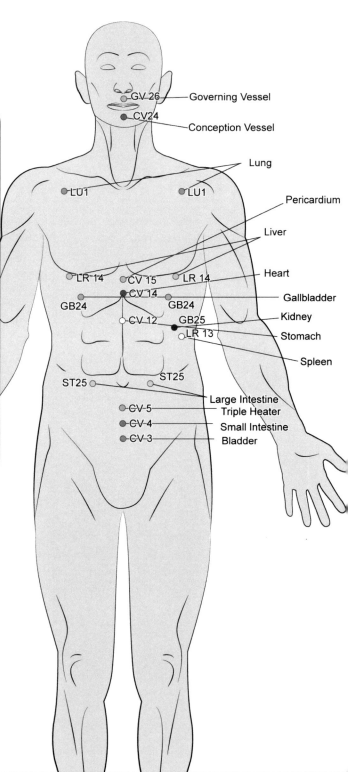

Table of Suggestions for Biogenic Support for Meridians – Table 8

The remedies mentioned here are a sample of the nutrients/herbal combinations that can be used. They are not a complete list! Contact suppliers for help in learning about the many remedies available and you'll feel more confident when you enrol on a nutrition module. For dosing, unless you are trained in nutrition or herbs do not exceed the manufacturer's recommendations.

Alarm Point	Nutrition	Comments
Central Meridian/brain Midline CV24 bottom lip	B complex Fish oils, Gingko Biloba extract, L glutamine, Folates, B12, CoQ10, Ashwagandha	Memory loss/dementia
	5 HTP, Vitamin D, L Glutamine Magnesium,	Depression
	B Complex NADH, Magnesium,	Anxious/stressed
	Eskimo 3, Co Q10, Gingko Biloba	Learning difficulties/memory
Governing Meridian Midline top lip	Amino Acids, protein	Rich in protein and nutrients
Circulation Sex/Pericardium **Midline on the sternum between the 4th & 5th ribs (between the nipples)**	Female glandular support remedies	Glandular support
	Blackcurrant seed oil, calcium D-glucarate, DIM, indole-3-carbinol	Perimenopause and menopause/symptoms
	Star flower oil (borage seed oil), Prostate phytonutrition	Male
	Omega 3 oils, Gingko biloba extract, Zinc, hawthorn	Circulation
	Magnesium glycinate, B complex, B12 Folate,	PMS symptoms
Heart **Midline just below xyphoid process**	Vit E, Fish Oils, Gingko Biloba, L Carnitine, Magnesium, D3, B complex, Hawthorn, coQ10	Family history of heart disease, circulatory disorders
Stomach **Midline halfway between the heart alarm point and the navel**	Piridoxal-5 Phosphate, Zinc, Digestive enzymes, HCl	Ensures good digestion
	B complex, Magnesium Glycinate, Bicarbonate remedies	B vitamins helps digestion and digestive juices, anxiety affects digestion
Triple Heater/Warmer (thyroid) **Midline, 1/3 of a distance between the navel and pubic bone**	Magnesium Glycinate, B complex, Iodine, Thyroid remedies	Thyroid support
Triple Heater/ Warmer(adrenals)	B Complex, Zinc, Magnesium, Vit C, Chromium, Adrenal support remedies	Adrenal support/ stress

Alarm Point	Nutrition	Comments
Small intestine **Midline, 2/3 of the distance between the navel and pubic bone**	Grapefruit Seed extract, Curcumin extracts, Probiotics, Herbal remedies designed for candida and parasite elimination	Suspected viral protozoa, parasite etc. infection
	L glutamine, Zinc, probiotics, Omega 3 fatty acids	Intestinal health
Bladder **Midline, just above the pubic bone**	Omega 7 oil, Magnesium, Serrapeptase Vitamin C, Pyridoxal 5 Phosphate	Urinary tract health
Lung **Bilaterally, at the junction of the shoulder and chest**	Zinc, Magnesium, Calcium, Vit C, Thyme, Fenugreek, Other herbals for lung health	Asthma/allergies/hay fever
Liver **Bilaterally, in line with the nipples between the 6th & 7th ribs**	Liver Support, Vit C, Magnesium, calcium D-glucarate, N-acetyl cysteine (NAC), Vit C, Milk Thistle, Curcuminoids,	Liver support
Gall Bladder **Bilaterally vertically below the nipple between 7th & 8th rib**	Herbs for gall bladder support (also think parasites), Digestive enzymes containing bile salts	Gall bladder support
Large Intestine **Bilaterally 1 ½ body inches either side of the navel**	Iron, L Glutamine, Marshmallow, Liquorice, Zinc, Fibre, Probiotics, Herbal combinations for bowel health	General Support
	Grapefruit Seed extract, Herbal Combinations for parasites	Suspected parasites
	Curcuminoids, Oregano, Pomegranate seed, Herbal combinations for candida	Suspected candida
Spleen/Pancreas **Bilaterally, the tip of the 11th rib**	Vitamin E, Vit C, Astragalus, Echinacea, Zinc	Immune system/spleen
	B complex, Digestive Enzymes	Digestion
	B Complex, Vit C, Chromium, Magnesium	Blood sugar handling
Kidney **Bilaterally , the tip of the 12th rib**	Magnesium Citrate, Vit E, B Complex, Vit C, Vit D3	Kidney support
	Probiotics, Potassium Citrate, Omega 7 oils, Cranberry, Colloidal Silver, Herbal combinations with antibiotic properties.	Suspected infection (Please seek doctor's advice)

Toxicity Talk

We will eventually become toxic if there are more toxic substances entering or staying in the body than are being eliminated. Toxins, whether they are endogenous (created by our bodies as by-products, spent hormones or chemicals), or exogenous (coming from outside our body either from what we imbibe, put on our skin, or breathe in from the environment) need to be eliminated from the body.

 Research how to reduce, where possible, the amount of toxins we get from our food and environment.

*It's important to ensure that our eliminatory organs are working for us. Here we're talking about – **The liver, kidneys, colon, lungs, skin, and the extracellular matrix (look out for this later!) See Fig. 38***

Address any toxic metals that may be showing in your testing procedures.

Address any troublesome pathogens – they too have to excrete their waste and that means an extra burden on the host! These pathogens include fungi, parasites, unfriendly bacteria or other organisms that are commensal (friendly, not harmful).

The Process of Detoxification and Elimination – Figure 38

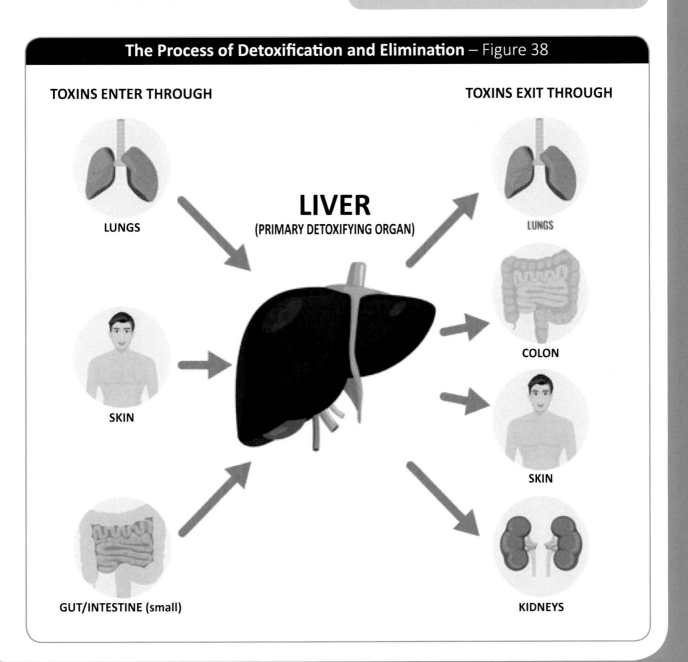

TOXINS ENTER THROUGH

LUNGS

SKIN

GUT/INTESTINE (small)

LIVER
(PRIMARY DETOXIFYING ORGAN)

TOXINS EXIT THROUGH

LUNGS

COLON

SKIN

KIDNEYS

Liver Support

The liver is a highly complex organ with many functions. The two functions we will briefly discuss are the liver's detoxification pathways, and bile production. **(See Fig. 39)**. I recommend that you study these in detail as they are linked to so many health issues.

Liver Detoxification Pathways

Two detoxification pathways to be aware of are known as Phase 1 and Phase 2 or First Pass and Second Pass metabolism. **(See Table 9)**. They are highly complex and there are (thankfully for us!) failsafe methods ensuring functions overlap – useful when genetic differences mean that some pathways just don't work as well as others. For example, some people can't tolerate even just a small glass of wine without being affected whereas another person can become drunk but never get a hangover. Some individuals smoke 20 a day all their lives and live to their 90's whereas others develop lung cancer on 5 a day. All of these sorts of people would likely be described as having normal liver function.

The concept of liver detoxification is the processing of waste products so that they become water soluble and therefore easily excreted by the kidneys and bowels. Simply put Table 9 shows how it works:

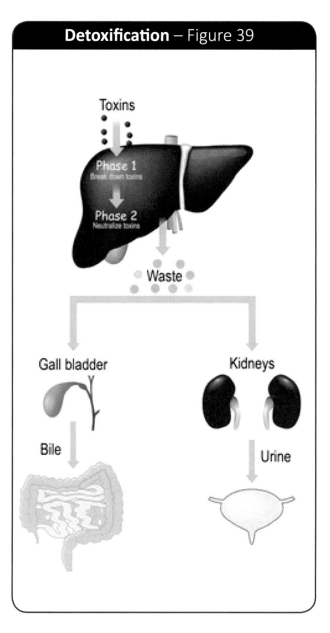

Detoxification – Figure 39

Toxins

Phase 1
Break down toxins

Phase 2
Neutralize toxins

Waste

Gall bladder

Bile

Kidneys

Urine

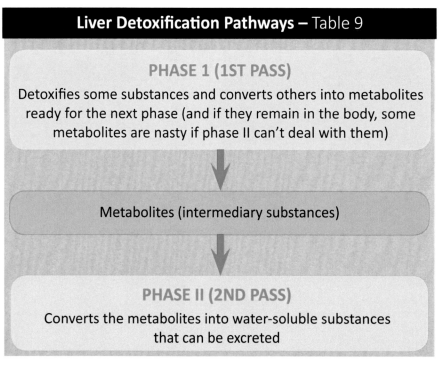

Liver Detoxification Pathways – Table 9

PHASE 1 (1ST PASS)

Detoxifies some substances and converts others into metabolites ready for the next phase (and if they remain in the body, some metabolites are nasty if phase II can't deal with them)

Metabolites (intermediary substances)

PHASE II (2ND PASS)

Converts the metabolites into water-soluble substances that can be excreted

For healthy detoxification, there needs to be a good balance between Phase I and Phase II

Properties of Bile

As well as emulsifying dietary fats, bile increases the motility of the bowel. In cases where the liver is not producing enough, transit time in the bowel slows down contributing to poor elimination of waste. Bile gives stools the brown colour, so if your client complains of pale stools, think of insufficient bile. This may be because the liver is congested, or the person is deficient in bile salts.

Bile serves as a means of excreting several important waste products from the blood. Spent hormones and other chemicals are secreted by the liver into the bile, so if bile is not flowing, these substances continue to circulate inappropriately in the system.

Testing Liver Function

Method 1:

The most direct way of testing for liver function is the use of test vials.

Liver Dysfunction (this is a 'blanket' test vial that covers various specific dysfunctions)

Specific test vials available include:

Liver detoxification pathways impaired

Liver congestion (bile)

Bile Salt Deficiency

OR

Method 2:

A bilaterally weak pectoralis major sternal muscle tested using a gamma II muscle test shows organ (liver) dysfunction. It is possible to place these muscles in circuit retaining mode and find a correction/remedy. Some sources say that this is an indication for heavy metal toxicity (Deal)

OR

Method 3:

1. Activate the biochemical finger mode and contact the liver alarm point. If the IM unlocks the liver needs biochemical support. Place these into circuit retaining mode (unlock).

2. Activate the finger mode for toxicity. **(page 61)**.This will **lock** the IM if the liver requires support for detoxification.

3. Take off the toxicity finger mode as you have this information. This means the IM will return to unlocked, which is easier to find the most beneficial support which will **lock** the IM. (When the supportive nutrition selected helps to increase chi, the 'Raise Vital Force Mode' will then **unlock** the IM).

Liver Detoxification Pathways Impaired
(See Table 9)

Useful Nutrition:

Selenium, zinc, vitamin C, beta carotene, B complex, quercetin, alpha lipoic acid or R-lipoic acid, NAC, milk thistle, dandelion, glutathione, DIM (di-indole methane from cruciferous vegetables), I3C (indole-3 carbinol also from cruciferous vegetables), cysteine. Broccoli and other cruciferous vegetables. Other sulphur-containing foods are eggs, garlic and onions

Protein is important as the phase II pathway needs amino acids to conjugate hormones and chemicals. Check using the 'protein deficiency' test **(Fig. 36 on page 37)**.

Liver Congestion – Bile

Using a castor oil pack placed over the liver area can help a congested liver. **www.edgarcayce.org**

Increase healthy fats in the diet such as avocado and coconut oil. Fats stimulate bile production.

Beetroot, celery, radish, berberis, dandelion root, fumitory, Oregon grape.

Bile Salt Deficiency

The body preserves bile salts by recirculating them several times before they are finally excreted in bile. People who have had their gall bladder removed or have been on a low-fat diet may show a deficiency.

Beetroot, celery, radish, Oregon grape, berberis, or proprietary brand digestive enzymes containing bile salts can help. Consider supplementing with the amino acid taurine, which is essential for making bile salts. ✓

Liver and the Thymus Tap Connection

This procedure was developed by Dr Walter Schmitt. He noticed that a previously strong pectoralis major sternal (liver circuit) would sometimes weaken after the thymus was tapped. This could be because:

- The thymus produces some cytokines – small proteins that are involved in cell communication. If the immune system is dysregulated, they could be inappropriately released signalling pain and inflammation.

- If the liver's detoxification system is overloaded, when the thymus is tapped any extra cytokines being released could stress the liver further.

Balancing the liver circuit will assist the liver to cope with its detoxification process, which in turn will help to reduce pain and inflammation.

1. Using a gamma II test, check individually both pectoralis major sternal muscles (tests for organ dysfunction). They should test strong in the clear. If not, rub the NL's, NV's or go through the 4 key finger modes and administer a correction.

2. Firmly tap over the thymus (over the manubrium) and retest both PMS's using a gamma II test again. If they now weaken, or they become hypertonic (check using a magnet), the extra production of thymus cytokines is affecting the liver.

3. Place the weak/hypertonic PMS's into circuit retaining mode (unlocked) and go to the visceral referred pain chart **(Fig. 40 on page 86)** and CL to find the areas that two-point (lock).

4. If you intend to add nutrition, find the remedy/ies which should lock the IM. Activate the 'Raise Vital Force' mode which should unlock the IM. Leave the nutrition on the body for the next step. ✓

5. Rub the visceral pain area that two-points.

6. Cancel the lock and recheck step 1.

Related Nutrition

The amino acid glycine. Glycine's cofactors are folic acid, manganese, B6, B2, sulphur, selenium and reduced glutathione.

Kidney Support

Method 1:
To identify any kidney imbalance, place a 'Kidney Dysfunction' test vial on the body. If the AIM **unlocks** and is a modality or priority, try one or more of the suggestions below.

OR

Method 2:
Activate the biochemical finger mode then CL the kidney alarm point.

If the IM **unlocks**, place into pause lock and check any of the suggestions below that **lock** the indicator muscle. Make sure that the remedy is energising for the client, activate the 'raise vital force' mode, which will **unlock** an IM when a suitable remedy is found.

Related Nutrition

Water is the transport that carries waste out of the body via the kidneys, so proper hydration is essential.

Soothing and healing herbs protect the delicate filtration system in the kidney tubules. For example, marshmallow, cordyceps, ginger, fumitory, self-heal, horsetail, nettle, N-acetyl cysteine (NAC), magnesium, vitamin D.

Complex homoeopathic remedies designed for kidney support.

Proprietary kidney support combinations from supplement companies.

After using one of the two methods for identifying the need for kidney support, test each of the realms by activating the four key finger modes. The mode that locks the IM will allow you to narrow down your search for the body's preferred correction.

Lung Support

This as an important naturopathic principle that is often overlooked. Breathing correctly allows toxins to be expelled via the respiratory system as we exhale so it is important to teach our clients how to do abdominal breathing on a regular basis. Not only does this help to release toxins via the out breath, but it reduces stress, reduces blood pressure, and slows the heartbeat.

Test the diaphragm muscle, the anterior serratus and the deltoids making the necessary corrections using the neurolymphatic and neurovascular points. Food rich in vitimin C are helpful.

 Instruct your client how to do abdominal breathing. Once they understand how to 'belly breathe' clients' can be shown how to gradually increase, over time, the length of each in breath, how long they hold their breath and the length of the out breath then holding their breath again, ensuring that the lungs are fully emptied before taking in the next cycle.

This subject should be researched further.

The Colon

As well as storing waste products ready for evacuation, the colon also removes and recycles excess water so that the stools are solid.

The waste products should not sit in the colon for too long as autointoxication can occur where the toxins are reabsorbed into the bloodstream. This means that the liver has to work even harder to clear the recycled toxins.

- Fibre is a great binder of toxins, particularly heavy metals, and should be part of any detoxification plan for your clients.

- Consider checking a test vial for 'beneficial bacteria deficiency' and supplement with an appropriate probiotic that balances intestinal flora.

- Check the quadriceps muscles, abdominals (small intestine) the hamstrings, tensor fascia latae and quadratus lumborum (large intestine) and correct if a priority/modality.

- Check and correct if necessary, the ileocaecal valve. An overloaded colon can cause this non-return valve to open, allowing toxic waste to back up into the small intestine where it can be reabsorbed. Also test and correct the Houston valve/rings if necessary.

- Ensure your client isn't constipated and is eating enough fibre for the toxins to be 'swept away' in. You may choose to supplement with psyllium hulls, apple fibre, chia seeds etc. There is a test vial for 'fibre deficiency' and the types of suitable fibre can be checked against this vial.

- There may be a case for giving your client digestive enzymes. A problem further up the chain or digestion can be a catalyst for slow transit time. **(See page 71)**

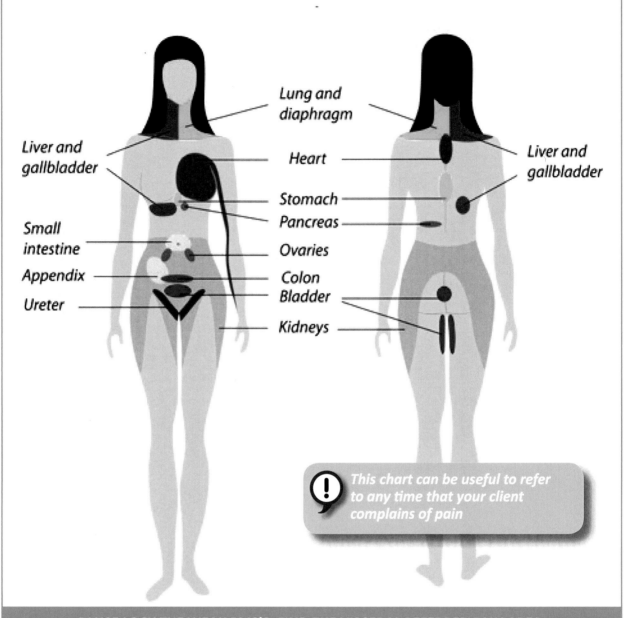

Visceral Referred Pain Chart (VRP) – Figure 40

Lung and diaphragm

Liver and gallbladder

Heart

Liver and gallbladder

Stomach

Pancreas

Small intestine

Ovaries

Appendix

Colon

Ureter

Bladder

Kidneys

This chart can be useful to refer to any time that your client complains of pain

PAUSE LOCK THE WEAK PMS'S, FIND THE VISCERAL REFERRED PAIN AREA (LIKELY LIVER AND GALL BLADDER) AND RUB THESE POINTS

The Skin as an Eliminatory Organ

Ways to improve the expelling of toxins via the skin include:

 Research the following:

Dry skin brushing daily.

Using a far infrared sauna.

Regular use of Epsom salt baths can draw out heavy metals and other toxins from the skin. It is also known for its exfoliating properties.

Extracellular Matrix

About 56% of the adult human body is fluid. About one third of this is in the spaces outside the cells. This extracellular fluid is in constant motion throughout the body. It is rapidly transported in the circulating blood and then mixed between the blood and tissue fluids by diffusion through the capillary walls. There are ions and nutrients in this fluid that are essential for maintaining cellular life. (Guyton) **(See Fig. 41)**

If lymphatic circulation is sluggish, the extracellular fluid becomes burdened with toxic waste from the cells, which should otherwise be transported to the kidneys for excretion. Clearly, it's bad news to have polluted waste languishing in our tissues.   From the naturopathic perspective extracellular matrix function is very important to address if the body is to have a chance to feed and cleanse itself.

There isn't a specific test for the extracellular matrix, but try a test vial for **Toxic Lymph.**

- A muscle balance, correcting underpowered muscles using neurolymphatic and neurovascular points is a great way to improve circulation and lymph flow.

- Check and address the retrograde lymphatic system (technique described on page 160).

- Test for homoeopathic remedies made by companies such as New Vistas, Heel and Energetix.
  Find out more about these.

- Regular body massages and skin brushing, will increase the movement of extracellular fluid.

- Cross crawl to improve circulation.

- Exercise, for example rebounding.

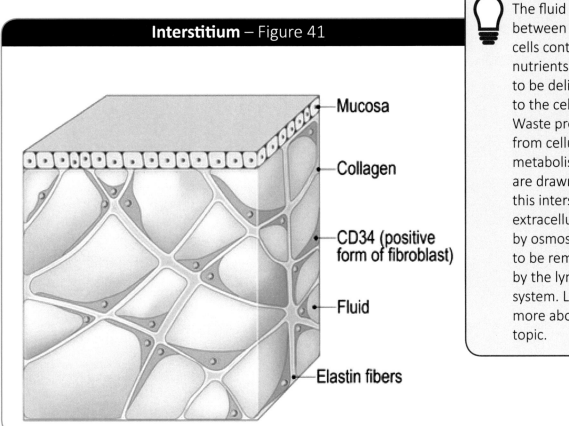

Interstitium – Figure 41

Mucosa

Collagen

CD34 (positive form of fibroblast)

Fluid

Elastin fibers

The fluid between the cells contain nutrients ready to be delivered to the cells. Waste products from cellular metabolism are drawn into this interstitial/extracellular fluid by osmosis, ready to be removed by the lymphatic system. Learn more about this topic.

Heavy Metal Toxicity

Minerals are 'double edged'. There are around 90 minerals that we are exposed to in ultra-trace amounts. In these quantities many are known to be beneficial but are usually toxic in larger amounts. For example, boron and vanadium have been used therapeutically in recent years, but they can both be toxic. Selenium was known for toxicity, but now is known for saving lives. The more we learn, the more we see that many minerals are valuable in ultra-trace amounts.

What are Heavy Metals?

Heavy metals may commonly be defined as those with a relative density is > 5g/ml. This does not automatically mean that they are toxic to the body since some heavy metals are essential nutrients, for example chromium, copper, iron, vanadium and zinc. However, all heavy metals can be toxic if concentrated enough. Note that many 'lighter metals' such as aluminium can also be toxic. For sources of toxic metals see **Table 10.**

Heavy metals			
Antimony	Gallium	Silver	Arsenic
Gold	Tellurium	Bismuth	Iron
Thallium	Cadmium	Lead	Tin
Cerium	Manganese	Uranium	Chromium
Mercury	Vanadium	Cobalt	Nickel
Zinc	Copper	Platinum	

Major toxic metals		
Al – Aluminium	As – Arsenic	Cd - Cadmium
Pb – Lead	Hg - Mercury	

Heavy metals such as lead, cadmium, nickel and mercury are exceptionally heavy and can accumulate in the body. They do not disperse without help.

Removing such metals from the body may take months. In the meantime, a client must avoid contact with cigarettes or any other smoke (cadmium), exhaust fumes (lead) and hair dyes (cadmium), household and beauty products and poor-quality Chinese herbs.

Mercury is not as heavy as some metals, but it is not as easily excreted as aluminium. It is ubiquitous in many manufacturing processes and of course it can be found in metal tooth filling.

Nickel will be picked up in food that is in contact with chrome plating.

Aluminium is not a heavy metal and will excrete easily, however more is often consumed than can be excreted.

Arsenic can be found in the water supply and contaminated foods. Absorption can be due to contact through the dermal layers, ingestion and inhalation.

How Big is the Problem?

We absorb more than we excrete.

Lead is still a problem in America – even after banning it from paint and petrol.

Metals are used on a massive industrial scale. Escape occurs during extraction of the metals in their own right, or from release of traces during the processing of other metals. Clouds of particles containing metals can move over thousands of miles with prevailing winds.

There are insufficient large-scale population studies.

NOBODY REALLY KNOWS!

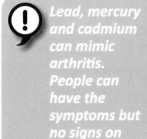

> **!** Hypertensives excrete 40% more cadmium in their urine than normotensive people

> **!** Lead, mercury and cadmium can mimic arthritis. People can have the symptoms but no signs on X-ray.

Effects of Metal Poisoning
(See Table 11 on page 91)

It can affect every system and every tissue.

It can cause or exacerbate almost every symptom.

Clients are worsened by multi-metal exposure.

Dr Rodney Adeniyi-Jones said,

❝ *The initial symptoms are usually attributed to something else! Therefore, check this when anyone is not showing signs of improvement.* ❞

 Note: *Children and elderly people are most at risk. Children absorb more in relation to exposure. Children have developing nervous systems that can be affected more easily. The elderly have many years of accumulation and highest levels, less effective liver function and have lower levels of protective nutrients.*

Sources of Metal Toxicity – Table 10	
Sources of Nickel	
Tobacco smoke	Electronic devices
Steel/metal alloys (jewellery, prosthetics)	Air/water/soil in/ around industrial areas
Hydrogenated oils	
Sources of Mercury	
Silver amalgams (dental filling)	Paints
Broken thermometers and barometers	Felt
Fresh and saltwater fish/shellfish	Grains/seeds treated with mercury fungicide
Tattooing	Fungicides
Fabric softeners	Adhesives
Mercurial diuretics/ointments/antiseptics	Floor waxes and polishes
Wood preservatives	Cinnabar (used in jewellery)
Some cosmetics	Film
Photo engraving	Plastics
Sewage sludge/sewage disposal	Air and water in and around industrial sites
Sources of Cadmium	
Paints (artist's/commercial/industrial)	Metals (metal plating)
Coloured plastics	Fertilizers
Fungicides	Antiseptics
Solder	Batteries
Petrol	Refined foods
Fish/shellfish	Coffee

Sources of Cadmium - continued

Meat (liver/kidneys)	Poultry
Grains	Dairy products
Cigarette smoke	Soil and air in/around cities and industrialized areas
Landfills	Sewage sludge
Waste incineration	

Sources of Arsenic

Insecticides	Weed killers
Ceramics	Glass
Paint	Wallpaper
Copper-smelting factories and soil from surrounding areas and downwind (sometimes for hundreds of miles)	

Sources of Aluminium

Cans	Foil
White flour	Some cheeses
Antacids	Sodium aluminium sulphate in baking powder
Aluminium cookware/cooking utensils	Buffered aspirin
Antiperspirants	Tap water
Food additives	Some infant formulas

Sources of Lead

Paint chips	Batteries (production and burning)
Dust in and around homes and buildings	Inks
Lead based paints	Solder
Leaded glass	Leaded petrol
Pottery glaze	Newsprint
Dyes	Plumbing (lead-soldered pipes)
Landfills	Ashes and fumes from burning oil-painted wood
Soil and air in and around industrialized areas	Drinking water
Sewage sludge	Waste incineration
Lead-soldered cans (from food)	

Effects of Metal Poisoning – Table 11

Al	(Aluminium) Mainly neurotoxicity: Alzheimer's, MND, dialysis dementia. suppression of cell mediated and humoral immunity, shortens life span, lung damage, kidney damage, memory loss, confusion, colic.
As	(Arsenic) Diaphoresis (sweating), metallic taste in the mouth, vomiting, cramps, garlic-like odour to the breath, diarrhoea, neural disorders., loss of hair, muscular weakness, tingling or burning extremities (degeneration of nerves – peripheral neuropathy), cirrhosis or fatty liver, death, kidney damage, death.
Cd	(Cadmium)Anorexia, sore joins, mouth lesions, dry and scaly skin, hair loss, weight loss, lung damage, hypertension, kidney damage, nutrient malabsorption, anaemia, antibody suppression, kidney and liver disease, decreased growth, low body temperature, fatigue, headaches, irritability, possibly prostate hypertrophy, high blood pressure.
Cu	(Copper) Irritability, low blood sugar, slow healing and sleeping after meals. This toxicity is common in vegetarians.
Pb	(Lead)Fatigue, irritability, abdominal pain, constipation, impaired coordination, gout, bone pain, anaemia, numbness and tingling in hands and feet, muscular tremors, hallucinations, memory loss, headache, loss of concentration, peripheral neuropathy, kidney degeneration.
Hg	(Mercury)Anaemia, anorexia, low temperature, drowsiness, headache, fatigue, insomnia, anxiety, depression, hypersensitive reflexes, kidney damage, joint pains, mental disturbances, tremors, weight loss, flu-like symptoms, high blood pressure, numbness, depression, colitis, stomach pains, mood swings, irregular heartbeat, eczema, ear nose & throat problems, metallic taste, alopecia, rashes, dizziness, gynaecological disorders, brain fog, multiple sclerosis, asthma, chest pains, birth defects, ME, susceptibility to yeast overgrowth, sore or burning mouth, mouth ulcers, swollen tongue.
N	(Nickel)Contact dermatitis, nausea, low blood pressure, oral cancer, intestinal or respiratory tract cancer, haemorrhages, brain degeneration, heart attack.

Heavy Metal Detoxifying Agents – Table12
Use Test Vials to identify toxicity. Treat in modality order

Herbs	Bayberry, barberry, cleavers, culvers, echinacea, butternut, silymarin, goldenseal, cilantro (always take with chlorella to avoid re-toxification), burdock, dandelion root, ginger, parsley and artichoke. Use herbal combinations, but if a person is sensitive, you may need to resort to individual herbs). Other important toxic metal 'sponges' are chlorella. It is advisable to take constantly for 3 – 4 months at a time.
Foods	Garlic, beans, onions, eggs, vegetables. Fasting increases the excretion of the heavier metals. Protein is very important because the liver uses the amino acids to conjugate toxins. A protein drink taken daily may be a good thing, particularly in the case of vegetarians or poor eaters.
Fibre	e.g. Guar gum, oat bran, pectin, apple fibre, psyllium husks, chia seeds, flax seeds (soaked)
Nutrients	R Lipoic Acid, MSM Sulphur (cysteine/glutathione synthesis), Vit C, N-acetyl cysteine, methionine, selenium, zinc, glutathione, taurine and methionine (protein). For long term prevention and protection, use high potency multivitamins and multiminerals. For aluminium toxicity consider magnesium and Silicon.
Other treatments	Chelation therapy (intravenous EDTA) reduces levels of all toxic metals and has many benefits when used for serious illnesses. It has been used since 1951.

How to Find and Address Heavy Metal Toxicity

If the biochemical finger mode and the toxicity finger mode shows, remember to test for heavy metals.

Test vials appear to be the easiest solution for testing heavy metals and prove to be reliable. Any that unlock an AIM, and are a priority or modality, can be addressed by finding the right supplements/herbs/foods. Test vials can be bought individually or as a set. There is also a 'blanket' test vial available called 'Heavy Metal Toxicity' (for more about test vials see page 63). However, I will describe another test devised by Dr Walter Schmitt. (Deal)

1. Test either the psoas or a PMC (pectoralis major clavicular division). They should test strong in the clear.

2. Position the limb across the midline and retest the muscle. If the muscle then weakens, this is an indicator that toxic metals are present in the body. To save repeated testing, this test could be entered into circuit retaining mode.

3. To find which metals are the problem, place the test vials on the body one at a time and retest as in step 2.

4. Any heavy metal vial that then **locks** the muscle, when tested in this position, is toxic for the client.

It is possible to carry out a correction using homoeopathic potencies of the heavy metal. This will certainly mobilise the metal in the body, but if the body detoxification pathways are not functioning well, then the metals will remain in the body but just be deposited in another area. So, it is imperative to support the organs involved in detoxification using nutritional/supplementation. **DO NOT TRY TO MOBILISE THE HEAVY METALS WITHOUT GIVING THE APPROPRIATE NUTRITIONAL SUPPORT.**

The body will do its utmost to protect itself from pathogens and xenobiotics (foreign substances that should not be in the body) and thus it's very good at compensating, so bear in mind that we, as kinesiologists, can miss a lot of cases of heavy metal toxicity in our practice. The body will store the metals in fat and pack them 'safely' away in tissue until they can be excreted. So occasionally it can be a challenge to coax the body into revealing that they are there. The endocrine system compensates for the toxic heavy metals in the system, mostly via the adrenals, thyroid and ovaries or testicles (Deal). So, we need to reveal these compensations in order to obtain a clear picture. Some clearing techniques are complicated, but in my experience using vibrational essences such as Bach Flower Remedies, Phytobiophysics Flower Formulas, other flower or gem essences work just as well. Dr Dietrich Klinghardt, an expert in the field of heavy metal toxicity, confirms that to successfully detoxify heavy metals from the body it is very important to address the emotional aspects of an individual alongside using supplements.

If you suspect that your client has a problem with heavy metals, **but your kinesiology tests are negative**, carry out the following:

If the Heavy Metal Toxicity Tests Don't Show

If suspected heavy metals do not change an AIM

1. Leave the test vial on the body or carry out the protocol above using the psoas or the PMC.

2. Place each box of vibrational remedies (Bach etc.) on the body and repeat the test.

3. If any of the boxes, then unlock the IM there is an endocrine compensation involved. There is something in the box that is supporting the body so that it's now safe for the body to reveal the metal toxicity.

4. Remove the box from the body and place each remedy in turn on the body until you find the one(s) that unlock the IM.

5. Leave the chosen remedies on the body with the test vials, or the psoas/PMC test, whilst you find the appropriate supplements to help the body to detoxify. Any appropriate ones will lock the IM. **(See Table 12)**

6. In order for the body to recognise the stored toxic metals, *it's very important for your client to take the chosen essences alongside the selected supplements.*

Amalgam Removal

"Mercury is a highly toxic heavy metal, which upon chronic threshold overload has been shown to produce and / or perpetuate symptoms in almost any organ system. It does so by nature of its devastating effects on the Functional Nervous System (the Autonomic Nervous System); the fact that it is a highly oxidative substance, which may enter the system in the elemental form but becomes oxidized easily, generating free radicals; and this highly persistent heavy metal binds to sulphur and other mineral binding sites inactivating enzymes, cellular membranes, cross linking proteins (ageing), and reducing the detoxification capacity and biochemical function of the person.

Research shows that 43 micrograms of mercury comes off each square centimetre of amalgam in water every 24 hours. In the absence of any specific detoxification methods, it is possible to excrete around six (6) micrograms in 24 hours.

> **!** *After finding the nutrition to deal with toxicity, and focusing on the eliminatory organs, you will usually find that the person's ability to excrete mercury will improve.*

Therefore, a person with only around three amalgams is absorbing 37 micrograms of mercury every day. Where does this mercury go? Most of it is inhaled. It is estimated that 80% of the mercury vapour inhaled enters the body thorough the lungs and is distributed to various bodily tissues and organs." (Biological Mercury -Free Dentistry (with references), n.d.)

In addition to the severity scale vials, a test vial that helps assess mercury excretory status can be employed. If clients test positive to this, the vial can be used to select appropriate nutrients and foods that can enhance mercury excretion (e.g. selenium, magnesium, B-vitamins, vitamin C, vitamin E, glutathione or glutathione precursors, fibre, garlic, water, etc.). Clients proposing to undergo amalgam removal might wish to wait until they test negative to this vial unless the amalgam removal is considered urgent, when, as always, it should be accompanied by the usual safety measures adopted by mercury-safe dentists.

Candida Albicans

Biochemical Finger Mode

Sometimes Friendly, Sometimes Our Enemy

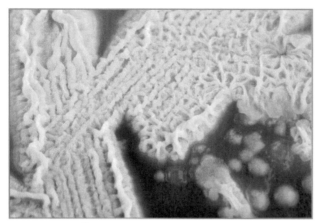

C. albicans cultured in a petri dish

Candida albicans is a fungus. It is normally a harmless member of the microbiome, but it can become rampant under certain circumstances. No one quite knows why we have *C. albicans* in our gut and on our skin, but it is thought that it could actually 'hold down the fort' if the microbiome is disrupted and beneficial bacteria are destroyed, for instance when we take antibiotics or our immune system is compromised in some way. Mycologists Prof Carol Kumamoto and Dr Jesus Romo from Tufts University, Somerville Massachusetts have been studying candida for years and explain that because its interaction with humans is so complex, sometimes it is friendly and sometimes our enemy. For example, they discovered that mice that carried *C. albicans* in their guts were protected from lethal doses of the bacterium Clostridium difficile.

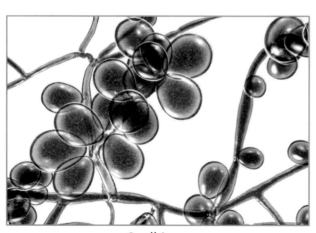

C. albicans

C. albicans can cause fatal infections if a person has a weak immune system. An extreme case of this would be individuals who are on immuno-suppressant drugs. The fungus can then change shape into elongated cells called hyphae that can then penetrate and destroy tissue creating inflammation. (see **Table 13** on page 96 for a list of symptoms). It reminds me of the story of a dear client I had a few years ago. She came to the clinic, looking very ill indeed, with a tooth infection. We did some kinesiology testing and strangely enough, her body's high priority was not the tooth infection, but appeared to be an overgrowth of candida. She was given appropriate supplementation but was advised to immediately go and visit her doctor as it was clear she was very sick. The outcome was that she actually had a type of blood cancer called myeloma. She was almost immediately hospitalised and treated with chemotherapy. As a result of her hospital stay, she was unable to take her supplements for the candidiasis. Whilst she was in hospital, she developed diarrhoea, but the doctors were unable to find the cause. Very sadly, on the day she was to be discharged, she suddenly died. Because it was an abrupt unexpected death there was a post-mortem. The cause of death was a massive invasion of *C. albicans* throughout her major organs. It appears the candida that we suspected was present before her treatment had spread uncontrollably, no doubt due to the chemotherapy. Because candida is so ubiquitous her stool tests did not pick this up.

Candida Auris

There is a new 'kid on the block' called *Candida auris.* This candida strain can be difficult to deal with as it can withstand anti-fungal drugs. It has now been detected in about 20 countries with no sign of stopping. It is known to survive in hospital rooms and is responsible for outbreaks due to patient-to-patient transmission. It creates biofilms, which are communities of microbes that create their own environment by protecting themselves in a glue-like substance. Biofilms protect bacteria and fungi from the effects of antibiotics or anti-fungal drugs and render them virtually undetected by the immune system. There is a biofilm test vial available.

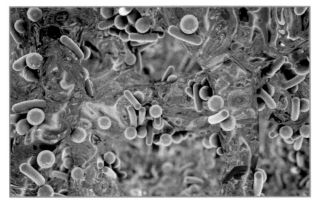

Biofilm of Antibiotic Resistant Bacteria. Rod-Shaped and Spherical Bacteria. Escherichia Coli, Pseudomonas, Mycobacterium Tuberculosis, Klebsiella, Staphylococcus Aureus, MRSA

Serrapeptase (a proteolytic enzymes that breaks down protein), Biocidin and a number of herbs, are known to be effective breaking down biofilms. Carbohydrates can exacerbate the development of biofilms so dietary advice is a reduced carbohydrate diet with avoidance of refined carbohydrates.

C. auris can be found in biofilms clinging to catheters and other implanted devices such as pacemakers, heart valve replacements and replacement joints. (Kumamoto & Romo, 2019).

We will probably be hearing a lot more about this bug in future, but the researchers are learning a lot from studying its cousin *C. albicans.*

C. auris

The most common biofilm-related candida infection is found in the tissues supporting dentures where the *C. auris* in biofilm attaches itself to the dentures. It is believed to provoke an immune response causing inflammation of tissue due to the release of pro-inflammatory cytokines. This candida biofilm occurs in 70% of all dental wearers (Tsui et al, 2016). The candida can then penetrate tissue. Antifungal drugs seem unsuccessful because as soon as the infected dentures are returned to the mouth, the infection sets up again.

(Williams and Lewis 2011).

Diseases Thought to be Related to or Affected by C.A (Chaitow, 1996) – Table 13

Candidiasis can be involved with these common symptoms

Candidiasis is very common. Here is a list of just some of the problems it can be associated with.

Fatigue	Abdominal Pain	Vaginal Thrush
Depression	Irritable Bowel	Vaginitis
Brain Fog	Indigestion	Jock Itch
Migraines	Gastritis	Oral Thrush
Persistent Headaches	Gas and Bloating	Anal Itching
Mood Swings	Mucous in Stools	Nappy Rash
Short Attention Span (particularly children)	Dry Mouth	Chronic Sinus
Panic Attacks	Sore Bleeding Gums	Cough
Craving for Sweets	Mouth Ulcers	Wheezing
Insomnia	Recurrent Sore Throat	Nasal Congestion Postnasal Drip
Tissue Inflammation	Weak Immune System	Hay Fever
Allergies to chemicals or foods	Chrohn's Disease	Hodgkin's Disease
Systemic Lupus Erythematosus	Scleroderma	Sarcoidosis
Chronic Respiratory Disease	Myasthenia Gravis	Autism
Alcoholism	Anorexia Nervosa/Bulimia	Multiple Sclerosis
Drug Addiction	Inflammatory Bowel Disease	AIDS
Rheumatoid Arthritis	Psoriasis	Eczema
Joint Inflammation	Recurring Infections	Fluid in Ears or Excessive Wax
Fungal Nails	Pre-menstrual Syndrome	Deafness
Athlete's Foot	Menopausal Symptoms	
Urticaria	Failure to Menstruate (Amenorrhoea)	Cystitis/Urethritis/ Kidney Infections
Skin Inflammation	Heavy Periods	Prostatitis Impotence
Mitral Valve Prolapse	(Menorrhagia) High Oestrogen levels	Lack of Libido
A result of chemotherapy	A result of radiotherapy	Diabetes

Addressing a Candida Imbalance

Use the following test vials or activate the candida finger mode (See Method 2 on page 103). Remember a finger mode is not universal and should not usually show 'in the clear'. Modes are meant to be used with reference to an imbalance.

Method 1 – Using Test Vials

1. Test the following vials and address in modality order the ones that unlock the AIM.

   a. Candida Toxins

   b. Candida

   c. Immune System Weak**

   d. Leaky Gut **

   e. Beneficial Bacteria Deficiency**

2. After tackling the most important imbalances, on the client's next visit, whether they showed on the previous session or not, check all of these vials again. These may test positive for a few months because of the candida overgrowth's obstinacy and new imbalances may emerge.

3. Use the 'complete mode' (see page xxii) with any negative test vials, that were previously testing as positive. If there is no more work to do at this time the IM will change to **unlocked**.

4. Now find the appropriate supplements or herbs that will resolve the imbalances you've discovered. It is important to use supplementation as a solution. The body's preferred supplements will **lock** the IM.

5. I like to use the 'Raise Vital Force' mode that helps me to identify supplements that will not be too tough for the client to deal with but should in fact increase their energy. If the supplement raises vital force, then with the supplement on the body and the mode, the IM will change from locked to **unlocked**.

**These imbalances are associated with many illnesses not just a candida overgrowth. The

detailed descriptions on how to resolve these issues apply to most illnesses.

> ***Please do not be tempted to solely balance out these test vials by placing them in pause lock and using finger modes to correct. This can cause the candida to be mobilised, but if the excretory organs are impaired this means the candida and its toxins will not leave the body but just migrate to somewhere else, which has been known to lead to serious problems.***

! Key Solutions

To have any great impact on candida overgrowth, it is important to address all of the following stages. Consider a diverse approach rather than addressing just one or two areas. Using just one approach only is much less likely to work.

Diet

Avoid making the diet too difficult for your clients so that they can stick to it. In my experience, as long as you address the major imbalances, a difficult diet just isn't necessary. The idea that yeast and mushrooms should be avoided is a fallacy. Many times I've had new clients who have been on a strict candida diet for years but as soon as they deviate from it their symptoms are back.

Best practice:

● Cut out all refined sugars and carbohydrates (anything white!).

● Avoid any food intolerances.

● Cut out alcohol as this also is converted into acetaldehydes.

● Eat plenty of garlic, onions, olive oil, herbs and spices, and of course green leafy vegetables.

● Contrary to popular belief, fruit does not create too much of a problem. However, eating only low fructose content fruits such as berry fruits, apricots, oranges, lemons, limes, grapefruit, kiwi, plums, gooseberries and cranberries may be necessary for some people.

Candida Toxins

Candida and other fungi, parasites and bacteria produce toxins. Experts consider that these toxins may be the underlying cause of infection and many of the symptoms that people suffer from. Two of these toxins are acetaldehyde and ethanol (yeasts convert sugar into alcohol not only during wine making, but in the body too!). The small intestine absorbs these toxins and they are carried via the portal vein to the liver for detoxification (poor liver – it's got enough work to do!).

If you're not sure where to start when you have a client showing symptoms of candidiasis, begin here!

✔ Look in the Detoxification section under liver, kidneys, skin etc (see pages 81-87). These systems need addressing so that the body can rid itself of the extra toxins that produced when the candida dies off. Bear in mind that if remedies are being given that break down biofilm, there is going to be a big influx of mycobacteria and other strains being released, so 'all hands need to be on deck'! Ensuring that detoxification pathways are functioning can in itself make a huge difference to your client's symptoms.

Check that supplements are well tolerated and will raise vital force.

If symptoms worsen, they could be suffering from candida die back symptoms. Bear in mind that if they have been asked to avoid caffeine, sugar or wheat, and their diet is normally rich in these, they may well be experiencing withdrawal symptoms (violent headaches, nausea, fatigue, shivering). The literature says that 50% of clients will get some of these indications. If your client calls you with any of these symptoms after eliminating these types of foods, advise the client to "stick it out" if they can for a few days

and check in with you again if symptoms persist.

This great naturopathic remedy really helps! You could make a handout for your clients.

Put **1 tsp mustard powder** into hot water. Use a

suitable size bowl for soaking feet in.

Soak a flannel in another smaller bowl containing a few drops of **lavender** oil with very cold or iced water. Soak feet in the hot mustard bath and at the same time place the cold flannel across the forehead, occasionally refreshing it in the lavender water.

A hot mustard foot bath *also relieves symptoms of a cold or 'flu or you could try it any time you feel exhausted.*

Addressing Candida Overgrowth

When addressing candida itself, it is advisable to gradually build up supplement dosage. If die-back symptoms persist, retest the client with the substances they are taking and, if you have one, recheck the test vial 'Candida Toxins', or re-test and support the eliminatory organs.   If this is well managed and treated in modality/priority order, then your client is unlikely to experience any die back symptoms.

It is particularly important to be cautious if the patient is suffering badly from asthma, eczema, depression or a serious illness.

Here are a few suggestionsof key remedies, but new things are being discovered all the time. This is a subject that needs constant updating:

Supplementation

- Formulas containing caprylic acid, which is a medium chain fatty acid, are known to inhibit the growth of candida hyphae in the gut. One source of this is coconut oil.

- Grapefruit seed extract has been shown to contain anti-fungal properties and discourage a biofilm because of its anti-adhesion properties.

- Oregano oil has similar properties to grapefruit seed extract.

- Promising lab tests in the petri dish (in vitro) have shown that spirulina as well as raw garlic are promising anti-fungals.

- Saccharomyces boulardii is actually a strain of yeast. However, it has proven very effective in inhibiting candida from changing form and suppressing its spread.

- Other herbs include pomegranate seed, artemisia, barberry, thyme, Japanese knotweed (polygonum cuspidatum).

- Biocidin and serrapeptase (proteolytic enzymes) are each recommended for helping break down biofilms.

Immune System Weak

If this test vial shows, the immune system needs supporting. There are many reasons why this could occur because the immune system encompasses the entire body. Some possibilities are:

- Thermal stress.

- Emotional stress: studies show that emotional stress reduces white blood cell count.

- A deficiency of friendly gut bacteria.

- Lack of nutrients that support a healthy immune system.

- Adrenal exhaustion (candida overgrowth may also cause hypoadrenia).

The immune system benefits from a positive attitude. The stresses in today's society, including reading the newspaper or watching the latest news bulletins on television conspire to encourage a negative outlook.

The immune system is adversely affected by negative emotions such as anger, fear and frustration. Bad dreams have a similar effect, as they also engage the emotions. It is said that the recall of five minutes of anger cause immune system depression for six hours. Research shows that unresolved anger could have a deadly impact on health. Using the techniques described in the section 'Matters of the Mind' will be beneficial on pages 37 - 56.

Typical factors which stress the immune system include:

Anxiety	e.g. Time pressure
Frustration	e.g. Unresolved conflicts
Hostility	e.g. Blaming others
Perfectionism	e.g. Lack of control
Guilt	etc etc...

Lack of self-esteem downgrades immune function. Attention to the thymus gland is extremely important, including the Thymus Tap (see overleaf).

'Concept shifting' causes further problems – it is better to do one thing at a time, allocating good time management, than to split time tackling several jobs concurrently.

My old friend and mentor Sherridan Stock has this to say:

"Virtually every nutrient known plays a role in the immune system, so nutrient deficiencies have to be assiduously sought and addressed.

Free radical overload is likely to damage the immune system, particularly the thymus gland. The highly respected duo, Murray and Pizzorno, state that 'Perhaps the most effective intervention in re-establishing a healthy immune system is measures designed to improve thymus gland function.' The antioxidants believed to protect the thymus from atrophy are carotene, vitamin C, vitamin E, zinc, and selenium.

The liver is the unsung hero of the immune system, and the immune-suppressing effect of liver impairment has repeatedly been demonstrated. Liver support may therefore be appropriate (see section on Detoxification on pages 82 - 84). Chemical toxins burden the liver and all attempts should be made to minimize exposure from toxic cleaning chemicals (a typical under-sink cupboard usually provides a good yield of these, which where possible should be jettisoned in favour of more natural products), body care products, medicines, food additives, and pesticides.

Fibre deficiency is worth correcting, since it is causally linked to around 20 diseases, and the aim should be to induce at least two bowel movements daily. (The astute surgeon turned epidemiologist, Denis Burkitt, once wryly observed "little stools, big hospitals; big stools, little hospitals.")."

Thymus Tap for Supporting a Weak Immune System

Situated under the protuberance of the breastbone just below the sternal notch (the manubrium), the thymus produces specific cytokines that are part of the communication structure of the immune system. Immune cells called T cells mature in the thymus. Tapping over the thymus seems to stimulate it to produce needed cytokines and T cells. The following technique was devised by Dr John Diamond author of "Life Energy". He maintains the thymus gland monitors and regulates the body's energy flow. Therefore, when there is an imbalance in energy flow, the Thymus Thump, or Thymus Tap, can help correct it. Dr Diamond says that the thymus gland is linked between the mind and the body thus when there is emotional or physical disturbance can cause the thymus gland to shrink and cause depletion in this vital life energy.

1. TL the manubrium. If an AIM unlocks:

2. Place together the fingertips and thumb and with these firmly tap over the manubrium in groups of 3's (dah dah dah) as this appears to be most effective. The thymus can be disturbed by lack of self-esteem, therefore repeating the affirmations 'I love myself' or 'all is well with the world' while thymus tapping is particularly beneficial. This can be given as homework for clients. Tapping around the thymus area in an anticlockwise direction is also a great balancing technique that can be done any time.

3. The muscle associated with the thymus is the infraspinatus. Check, and correct if necessary (see Endocrine system on page 217).

Supplementation

There are masses of nutritional supplements that support the immune system. Any supportive nutrition will cause the IM to lock when placed with a 'Weak Immune System' test vial. Then check the remedies with the 'Raise Vital Force' mode. The ones that raise vital force will then unlock the IM.

For example, test:

- The **mushroom 'family'** of supplements such as reishi, cordyceps, maitake

- Vitamins **A, C and E**

- Vitamin **D**

- The minerals **selenium, zinc, iodine (thyroid function), magnesium, iron.**

Leaky Gut

The lining of the gut is very special. It has to stop invaders from entering the body via the walls of the intestines but still allow the 'good stuff' to enter. For this reason, the cells in this lining are packed very tightly together and the spaces between the cells are referred to as 'tight junctions. **(See Fig. 42)**

An invasion of pathogens such as candida and other parasites and bacteria, triggers inflammation to occur which causes the junctions open up and allow pathogens and undigested food etc. to enter. This can cause an abnormal immune reaction.

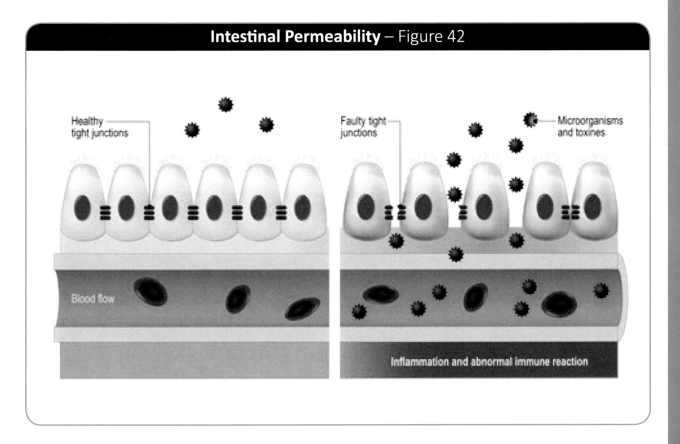

Intestinal Permeability – Figure 42

Healthy tight junctions

Blood flow

Faulty tight junctions

Microorganisms and toxines

Inflammation and abnormal immune reaction

1. Ask your client to avoid foods that they have an intolerance to, as these can inflame the gut.

2. Test nutrients known to heal a leaky gut see key points below.

Supplementation

- Marshmallow Root is soothing and calms the inflamed tissue.

- Liquorice extract.

- Slippery elm is mucilaginous and sooths and heals.

- Ginger.

- Aloe vera.

- The amino acid L-glutamine.

- Omega 3 essential fatty acids are anti-inflammatory.

- Zinc helps tissue to heal.

- Butyric acid (a short chain fatty acid found in butter, ghee and coconut). Be warned when you take the lid off the supplement pot, it smells a bit like vomit! This is its natural odour; the supplement hasn't spoiled, and the smell will dissipate. Butyric acid calms the digestion and aids healing.

- Probiotics.

- Fibre - if the gut is extremely inflamed start your client with steamed vegetables and fruit and perhaps slippery elm. Other sources include chia seeds, flax seeds, hemp seeds and psyllium.

- Digestive enzymes will help to break down food before it enters the intestines. This should minimise the risk of undigested food causing inflammation in the gut.

Beneficial Bacteria Deficiency

There are many strains of lactobacillus, acidophilus and bifidobacteria that may reside in the gut. Research shows that different strains yield different properties. Testing will determine which brand/combination will suit your client. To rebalance gut flora, consider the following:

- Cultured vegetables such as kimchi and sauerkraut.

- Kefir – there is water kefir and kefir made with milk. The kefir made with dairy does contain a greater range of probiotic strains (milk-based kefir can be taken by some dairy intolerant clients but test first).

Summary

When using the test vials, ensure you work with the modalities first. You will have noticed that there is some crossover in the suggested supplements. Many of them have multiple uses so you may find that you are addressing more than one area of concern at any one time.

Length of Treatment Time

The majority of people will feel much better after four weeks. Candida overgroth generally takes 8 - 12 weeks to normalise, longer in more difficult cases. The person needs to steer clear of sugar for at least 6 months. The client themselves will generally find their own level and, sometimes make their own mistakes and learn from them! All of the stages of treatment can be addressed at the same time as long as they test as a modality or priority. If your client has limited finances you can carry out the protocol in stages, which may just mean that they will need to take supplements over a longer period of time.

Other Considerations

- **The Heavy Metal Connection:**
  Dr Dietrich Klinghardt emphasises the link between mercury toxicity and the proliferation of unwanted fungal and parasitic overgrowth and stresses that **heavy metals should be addressed and corrected as a priority**. (see page 92)

- **Ileocaecal valve** dysfunction should be checked: Toxic waste being regurgitated into the small intestine could be a cause of intestinal dysbiosis (the wrong kind of pathogens in the gut). (see page 118)

- **Digestive insufficiency:** Hypochlorhydria, pancreatic exocrine insufficiency, and bile insufficiency all predispose to candidiasis. Hypothyroidism causes all three. Test and balance the digestive system and endocrine systems. (see page 70)

- Check **psychological conflict** and correct if necessary (see section Matters of the Mind') see page 41. The correction for this is tapping SI 3. The Chinese say that the small intestine 'sorts the pure from the impure'. If the energy of the small intestine is out of balance this will affect the intestinal milieu. This could be an important factor in gut health.

- Check **Ridler's Reflexes** for any nutritional deficiencies. Especially zinc, which helps balance elevated copper levels. (see pages 67 - 69)

Method 2 – *Testing for Candidiasis Without Test Vials*

The remedies and information described under method 1 still apply here.

1. An AIM will unlock when the client either sniffs bleach or ammonia (available as a cleaning fluid).
   If the test is positive to either or both of these substances, this indicates that there is a candida overgrowth problem. A copper supplement will usually unlock an AIM because candida sufferers typically have high copper levels (and subsequently low zinc). (Deal)

2. Put into circuit retaining mode (pause lock) the unlocked IM.

3. Test your selection of remedies. Give your client the ones that test as a priority or modality and raise vital force.

4. Test and address any imbalances in the eliminatory organs as discussed in the Detoxification section of this manual. (see pages 81 - 87) You can then be confident that the body can deal with candida toxins.

Method 3 – *Using the Candida Finger Mode*

A finger mode activated in the clear should not show. Finger modes are used in relation to an imbalance that we have in circuit.

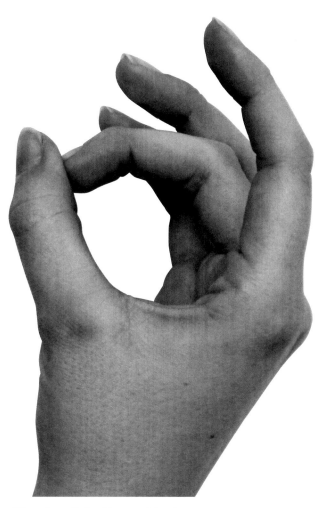

The Candida Finger Mode

Middle fingertip placed halfway down the thumb pad i.e. halfway between the biochemical finger mode and priority mode.

1. Place a lesion into circuit retaining mode (e.g. a skin lesion or an area of pain or discomfort) or ask the client to think of a symptom, for example fatigue or low mood. The IM will now unlock.

2. Activate the candida finger mode. If the IM locks, candida is involved with the imbalance. (You could also use the candida test vial in this manner to test for a link to the symptom).

3. If you are now going to look for remedies, remove the finger mode so that your IM returns to unlock. This makes it easier to find the correct remedies which will then **lock** the IM.

4. Any remedy that increases vital force will **unlock** the IM when the 'Raise Vital Force' finger mode is activated.

5. As in method 1 and 2, test and correct any imbalances in the eliminatory systems (candida toxins), leaky gut, beneficial bacteria deficiency and immune system.

Microbiome Finger Mode (Andrew Verity)

Middle finger pad to thumb, placed on the lateral crease of the distal joint of the ring finger.

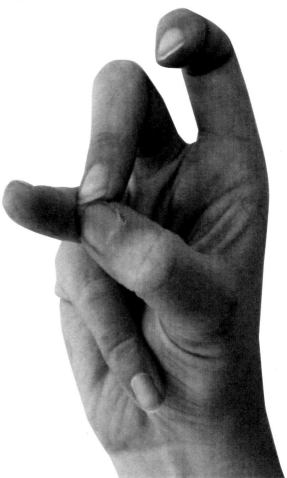

The microbiome is a term coined by Joshua Lederberg to describe "the ecological community of commensal, symbiotic, and pathogenic microorganisms that literally share our body space."

It is a sub-mode of the biochemical finger mode and if it two-points to any lesion, will tell you that a disturbance in the microbiome is contributing to the problem online. This mode applies to the whole microbiome. The microbiome in the gut greatly contributes towards maintaining a healthy body microbiome therefore if this mode shows check for imbalances relevant to gut health. Consider pre or probiotics for beneficial bacteria, resolving toxicity, identifying food intolerances, and addressing candida or parasites, etc...

Intestinal Parasites

Parasites are vermin that steal your food, drink your blood and leave their excrement that can result in it being reabsorbed back into your bloodstream.

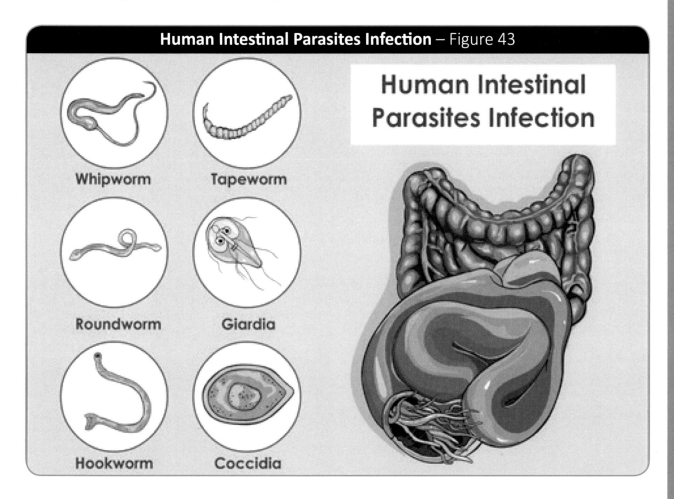

Human Intestinal Parasites Infection – Figure 43

Human Intestinal Parasites Infection

Whipworm

Tapeworm

Roundworm

Giardia

Hookworm

Coccidia

Parasites feed on the undigested food residue on the walls of the gastrointestinal tract. They vary from a fraction of an inch to thirty feet in length. **(See Fig. 43)**

There are several classes of parasites:

- **Pinworms:** These feed on refined carbohydrates and live in the rectum and sigmoid areas.

- **Hookworms:** Feed off blood, attaching themselves to intestinal walls.

- **Roundworms:** From animal faeces.

- **Tapeworms:** From undercooked meat.

- **Liver Flukes (Trematodes):** Freshwater fish, watercress (contaminated streams or lakes).

- **Giardia Intestinalis:** Water borne organisms with a flagellum (the tail that propels them), from inadequate water purification.

- **Protozoa:** These are single celled organisms that can move independently. They feed on organic matter, organic tissue or other organisms. Examples of those that can inhabit humans include *Blastocystis hominis, Entamoeba histolytica* (can cause traveller's diarrhoea), *Cryptosporidium* (coccidia) – dog or cat faeces, *E. coli, Dientamoeba fragilis* (a major cause of traveller's diarrhoea)

You can get worms from pets, going barefoot, fruit/vegetable infested with eggs, undercooked meat, and overseas travel.

For symptoms of parasitosis see **Table 14 overleaf.**

Symptoms Which May Be Linked to Parasitic Infestation – Table 14		
Fever	Abdominal Pain	GI Inflammation
Cough	Diarrhoea	Weight Loss
Asthma	Constipation	Weakness
Hives	Liver enlargement	Failure to thrive (children)
Itching with no rash	Nausea and/or vomiting	Fatigue
Migraines	Bloating & belching	Anaemia
Irritability	Anal itching	Arthritis
Cholecystitis (gall bladder inflammation)	Small intestine problems could be related to Giardia	Knee problems - protozoa e.g. Blastocystis can be found in synovial fluid. Think of in cases of knee problems
B12 Deficiency		

Testing for Parasites

You'll notice that there is some overlap with the candida protocol. You will still address the detoxification pathways, leaky gut and beneficial bacteria deficiency. (see pages 82 - 87 & 101-102)

Method 1 – Using Test Vials

1. With an AIM, place the individual test vials on the body. Some examples of these are parasite box sets and there are also individual 'blanket' test vials such as:

   - Intestinal Nematodes
   - Intestinal Protozoa
   - Intestinal Trematodes

2. Find the modality and address first.

3. Find the priority supplement/herbs that lock the IM.

4. Check if the chosen supplements will increase vital force. With the remedy/ies and the test vial on the body, activate the 'Raise vital force' mode, which should **unlock** the IM.

Method 2 – Using the Parasite Finger Mode

The protocol is the same as using the candida finger mode. This mode is for any type of parasite. It will not tell you whether it is nematodes, protozoa or trematodes, but you can still find the suitable supplements/herbs/homoeopathy to help the problem.

1. Identify the lesion that you want to check for a parasite connection. In this example, we'll say a swollen painful knee.

2. Ask your client to TL the painful area. The IM will unlock.

3. Activate the parasite mode which is **the thumb and little fingertip placed together over the top of the other three fingers**. The IM will now lock if there is a parasite link.

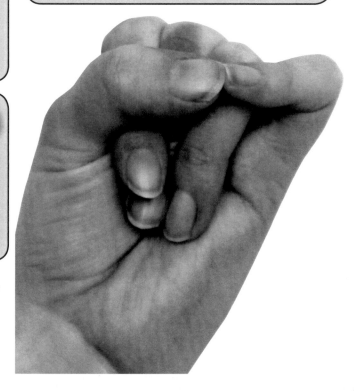

4. Remove the parasite mode so that you are back to an **unlocked** IM.

5. Find the remedy which should **lock** the IM.

6. Activate the 'Raise Vital Force' mode, which should now **unlock** the IM if the remedy does so.

Remedies for Intestinal Parasites

- Black walnut hull tincture (for systemic infestation, tapeworms).

- Cloves (for Intestinal eggs or cysts).

- High potency garlic or raw garlic, pomegranate peel extract, pumpkin seeds.

- Biocidin.

- Artemisia (wormwood), cryptolepis (protozoa), boneset [eupatorium perfoliatum] (protozoa), andrographis (worms), thyme (hookworms), oregano, tribulus, grapefruit seed extract.

- Quassia (protozoa).

- Colloidal silver (protozoa).

- Combinations available from supplement companies.

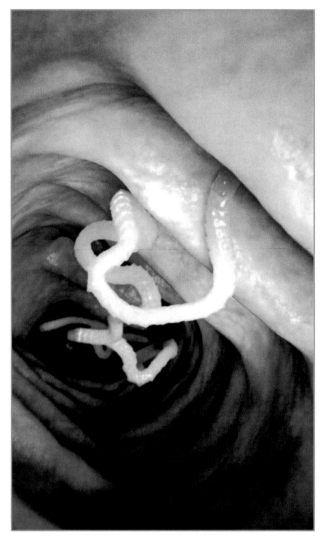

Image of Tape Worm in ingestive duct

Image of Thread Worm in intestines

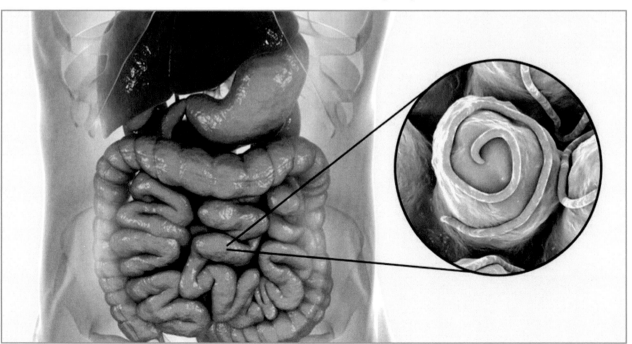

Other Considerations

- **Check for digestive insufficiency.** If digestive secretions are optimal, eggs and protozoa are likely to be destroyed in the stomach. Parasites can slip through the net when HCl and pancreatic enzymes are deficient. A sure sign of HCl deficiency in these circumstances is an itchy anus (pruritus ani). This can happen because parasite eggs are not destroyed in the stomach (lack of bile salts can also cause pruritus ani). The wrong pH in the stomach can have a knock-on effect in the large and small intestine which then creates an environment that parasites thrive in. HCl and digestive enzyme supplementation is also a preventative measure to stop re-infection. If travelling abroad to a country known for its lack of hygiene, check for this and address it before leaving. It's worth taking digestive enzymes anyway as a prophylactic whilst there. (Pages 70-71)

- **Ensure that detoxification pathways are optimal.** (Pages 81-87)

- **Beneficial bacteria.** Encourage friendly bacteria to address the microbiome. Avoid giving the prebiotic fructo-oligosaccharides, (found in onions, leeks, chicory, asparagus, tomatoes, wheat, bananas and other fruit and vegetables) as it is thought that they may be used as food by parasites. They can exacerbate the symptoms of irritable bowel syndrome. (Page 102)

- **Leaky gut**. Address a leaky gut (as for candida). (Page 101)

- **Avoid sugar and refined carbohydrates.** Instruct the client to avoid refined carbohydrates whilst on this protocol as parasites thrive on sugars.

- **ICV.** Check and correct ICV (and Houston valve) as parasites can congregate around the valve. (Pages 118 - 134)

 Address any emotional connection.

Dr Terry Franks submitted a paper to ICAK (International College of Applied Kinesiology) showing that individuals susceptible to parasite infections often presented with a trauma in early childhood, particularly between the ages of 4-6. He showed that diffusing any unresolved trauma resulted in recurring infections stopping.

Case History of Parasites and the Emotional Connection

The last point reminded me of a case that I saw some years ago. The Hospital for Tropical Diseases had diagnosed a new client with Blastocystis hominis. This client had received conventional treatment for this protozoon and was currently taking some natural remedies that kept the symptoms under control (Blastocystis hominis can be tenacious!). He came to see me because he was getting married and he wanted to finally get rid of the abdominal pain he was still suffering. My remit was to help him resolve this. What was interesting, when kinesiology testing was carried out, his body did not want anything biochemical – not surprising since he had taken almost every remedy under the sun! So, when the emotional finger mode came up as the priority, I wasn't concerned that an antiparasitic remedy was not selected and that he just required a gem essence. When he returned a month later, he reported that all his abdominal symptoms had completely gone. The remedy that he was given turned out to be one that dealt with early childhood traumas. He couldn't recall that he had experienced any, but the remedy worked all the same.

Understanding Insulin

Biochemical Finger Mode

Test vials: **Pancreas Dysfunction (Endocrine), Blood Sugar Low (Hypoglycaemia)**

How many of our clients are pronounced healthy by their doctor despite having sinus troubles, postnasal drip, colds, viruses, allergies, constipation, dandruff, poor circulation, fatigue, blotchy skin etc.? The emotional troubles which brought them to see us in the first place are still unexplained and they complain of feel nervous, irritable, sleepless, tired, edgy and subject to uncontrollable fits of temper, difficulty in concentrating, hypochondria, and a completely unjustified constant feeling that "something terrible is going to happen". They can't stand crowds, lifts or supermarkets. They're often told, "it's all in your mind, go and see a counsellor and take an antidepressant". Sometimes they report that they have had counselling, but it hasn't helped them. Any of that sound familiar?

Consider Blood Sugar Handling Problems

The following conditions will lead you to check for blood sugar handling problems.

- Anxiety attacks
- Unpredictable and apparently out of the blue panic attacks that your client feels are unjustified
- Depression for no apparent reason
- Epilepsy
- Schizophrenia
- Agoraphobia
- Tinnitus
- Obesity, with an uncontrollable addiction for sweets
- Obsessive-Compulsive behaviour

> **!** *Remember that hypoglycaemia can masquerade as a hundred physical diseases from epilepsy to gastric ulcers and can embellish the symptoms with a simulation of neurosis or psychosis.*

- Multiple allergies
- Difficulties with short-term memory and concentration
- Repeated vaginal yeast infections
- Depersonalised feelings (feeling spacey and not there)
- Blurred vision (the brain and retina are first affected by lack of glucose)
- Feeling hungry more often than is normal

The most common denominators behind these symptoms are a diet rich in refined carbohydrates, excessive smoking or drinking, and stress. Physical stress such as over-training can also cause symptoms. (Described in Martin Budd's book *Low Blood Sugar*)

> **❝ The most pervasive and underrated poison is simple sugar in our daily diets. ❞**
>
> **Dr Marilyn Glenville**

Some medications will cause blood sugar levels to fluctuate and if this is an issue, your client should discuss this with their doctor. We're talking here about sub-clinical hypoglycaemia, not the type of low blood sugar caused by a conditions such as stomach and small intestine surgery, a tumour causing excess insulin production, or a diabetes type 1 sufferer who has miscalculated his/her insulin injections and balance of food intake. Having said that, it's interesting to note that when a diabetic has a 'hypo', they can become exceedingly angry and unreasonable, confused and dizzy. It is common for people to pass them on the street, rather than helping them, thinking they are drunk. Could hypoglycaemia in a milder form be responsible for family breakups, criminal behaviour and some situations of domestic abuse etc.?

After you've discussed blood sugar handling with your client, they may decide to visit their doctor. Even with obvious symptoms that are ameliorated by food, fasting blood sugar tests often come back normal, which is a range of

4.0-5.4 mmol/L. This is just a 'snapshot' and will not consider any abnormal glucose level fluctuations over a period of time after eating or during fasting. The most accurate way of testing blood sugar handling is a glucose tolerance test. Blood glucose is measured in a specific way over a 6-hour period. When plotted on a graph, blood glucose levels can be seen to do strange things over a longer time interval. The results need to be read by someone who knows what the implications of the graph's variations mean, and how they relate to symptoms.

Different graph shapes, denoting how the body handles blood sugar, tell us what symptoms the client is likely to be experiencing. Doctors do not go into this, so generally, unless the doctor suspects that there is a serious problem, these tests don't help very much.

How Can Eating Sugar Cause Blood Sugar Levels to Drop?

When we eat any form of carbohydrate, (e.g. potatoes, bread, rice) the body converts them into sugars. Cells need glucose for energy production, especially brain cells. When glucose enters our bloodstream, insulin is secreted by the pancreas and promotes the uptake of glucose into the cells where it is used as an energy source. If we have more glucose available than our body actually requires at the time, insulin triggers the uptake of glucose into the liver where it is converted to glycogen. As glycogen can be readily converted back into glucose, our muscles also store glycogen so that we have fuel ready for action if needed. When we overindulge in refined carbohydrates, on a regular basis, the pancreas gets a "trigger happy" response by secreting too much insulin; consequently, too much glucose is removed from the bloodstream. This creates the situation where the nerve cells and brain cells receive an initial boost of energy and give a feeling of wellbeing followed by being starved of this essential fuel when blood levels crash. As a result, the body craves for something sweet to elevate blood sugar levels again. The vicious circle begins again – too much sugar is eaten, and again the pancreas overcompensates, and becomes reactive.

Dysglycaemia

Too much sugar in the blood can cause insulin to rise to high levels over and over again, which ultimately causes insulin resistance (when cells stop responding to normal amounts of insulin). This can lead to diabetes or other symptoms of metabolic syndrome in some cases, but also contributes to fluctuating blood sugar levels in those who are not considered diabetic.

How Does Stress Affect Blood Sugar Handling?

As we have just discussed, the pancreas releases the hormone insulin to lower blood sugar levels when they are too high. The other side of the balance are the adrenal glands. They react to low blood sugar by releasing hormones (glucocorticoids) to instruct the liver to release glycogen, thus raising the glucose levels again. When we are under physical or emotional or mental stress, the adrenal glands answer that call by 'ordering' more glucose into our bloodstream ready to be used as energy, preparing us for fight or flight. If we do not "fight or run", which normally we don't, the pancreas then has to order the sugar back to the liver again by secreting more insulin. This vital and delicate balance of blood sugar is maintained between the pancreas, the liver and the adrenal glands.

Hold the leg just above the knee and push it straight down towards the couch while the client resists

1. Client raises their left leg. Hold the leg just above the knee and push it straight down towards the couch while the client resists. **(See Fig. 44)** It should test strong. If muscle is weak, it is usually as a result of weak abdominal muscles and occasionally the quadriceps. Use the abdominal NL strengthening points (insides of the thighs) or spread the sagittal suture a few times on inspiration (See page 175). If this fails to strengthen the raised left leg, stimulate the NL for the quadriceps (along the border of the rib cage).

2. Bend the right leg at the knee so that the sole of the foot is flat on the couch.

3. In this position, ask the client to raise their left leg again and repeat step 1. If the left leg, which was previously strong, now weakens, there is a hypoglycaemia issue.

4. To double check results, place sugar between the lips or on the body and repeat step 3. This should cause the left leg to become strong again.

5. The test in step 3 is best placed in pause lock as repeated testing is not easy for the client to maintain. Find the nutrition that locks the IM and raises vital force (unlock). You can then remove the nutrition and check the 4 finger modes to find the body's preferred correction.

6. Place the nutrition back on the body whilst you make the correction.

 *Find the nutrition needed before making a correction.*

Diet and Nutrition

This requires further reading

- Someone with blood sugar fluctuations should not skip meals. Meals should contain protein with carbohydrates kept to a minimum.

- Dietary fibre and good fats such as avocado and coconut oil help slow down transit time so that sugars are not absorbed too quickly in the small intestine.

- If symptoms of low blood glucose are severe, initially eating a protein-only snack between meals may help until blood glucose levels are in a better balance.

- Avoid sugar, honey, alcohol, caffeinated drinks, smoking, recreational drugs, refined carbohydrates.

- Chromium, High dose B complex, Vitamin C, Magnesium, Liquorice, Angelica, Cordyceps and Dandelion Root.

Other Considerations

Check Blood Chemistry, adrenals and liver (detoxification section). Address poor digestion if this is a problem. (See pages 13, 213, 82 & 70)

Notes

Notes

Structural Imbalances and Corrections

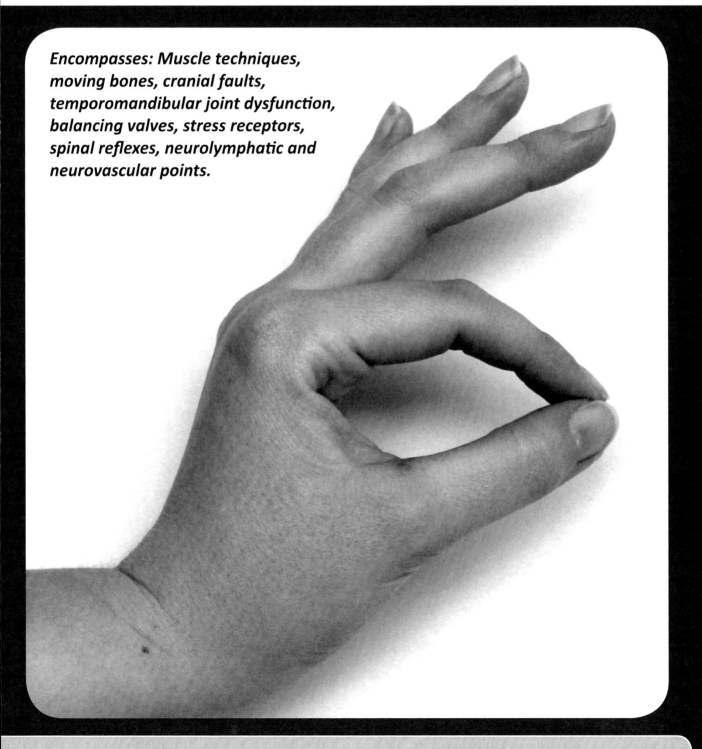

Encompasses: Muscle techniques, moving bones, cranial faults, temporomandibular joint dysfunction, balancing valves, stress receptors, spinal reflexes, neurolymphatic and neurovascular points.

Table of contents

Ileocaecal Valve (ICV)Syndrome

Structural Finger Mode (may also show as Biochemical)

Anatomical Position of Ileocaecal Valve – Figure 45

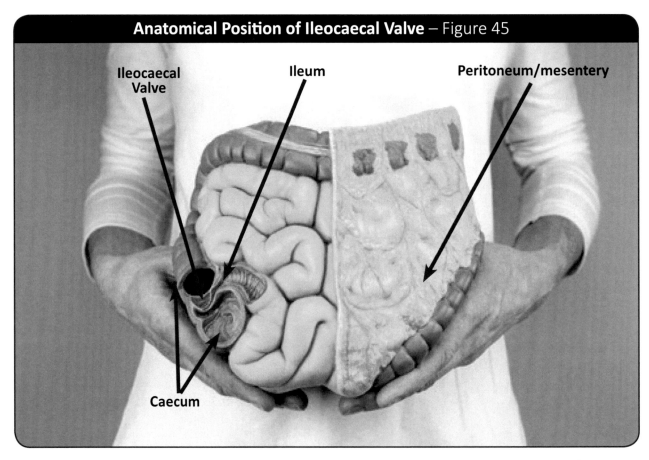

Ileocaecal Valve · Ileum · Peritoneum/mesentery · Caecum

The ICV was once thought to be simply a one-way valve that stays closed to retain the partially digested food chime in the small intestine **(See Fig. 45)** so that nutrients and water can be absorbed before being excreted. The valve comprises of two muscles and functions under autonomic nerve control. It is partly controlled by the vagus nerve and neural factors such as the enteric nervous system (ENS). The ENS lies in the gut wall, beginning at the oesophagus and ending at the anus. There is an emotional factor that also influences the valve; the "gut reaction" to stress affects its function. Many other factors appear to affect the ICV such as reflexes resulting from irritation of the gastrointestinal tract, the kidneys or the peritoneum. These can cause intense contraction and even cause delay or even completely stop movement in the transit of intestinal content through the ICV. The secretion of the hormone gastrin from the stomach increases contraction of the small intestine which in turn causes the ICV to relax (Guyton). Gastrin secretion is affected by HCl production, so we should address that too.

The ICV acts like a non-return valve and prevents matter in the colon, now destined to become faecal, from returning back through the valve to be reabsorbed by the small intestine's villi. The ICV should not open except when chyme is ready to pass through from the small intestine. The pressure of the peristaltic action of the large intestine helps keep the valve shut. If it opens inappropriately the person can be continuously poisoned by toxins giving rise to many unpleasant symptoms. This is a dynamic process. Sometimes the valve **should be open** and sometimes it **should be closed**. When an ICV tests positive on muscle testing, the valve could be working out of sync.

If in spasm, or neurological input from the sympathetic nervous system is excessive, the valve stays open and leaks. If flaccid, without tone (parasympathetic dominance), it stays shut causing putrefaction in the small intestine due to delay in proper transit time (Guyton). The main difference in symptoms between and open and shut ICV is, that when the valve is inappropriately closed, symptoms are worse in the morning and better for moving about (moving helps intestinal peristalsis). (Walther D. , Ileocecal Valve Syndrome, 1988) (Knowlative)

Examination and treatment of the ICV syndrome was first introduced by George Goodheart in 1967 and correcting this dysfunction has helped thousands of people. You will come across clients with ICV syndrome a lot in your clinic because it's such a common problem **(see Table 16 overleaf)**. The results, when this valve starts functioning properly, can be stunning. You first correct the valve and your client says, "what's an ileocaecal valve?" You explain. The next time they visit they might say, "My ICV has gone again!" They experienced such relief from your correction, they now know straight away when it needs re-setting.

Sometimes the results can be witnessed immediately. I had one gentleman who suffered from abdominal pain. He would describe it as 'horseshoe pain' because it covered an area of that shape. Clearly it was a very unhappy large intestine. As well as pain, he would feel really unwell and visibly go pale and sweaty. He had a chronic ICV problem that took quite a number of sessions to sort out (what was I missing as the underlying cause despite trying

all manner of corrections?). As soon as I opened the door to him, I would know when his ICV was in dysfunction just by looking at him – and so would he of course! What was so amazing was that almost immediately after carrying out the ICV treatment, his colour would return to normal and he would feel much better.

Another client presented with chronic diarrhoea. One of the main priorities was the ICV. However, it showed only as a hidden valve, so was a hyoid-related problem (see notes for hidden valves on page 127). The hyoid was corrected, and this resulted in the resolving the ICV problem and the full treatment was not needed. She reported that her diarrhoea had completely cleared up as a result. Having previously never heard of the ICV, I was amused when she came for her second visit and said "My ICV's gone again!".

The important thing that I have learned is that there are a lot of underlying issues that could be at the root of a dysfunctional ICV and Houston's rings such as the wrong foods, the microbiome, neck muscle tension impinging on the vagus nerve, psychological stress etc. etc. **(See Table 15)**. Pressing on the valve is probably only a very temporary effect that will make your client feel better for a while. In the meantime, search for the cause.

Predisposing Factors to ICV Syndrome – Table 15	
Poor diet, irregular meals.	Hypoglycaemia is often concurrent.
Diet too high in fibre, raw foods and fruit.	Lack of proper toilet training.
Allergies to commonly consumed foods.	Lack of exercise.
Gut flora disturbance and infestation of undesirable bacteria and fungi.	Emotional shock or trauma.
Parasites.	Continual emotional strain.
Adrenal insufficiency.	Psoas dysfunction and kidney meridian imbalance.
Low stomach hydrochloric acid causing the bowel to be too alkaline -open ICV.	The bowel is too acid – closed ICV (pancreatic enzymes may help improve alkaline production).

The client will not always complain about bowel function

These are not put forward as a complete list, but the following give some idea of the diversity of effects people can suffer.

List of Possible Symptoms of Autointoxication – Table 16	
Migraines and headaches.	Catarrh, colds are the body's attempt to clear toxins.
Stiff neck from toxins in a weak upper trapezius.	Pseudo sinus infection, postnasal drip.
Shoulder pain and shoulder joint pain, pseudo frozen shoulder.	Dark circles under the eyes, also a sign of kidney stress.
Elbow pain, pseudo tennis elbow.	Tinnitus.
Chest pains, the person might think feels like heart pains.	Allergies are aggravated by the immune system weakening.
Sudden thirst.	Dizziness.
Digestive disorders, indigestion, nausea.	Sudden low back pain - "I only bent over to pick up a pencil".
Pseudo hypochlorhydria.	Constipation, diverticulitis, "sludging up" of the bowel.
Chronic fatigue.	Nervous debility, depression.
Skin problems.	Arthritis or knee pains, small joint pain
Abdominal pain, "grumbling appendix", groin pain.	Bowel gas, distension of belly
Heart arrhythmia.	Worse for sleeping late (closed ICV)
Carpel tunnel syndrome.	Intervertebral disc problems (often accompanied by a feeling of right leg giving away and groin pain).

Tests involved with the ICV

> An active ICV involvement will always respond to challenge testing with an AIM if the tester presses in various directions into the area halfway between the ASIS and the navel on the right side. **(See Fig. 47 overleaf).** I usually use a sustained/ static challenge rather than TL over the valve because that will instantly give me the direction of correction that the valve needs to be pressed (as always, assuming it is a modality or priority).

Challenging the ICV

Discrepancies may be found in various kinesiology manuals on how to challenge the ICV. Going back to grass roots, a sustained, or static challenge (see glossary on pages iv & v) will give us information about the direction in which a correction should be made.

The principles are:

- When testing a **weak** muscle that is related to a presenting problem, pressing and holding, for example, a subluxated bone or valve in the direction it needs to go will strengthen the muscle. (Walther) (Frost).

- If working from an accurate indicator muscle, correction is made in the **opposite** direction to the positive sustained challenge.

- If the client TL's over the valve and the IM unlocks, then makes a sustained tug over the valve, the direction of correction is the one that causes the indicator to change (lock). The simplest way to do this is to enter the TL into pause lock. Testing with the unlocked muscle, challenge for the direction of correction, which will cause the IM to lock.

It will only TL if the ICV is a priority. Incidentally, if the client is switched, you could be dealing with a Houston's valves problem on the left! So, always check centring. A hyoid imbalance (see section on electromagnetics on page 9) could hide the problem and if ionisation hasn't been checked (page 15) TL with palms up if it doesn't show when testing with the palm facing down.

How do I Know if the Valve is to be Treated as Open or Closed?

If the valve needs be addressed as closed, the psoas will be hypertonic/over-facilitated, and the sedating points will not weaken the muscle.

If the valve is 'open', the psoas will either be weak in the clear, or if it is strong, will weaken when the sedating acupressure holding points (AHP) K1 & Liv1 are touched simultaneously. To do this, the practitioner contacts the two AHP's, then test the psoas immediately following.

Other Diagnostic Checks

As you examine your client kinesiologically, you may come across one or more of following signs that may lead you to think there is an ICV problem that needs checking.

- The iliacus, quadriceps, fascia latae, hamstrings or quadratus lumborum will often be bilaterally weak. A weak psoas or iliacus on the right my indicate an open valve.

- Soreness on palpation on the right side of C3, T4-5, or L1

- The gleno-humeral joint is tender (the hollow between the head of the humerus and just below the clavicle)

- If the acupuncture point Large Intestine 4 **(Figs. 49 & 50 on page 124 - 125)**. is tender when rubbed, this indicates there may also be a gall bladder issue.

- When palpating the colon, a sloshing noise is noted.

- There is bulging or engorgement and tenderness of the tissues of the lower right abdominal quadrant.

- There is a lesion at L1/L2. To correct see pages 142 - 146.

- The back molars congested or impacted, hence a TMJ connection (the neurologically connected tooth is the right lower wisdom tooth).

- Right metatarsal arch and foot reflexes for the intestines are sore or sharp.**(See fig.46 overleaf)**

Nutrition

Remember to check nutrition before making your corrections. **Chlorophyll** is good for these clients as are dark green leafy vegetables. **Spirulina** is rich in chlorophyll. **Aloe Vera** can also help settle the valve. HCl or digestive enzymes may help to correct any pH imbalances in the colon. Calcium may be indicated for a closed ICV. Consider absorption of calcium by checking for hydrochloric acid deficiency (Ridler's reflexes see page 68).

Full Treatment

Simply stated, this treatment stimulates afferent neurological connections so that the brain is alerted to the imbalance, it then sends efferent messages to synchronise the mechanisms controlling ICV function. To make the procedure easier to follow, start at the extremities of the body and correct all the reflexes in a sequence going towards the head. You could test each point individually and only correct those that have a positive CL, but this would make carrying out the procedure laborious. So, all corrections are carried out as a series whether active or not.

1. **FOOT REFLEXES**

   Massage the reflexes for the large and small intestine and the ICV as per reflexology chart (Fig. 46).

2. **THE FOLLOWING ACUPUNCTURE POINTS ARE THEN STIMULATED**

   Figs. 48, 49 & 50 Rub **Bladder 58**, **Kidney 3, 5, 7** and then **Kidney 10**. K 10 is just medial to the popliteal crease and between the two tendons. **Gall bladder 31** see **Fig. 50** is found by placing the client's hand with the fingers slightly bent at the centre of the lateral midline of the thigh on the same side. *(Go to knowlative. com – the site for kinesiologists, where you will find detailed acupuncture charts. Sign up is free)*

3. **THE FRONT NEURO-LYMPHATICS** for the muscles involved are rubbed: The upper trapezius, tensor fascia latae, hamstrings, iliacus, psoas and quadriceps. see **Fig. 48** Work upwards towards the head. *(Go to Knowlative.com)*

4. **BALANCING THE VALVE** Apply firm but gentle pressure within your client's tolerance level. Challenge (sustained) the valve in different directions until the IM unlocks. (**See Fig. 47**) Apply pressure in the opposite direction to the positive challenge. Hold this position until discomfort abates. Altering vector of compression slightly may help to facilitate the valve to normalise.

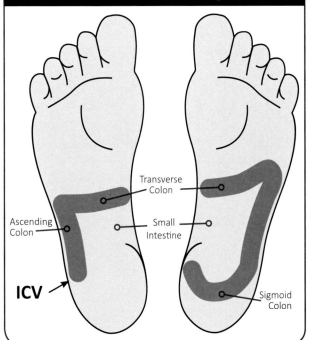

Foot Reflexes Chart – Figure 46

Transverse Colon

Ascending Colon

Small Intestine

ICV

Sigmoid Colon

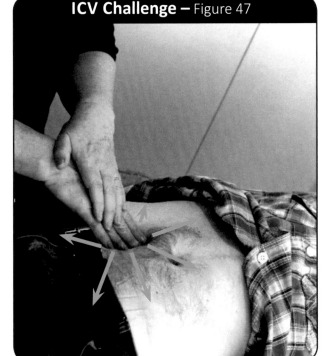

ICV Challenge – Figure 47

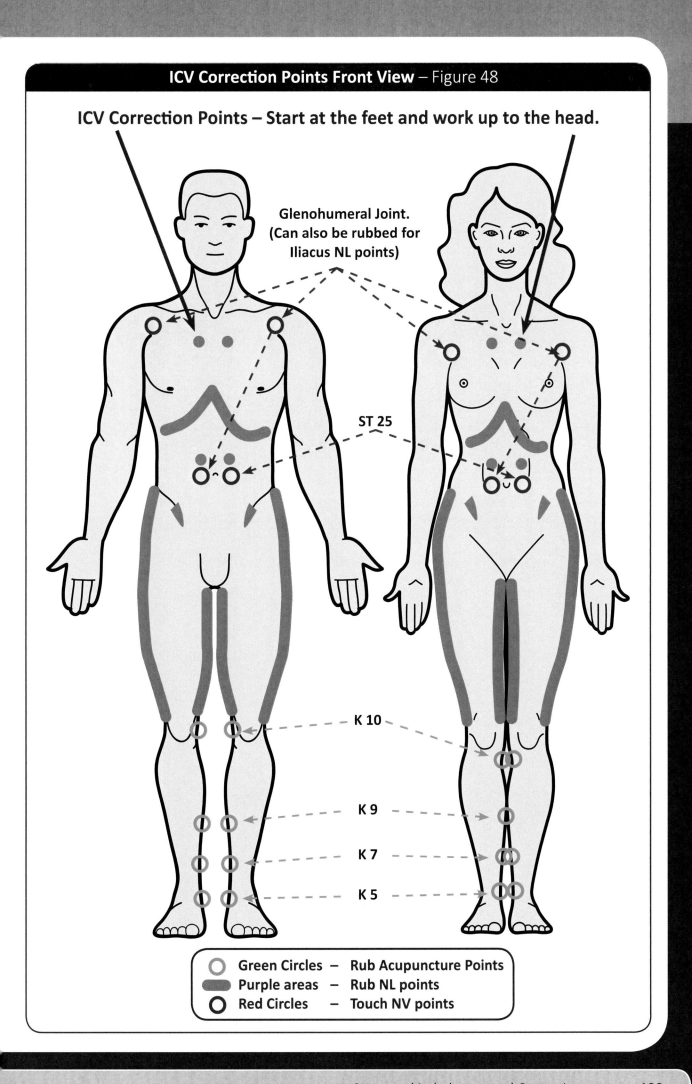

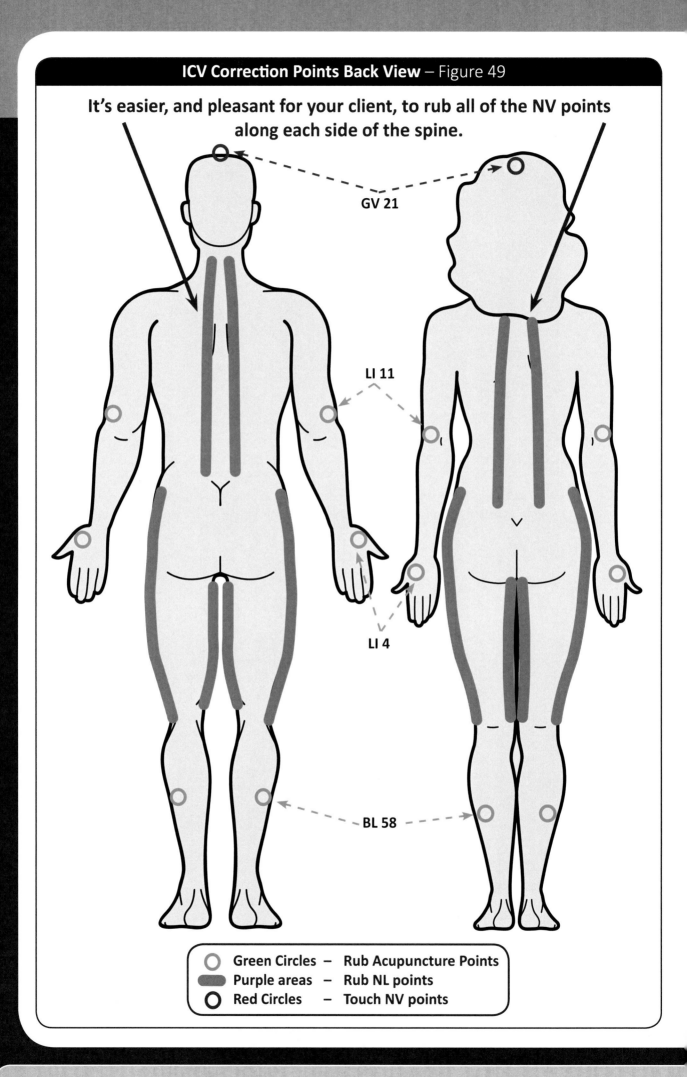

ICV Correction Points Back View – Figure 49

It's easier, and pleasant for your client, to rub all of the NV points along each side of the spine.

GV 21

LI 11

LI 4

BL 58

○ Green Circles — Rub Acupuncture Points
▬ Purple areas — Rub NL points
◉ Red Circles — Touch NV points

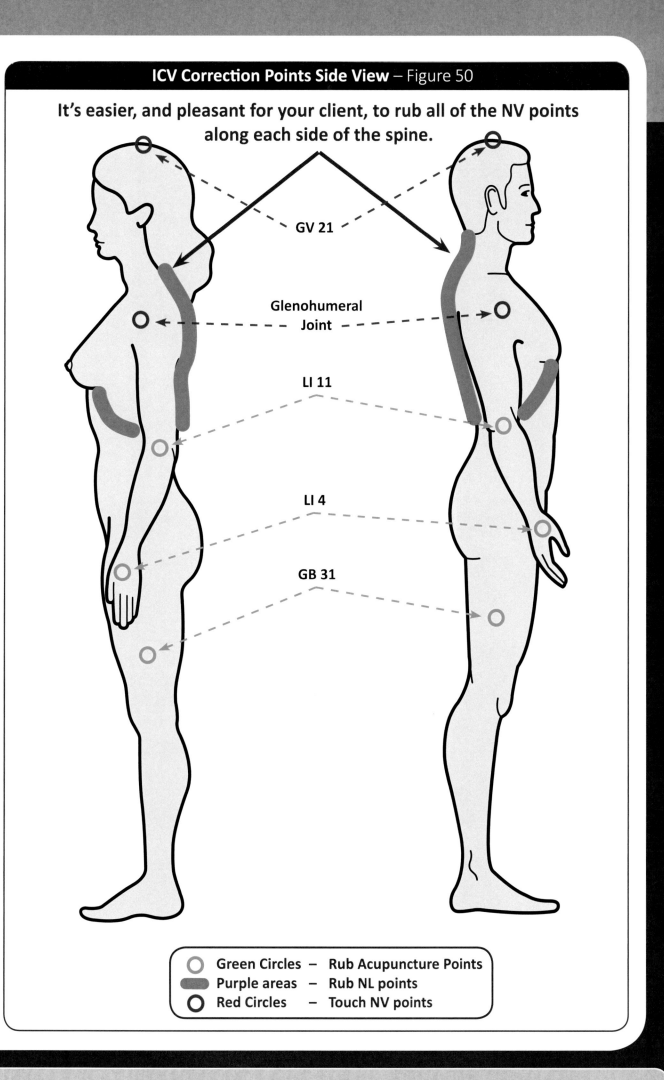

ICV Correction Points Side View – Figure 50

It's easier, and pleasant for your client, to rub all of the NV points along each side of the spine.

GV 21

Glenohumeral Joint

LI 11

LI 4

GB 31

○ Green Circles – Rub Acupuncture Points
▬ Purple areas – Rub NL points
◯ Red Circles – Touch NV points

5. The zygomatic cranial fault; to correct this, **compress the zygomatic arches** (cheekbone) by pressing with your thumbs into the skin over each zygoma under the orbits of the eyes. Keeping this pressure, quickly flick both thumbs downwards towards the feet (Van Rumpt thrust). This is a 'directional non-force technique' (DNFT) developed by Dr Richard Van Rumpt. "It is a method of making a chiropractic analysis by skin reflexes and a thumb contact adjustment thrust, a little deeper than skin deep. The term, "Non-Force" is used because it is non-force compared to some chiropractic techniques" (DNFT Chiropractic, 1987). Treatment for a closed ICV, **(See Figs. 48, 49 & 50).**

6. **SPINAL NEURO LYMPHATIC POINTS Massage these at C3, T4-5, L1-2**. (In clinic I usually rub either side of the whole spine as this is a pleasant thing to do for your client). **(See Fig. 49)**

7. **NEURO VASCULARS** Touch over the valve and simultaneously contact lightly **ST25 on the right, the left glenohumeral joint, then and the vertex, GV21. (See Figs. 48 & 49)**

8. ACUPUNCTURE POINTS ON THE ARM **Stimulate LI4*** at the web of the thumb and forefinger, and **LI11** on the outside crease at the elbow, just medial to the lateral epicondyle. **(See Figs. 49 & 50)** ** Please note there is some controversy in the acupuncture community regarding the treatment of LI 4 during pregnancy. It is therefore best avoided in this instance.*

CLOSED ICV

The closed ICV is encountered relatively rarely. The extra NV is the parietal eminence. Carry out a Van Rumpt thrust (see open ICV protocol), this time stretching the zygomatic arch (cheekbone) apart across the cheekbone from front to rear towards the ear.

The person may need calcium (Test for low

HCL using Ridler's points (pages 68 & 69) in case absorption is the issue), phosphorous, chlorophyll, vitamin D.

A closed or spastic ICV presents with any of the same symptoms as the open with the addition that the person will often complain of not being able to sleep on in the morning. If they do sleep longer, they complain of feeling really unwell until they "work it off". The longer they are up, the better they become. This person will often be very tense. Look out for this with people who don't answer the 'call of nature' because of their jobs – lorry drivers and hairdressers for instance.

Other pointers are:

Weak rectus abdominus on the right, hypertonic quadriceps, hypertonic psoas (to test for this, have the client bring a knee to the chest and see if the other straight leg rises from the table). Also, as mentioned earlier, contacting the sedating points K1 and Liv1 will not weaken the psoas.

HOUSTON's VALVES

The Houston's valves, or Houston's rings lie between the descending colon and rectum. Transverse folds were first described by Irish–British anatomist John Houston, curator of the Royal College of Surgeons in Ireland Museum, in 1830. They appear to be peculiar to human physiology: Baur (1863). The transverse folds of rectum (or Houston's valves) are semi-lunar transverse folds of the rectal wall that protrude into the rectum, not into the anal canal as that lies below the rectum. Their use seems to be to support the weight of faecal matter, and prevent its urging toward the anus, which would produce a strong urge to defaecate. (Wikipedia, 2019)

The Houston's valves will CL and challenge in the same position as the ICV but on the left side instead of the right.

The treatment is as above. Any points that are worked on the right side only, are worked on the left side instead. Symptoms of dysfunction are gas, bloating, ineffectual urging, constipation and/or haemorrhoids. People who are likely to suffer from a dysfunctional Houston's valves are people who ignore the signals that they need to open their bowels e.g. hairdressers, professional drivers, shop assistants.

Additional Information on the ICV

- Environmental stress and improper food combinations 'blow' the valve. If the tester finds that every person they treat shows an ICV problem, then suspect that the tester themselves has the problem.

- A hidden ICV problem does not show on TL, only by a challenge. This does not necessarily mean that it is not a priority. What it does mean is there is likely to be a connection with a hyoid imbalance.

- A definite crease below the lower eyelid indicates a chronic ICV condition.

Hidden Valves

ICV dysfunction may only show when the eyes are closed or when certain foods are placed in circuit. There could also be an ileal brake or gastro-colic reflex problem (See overleaf).

There is a hyoid connection with the ICV. This is perhaps because of the location of the tenth cranial nerve, the vagus nerve, which runs through muscles attached to the hyoid. It receives sensory information from the organs of the neck. The vagus and its branches run from the brain right down to the colon and plays a critical role in the muscles of the tongue, speaking and swallowing as well as in digestion (See page 131).

1. With two hands, client TLs over the valve.

    If the indicator changes when the left hand is touching the skin over the valve, there is a right brain and hyoid problem.

    If the indicator changes when the right hand is touching the skin over the valve, there is a left-brain and hyoid problem.

2. Proceed by correcting the hyoid (See section on Electrical Imbalances and Corrections on page 9) in the normal way.

3. Repeat step 1 which should now be clear. Now the ICV will either CL normally or be resolved - if it is compensatory to the hyoid.

Self-management of Ileocecal Syndrome

- Water: the only substance taken orally that does not require digesting. Several glasses should be drunk daily in between meals, up to a ¼ hr before, and not until 1 hr after meals.

- Avoid stimulants & irritants: tea, coffee, alcohol, carbonated drinks, black pepper, curries and other highly spiced foods.

- It's important to chew food thoroughly to ensure proper digestion.

- Avoid roughage for two weeks: raw food can constitute an irritant to the bowels.

- Eat yoghurt, kefir and fermented vegetables or take probiotics: sufficient quantities of lactobacillus acidophilus either as a preparation or in yoghurt – preferably goats, will assist in the re-establishment of the proper intestinal flora.

- Exercise: regular moderate exercise helps restore tone to the bowel.

- Allergens: avoid any foods to which the person is known to be sensitive. Allergens could trigger a faulty valve.

- Neurovascular point: lightly touch over the valve area after eating and after opening bowels.

- If symptoms occur the client can apply a cold pack to the ICV/Houston's ring area.

- Push up towards left shoulder on right lower abdominal quadrant area. This can be done with the head of a plastic water bottle, or similar.

- Rub along the bicipital groove on the upper arm and the glenohumeral joint on the right side of body (for ICV) **See Fig. 48** on page 123.

More on Peristalsis

Structural Finger Mode or may show as Biochemical

Ileal Brake Challenge for Fats
(Walter H Schmitt)

The ileal brake mechanism has the effect of slowing down peristalsis (the wave-like movement through the digestive tract) to allow better digestion of fats before moving through to the colon. Fatty acids in the digestive system stimulate the enteric nervous system (ENS) to decrease peristalsis to allow the fats to be absorbed in the small intestine first. The ileal brake reflex is a normal response as it prevents undigested fats from moving into the colon. The presence of undigested fats in the ileum stops the ICV from opening i.e. it puts the brake on peristalsis. If the ICV opens when fat absorption is incomplete, there will be fat in the stools and the stools will float (steatorrhea). If undigested fat is allowed to pass into the colon, this also creates a milieu for unfriendly gut flora. The ICV should remain closed until the fat has been properly digested. If fat digestion is incomplete, the ileal brake reflex causes the ICV to remain closed eventually causing constipation.

The aim of this protocol is to stimulate the reflexes for the liver and gallbladder and pancreas (lipid enzyme production) so that fat can be properly digested. The ICV can then open appropriately to allow properly digested fats through into the colon.

1. Test the ICV (page122). If it is a positive test and a priority/modality, carry out a correction. If the ICV test is negative, go to step 2.
2. Ask the client to TL the ICV area. The IM should remain **locked**.
3. Place on the body some form of 'good' fats for example flaxseed oil, olive oil etc. If the IM now unlocks the ICV is opening to the fat challenge when it should be closed, that is the dynamics of the ICV are disrupted due to poor fat absorption.
4. Enter the ICV TL and the 'good' fat into circuit. If there is an ileal brake involvement the IM will **unlock**.

5. Identify any nutrients that negate the positive challenge, for example pancreatic enzymes, pancreatin, zinc, digestive enzymes containing bile salts, magnesium, or liver support herbs (IM will lock on appropriate remedies).
6. With the oils (step 3) still on the body, contact the following treatment points and rub the active ones that two-point (**lock**) the IM.
   - Neurolymphatic points for liver, gallbladder and pancreas.
   - Alarm points for liver gallbladder and spleen meridians.
7. Recheck step 3.

Ileal Brake Challenge for Carbohydrates (CHO)

Many clients come with digestive problems. A common imbalance is the inability to digest carbohydrates properly. The symptom is usually severe bloating. The problem lies with the small intestine (SI) where carbohydrates are rendered into absorbable sugars. If this process is not completed here, the remaining carbohydrates ferment causing the small intestine to distend. One of the actions that control the opening and closing of the ICV is the difference in pressure between the ileum (in the small intestine) and the caecum (in the large intestine). So, with increased distension in the small intestine, the ICV is going to open whether CHO digestion is complete or not. Then we have the problem of toxic waste from the large intestine entering the small intestine and being reabsorbed, which makes the problem worse.

This protocol addresses carbohydrate intolerance by simultaneously correcting the small intestine and the ICV.

1. Check ICV function and correct if necessary.
2. Place some form of carbohydrate in the mouth, e.g. a sugar cube, white flour, white rice.
3. With the CHO still in the mouth, recheck the ICV. If the IM now unlocks the carbohydrate is causing an open ICV.

4. Whilst the person still has the carbohydrate in the mouth, CL the neurolymphatics for the small intestine (quadriceps NL and the NL for the abdominals) and/or the SI alarm point. Rub the correction points that two-point (**lock** the IM). ✔

5. With the CHO still in the mouth, recheck the ICV which should now test correctly.

6. Ask your client to consider reducing carbohydrates in their diet.

Gastric-Colic Reflex

If peristalsis is working correctly, when we have just eaten a meal our full stomach will trigger the large intestine to move waste along more quickly increasing the urge to empty the colon. This makes perfect sense – we eat a meal then get rid of the waste from a previous meal. When this mechanism is not functioning at its best, constipation can ensue as bowel contents build up. This protocol ensures that peristalsis is optimal throughout the digestive tract by treating the stomach at the same time as activating the ICV and Houston's rings. If this test

Visceral Referred Pain Chart (VRP) – Figure 51

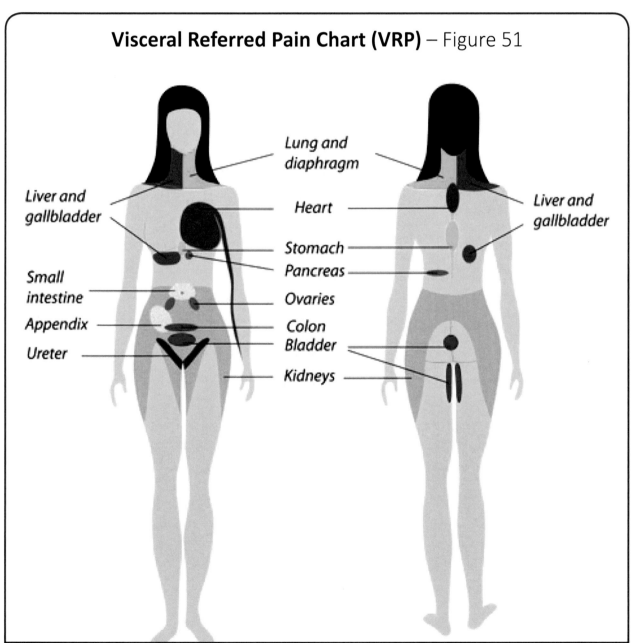

Liver and gallbladder
Lung and diaphragm
Heart
Liver and gallbladder
Small intestine
Stomach
Pancreas
Appendix
Ovaries
Ureter
Colon
Bladder
Kidneys

To challenge a VRP area, test an AIM whilst either rubbing the VRP are (mechanoreceptor activation) or pinching the area (nociceptor activation). These challenges seem to indicate the relative sympathetic-parasympathetic status of the organ itself.

is positive, this is an indicator of colonic dysbiosis (unhealthy gut bacteria) due to poor fatty acid metabolism (see also Ileal Brake Challenge).

The researcher Stephen Gangemi DC understood that the root of many clients' complaints is ICV syndrome. He found that even though individually the ICV, Houston's valves and stomach reflex tests were negative, testing them simultaneously often revealed a hidden problem (I wish I'd known this when treating my 'horseshoe pain' client! see page 119). Making a correction in relationship to each other was shown to alleviate the symptoms of this condition.

1. Test the ICV and the Houston's valves and make any corrections necessary. **(?)**

2. Correct the stomach reflex challenge. If either rubbing or pinching the VRP **(See Fig. 51).** for the stomach (turquoise area) changes an IM, make the following correction:

    If rubbing the VCR unlocks an IM, carry out Injury Recall Technique (see General Techniques section on page 205) whilst contacting the stomach neurolymphatics (NL's) (pectoralis major clavicular- PMC). This may increase sympathetic nervous system (NS) activity in the organ.

    If pinching the VCR unlocks an IM, rub the NL for the stomach (PMC). This may stimulate parasympathetic NS activity in the organ.

3. Now that all 3 points are clear, challenge all 3 points together. This can be done by the client challenging by pushing on their own ICV and Houston's valves and the practitioner challenging the stomach reflex by either rubbing or pinching the anterior stomach VRP area. If an AIM unlocks, place all 3 challenges together into circuit retaining mode. **(✓)**

4. With all 3 challenges in circuit, carry out the appropriate correction on the NL for the PMC described in step 2.

5. Retest step 3.

Balancing the Vagus Nerve

Structural Finger Mode

The vagus nerve is the tenth cranial nerve and interfaces with the parasympathetic control of the heart, lungs, and digestive tract **(See Fig. 52)**. The right and left vagus nerves are normally referred to in the singular. It is the longest nerve of the autonomic nervous system in the human body. The vagus nerve supplies motor parasympathetic fibres to all the organs (except the adrenal glands), from the neck down to the second segment of the transverse colon. The vagus also controls a few skeletal muscles in the neck (Wikipedia). This means that it is involved in the many processes of digestion including swallowing and the synchronisation of the valves serving the stomach, small intestine, and colon.

During emotional stress, excessive activation of the vagal nerve can be caused when the vagus overcompensates (parasympathetic) for a strong sympathetic nervous system response.

Test for vagus nerve involvement if your client presents with medically unexplained symptoms such as:

- An idiopathic (no known cause) cough
- Diarrhoea or constipation when under stress
- Indigestion
- Loss of bladder control when stressed
- Frequent fainting (vasovagal syncope)
- Tachycardia (abnormally rapid heartbeat) or arrhythmia (irregular heartbeat)

Vagus nerve balancing should always be considered whenever your client presents with digestive problems.

The Brain-Gut Axis and the Microbiome

The balance of gut microbes (microbiome) and the foods we eat affect the brain and behaviour. The vagus plays a part in this.

Microbiome → **Gut-Brain Axis** → **Vagus Activation** → **Neurochemistry Changes**

This technique is modified from Quantum Neurology ®, developed by Dr George Gonzalez, www.quantumneurology.com.

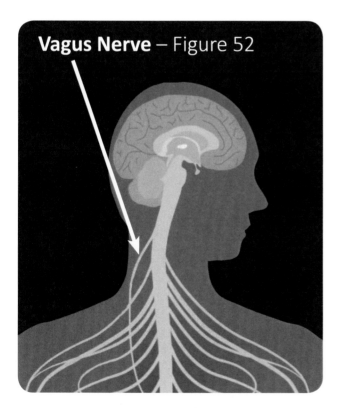

Vagus Nerve – Figure 52

1. The following muscles share circuits with organs that are affected by the vagus. Correct any that test weak in the clear.

   - **Pectoralis major clavicular**
   - **Subscapularis**
   - **Latissimus dorsi**
   - **Abdominals**
   - **Hamstrings**
   - **Fascia latae**
   - **Popliteus**
   - **Pectoralis major sternal**

2. CL very lightly over the carotid sinus by placing your hand over on side of the lateral side of the neck (the vagus nerve is close to this area) and enter into circuit retaining mode. It will not change the indicator, which will usually remain locked, but it will mean that you now have free hands to recheck the muscles in step 1.

3. Retest the muscles in step 1 on the same side of the body as the carotid sinus in circuit. If any of them now test weak there is a vagus associated issue on that side.

4. Cancel the lock.

5. Repeat step 2 & 3 on the opposite side.

---

6. Contact again the lateral side of the neck that showed as positive in steps 2 & 3 and enter it into circuit retaining mode. The example given here is for the right side.

7. Gently but firmly push together with your fingertips the right shoulder (in the region of the PMC) and halfway along the rib cage. With your fingers kept in the same position, tug the same spots apart whilst your client coughs at the same time. **(PUSH TOGETHER THEN PULL APART WITH COUGH)**. **(See Fig. 53)**

8. Carry out the same process as step 7 but place your fingers in the epigastrium area and just above the pubis. Again, push these two points together, then tug them apart whilst your client coughs. **(PUSH TOGETHER THEN PULL APART WITH COUGH)**

9. Cancel the lock

10. If the vagus nerve tests on the other side (e.g. left) in steps 2 & 3 were positive, repeat steps 6 - 9 on left shoulder and left ribcage etc.

11. Run a laser pointer over the brain stem area just below the occiput (suboccipitalis muscles) whilst the client stimulates the vagus nerve by swallowing – drinking water through a straw is ideal.

12. Repeat step 6 and then step 2. All indicators should now be clear. (Prestwich)

Step 7 & 8 Vagus Correction – Figure 53

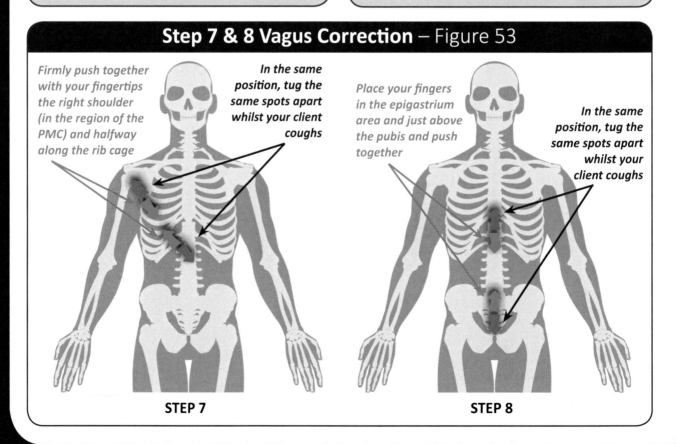

Firmly push together with your fingertips the right shoulder (in the region of the PMC) and halfway along the rib cage

In the same position, tug the same spots apart whilst your client coughs

Place your fingers in the epigastrium area and just above the pubis and push together

In the same position, tug the same spots apart whilst your client coughs

STEP 7

STEP 8

Chronic Valves

Structural Finger Mode

This technique is a Neural Organization Technique (NOT) procedure which was devised by the late Dr Carl Fererri DC. Neural Organization Technique is a specialised branch of Kinesiology which works through the central nervous system to restore structural, bio-chemical, and emotional balance. This discipline works with neurological priority systems. It uses acupressure, reactive muscle monitoring and co-ordinated respiration to address areas of concern. For more information about this excellent system visit www.neuralorg.com or www.neuralorganizationtechnique.org.

I have used this technique many times over the years and found it quick and highly effective in synchronising the valves of the digestive system. It forms part of a complex used in NOT to address the temporomandibular joint (TMJ) in relation to the neurological sequencing of digestive function. If this sequence is out of sync, more energy is needed to compensate for the imbalance which means that the body can give less attention to other functions that may be occurring at the same time.

Some actions that the TMJ performs, such as biting on food and chewing, trigger the valves, which must respond to this stimulation. The ileocaecal valve is controlled by left TMJ activity. Simply put, the pyloric sphincter is reactive to the ICV, and the Houston's valve is reactive to the cardiac sphincter. Dr Ferreri says that a particular action of an active TMJ, during biting down on a food substance, is to cause an active closure of these valves (as opposed to a natural state of closure). This seals the gut at the valves, which initiates peristalsis (so chewing gum clearly isn't a good idea as this would totally confuse the digestive process!).

Because the TMJ is affected by the fight or flight mechanism causing physical and emotional and systemic stress, TMJ dysfunction can cause the inappropriate signalling to the valves causing them all to contract and effectively stop peristalsis until the stress at hand is dealt with. The valves eventually fatigue causing insufficiency.

The valves involved are the ICV, the pyloric sphincter, the cardiac sphincter, and the Houston's valve/rings. The procedure involves a Van Rumpt-type technique over the valve areas together with the neurolymphatic and neurovascular points for the tensor fascia latae, which is a muscle associated with the colon. The gluteus medius is used as an indicator because of its association with the TMJ.

1. Using the gluteus medius as your IM. Ask your client to place their fingertips on both temporom-andibular joints (TMJ). The IM should remain locked. Then check further for TMJ dysfunction and hyoid dysfunction by asking your client to keep the TMJ contact and then test the gluteus medius with the client's:

    a. Mouth open

    b. Biting teeth together

    c. Chewing motion

    d. Swallowing (check hyoid,C1,C2,C3)

    If any of these tests unlock the IM, correct the TMJ and the hyoid for swallowing first before moving to step 2.

2. Ask your client to place the fingers of their right hand on the left TMJ and test the right gluteus medius. If the indicator unlocks there is a chronic valve imbalance.

3. ***Your client needs to keep contacting the left TMJ during the whole process.***

4. With a firm pressure, pull the ICV downwards (inferiorly) towards the right leg and the push inwards (posteriorly). **(See Fig. 54 overleaf)**

5. Push inwards (directly posteriorly) and then screw or twist your fingers into the pyloric valve. This is located approximately 1" above and 1" to the right of the navel.

6. Press into and pull down (inferiorly) the cardiac sphincter situated just under the xyphoid process.

7. Pull the Houston's valves downwards (inferiorly) towards the right leg and the push inwards (posteriorly). ✓

8. Rub the neurolymphatic points for the tensor fascia latae (TFL) on the lateral surface of the thighs down to just below the knee.

9. Hold the neurovascular points for the TFL situated on both sides of the head on the parietal eminences.

Step 4,5,6,7 Chronic valves – Figure 54

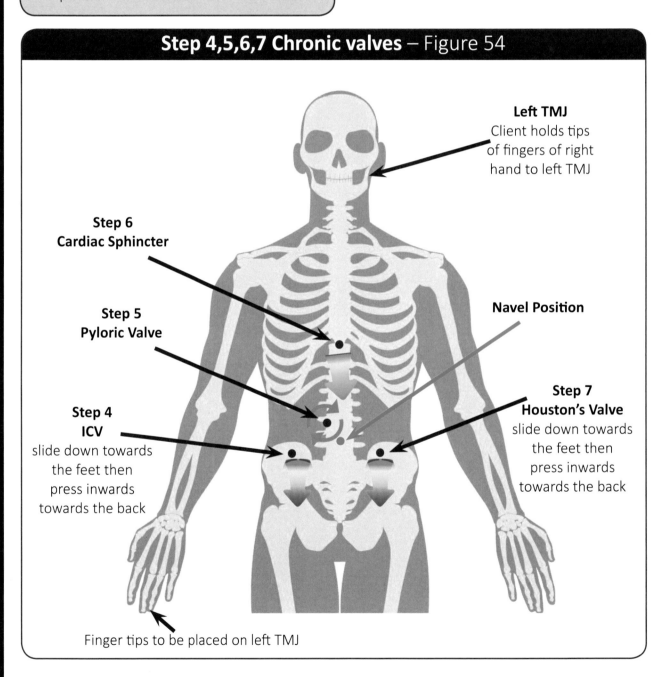

Left TMJ
Client holds tips of fingers of right hand to left TMJ

Step 6
Cardiac Sphincter

Navel Position

Step 5
Pyloric Valve

Step 7
Houston's Valve
slide down towards the feet then press inwards towards the back

Step 4
ICV
slide down towards the feet then press inwards towards the back

Finger tips to be placed on left TMJ

Sub Clinical Hiatal Hernia

Structural Finger Mode

Hiatal Hernia – Figure 55

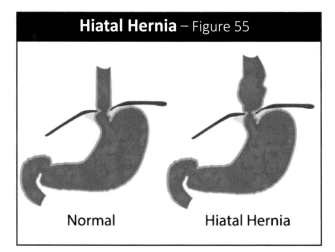

Normal   Hiatal Hernia

A hiatal hernia is a weakening in the diaphragm where the oesophagus passes through it. A small portion of the stomach can protrude through this hole which renders the cardiac sphincter unable to prevent the contents of the stomach regurgitating back into the oesophagus **(See Fig. 55)**. This causes burning and discomfort, particularly when bending forward or lying down. Very slight impingement of the stomach can cause indigestion. Stress can cause the diaphragm to tighten which can create pressure on the oesophagus. This protocol helps release any impingement that the diaphragm is causing.

1. With the client relaxed, push up under the rib cage on the left side near the xyphoid process of the sternum (use firm pressure – a light touch is the test for HCL deficiency). If the indicator unlocks, this suggests that the top of the stomach has slipped up through the opening in the diaphragm and may be pinched and irritated. This may create chest pains, 'heartburn', and difficulty breathing.

2. Have the client stand up against a wall. With the client relaxed, work your fingers up under the xyphoid process and pull downwards sharply a few times all along the costal border (the border of the ribs - **See Fig. 56**). When the diaphragm feels tight, it is beneficial to pull downwards and hold position until muscles start to relax, and the client no longer feels discomfort. Sometimes this can be quite painful since the area, if irritated, will be sore on palpation. Therefore, go gently at first and gradually build up the pressure as the client relaxes.

3. Rub firmly, horizontally **(See Fig. 57 overleaf)**, on the front and back of the lower edges of the ribs simultaneously. You are rubbing along the diaphragm's insertion.

Step 2 Hiatal Hernia Correction
Figure 56

Pull downwards sharply a few times all along the costal border

> **!** *Notice that the diaphragm has its origin in the same area as the psoas, which could also be involved. Check the psoas muscle and correct if necessary. They can be reactive to one another*

Step 3 Hiatal Hernia Correction
Figure 57

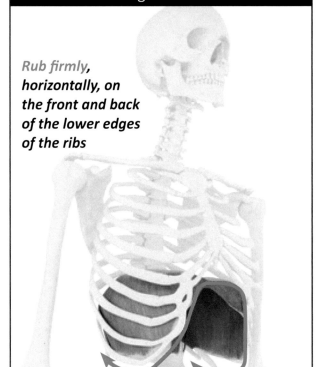

Rub firmly, **horizontally, on the front and back of the lower edges of the ribs**

Step 4 Hiatal Hernia Correction
Figure 58

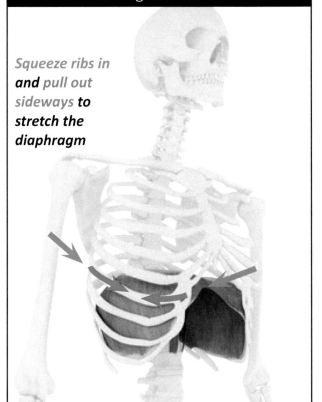

Squeeze ribs in **and** *pull out sideways* **to stretch the diaphragm**

 Ask clients to: *Watch their posture when eating.*

Restrict the size of their meals and chew their food well

Ensure that they are not constipated

---

4. To stretch the diaphragm, stand to one side of the client, placing one hand in front, below the xyphoid, and the other hand at the back of the ribs on the same side of the spine. Pull firmly with both hands, as if squeezing the ribs together and pulling them out to the side, **(See Fig. 58)**. Repeat on the other side of the rib cage.

5. Rub the NL for the diaphragm, which is along the sternum. Simultaneously hold the other hand over the three NV points at GV 17, 19 and 21 these are located at mid-occiput, vertex and crown respectively. Then rub the back neuro-lymphatic point for the diaphragm near the spine right side only T10. (See knowlative.com).

6. Retest as in step 1.

Nutrition

Constipation can cause or exacerbate a sub clinical hiatal hernia. This is because a full colon will push upwards disturbing the stomach, which in turn can then press upwards on the diaphragm. It is very important that constipation is addressed so that this protocol holds.

Test the Ridler's points for HCl and/or digestive enzymes. They may need to be taken together with B Complex and/or the amino acid L glutamine. **If your client has oesophageal reflux do not give HCl.**

Other Considerations

Check for psoas involvement.

Look for sub clinical hiatal hernia in asthmatics as in some cases it can greatly relieve their symptoms. After treatment test whether they need to take digestive enzymes or HCl supplements.

Lateral Atlas

Structural Finger Mode

The atlas, the first vertebra in the spinal column, is unique in structure. The bone is flat and ring-shaped and has no vertebral body which means that it can constantly adapt and shift position to maintain the sensitive balance between the head and neck **(See Fig. 60)**. It is called the atlas because it supports the skull after Atlas, the Greek god who was supposed to support the heavens on his neck and shoulders. The atlas is also referred to as C1.

The late Dr Alan Beardall often discussed the adaptive nature of this vertebra. He would explain that the because the vagus, the 10th cranial nerve can be easily trapped by atlas misalignment, anyone who continually eats foods that they are allergic to, can never maintain a stable atlas. This is because the vagus nerve provides parasympathetic innervation to the stomach and intestines. So, if clients continually complain of neck problems that keep coming back after repeated treatments, consider whether food allergens might be the underlying problem. Almost a century earlier Dr Head had observed that "organs innervated by the vagus nerve would often refer pain to cutaneous zones related the cervical spinal nerves". (Williams, 2011)

Atlas misalignment can be an underlying cause of many problems in addition to allergies. Headaches, temporo-mandibular joint pain, neck pain, lower back pain, scoliosis (twisting of the vertebral column) to name a few. **(See Fig. 59)** The lateral processes serve as attachments for muscles that assist in turning the head and shoulder blades. Therefore, check for this often!

Procedure for Aligning Atlas

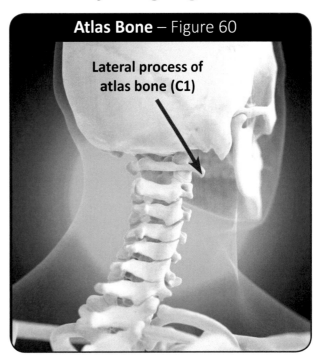

Atlas Bone – Figure 60

Lateral process of atlas bone (C1)

This is a cranio-sacral technique. Energy is 'drawn' between the fingers placed on the opposite side of the head and the process of the lateral atlas allowing the tissue and bone to naturally move into the correct position.

Cervical Spinal Issues – Figure 59

Scoliosis

Atlas Misalignment

Lower Back Problems

1. Whilst testing an AIM, the client in TL's the lateral spinous processes of atlas each side of the neck in the soft spot behind the ear. If indicator unlocks on either side, or both sides, proceed as follows:

2. If both sides are imbalanced, hold the modality mode or priority mode as a filter and then retest to see which side is priority. The one that **unlocks** the IM is the modality.

3. The practitioner contacts the involved side simultaneously with the **opposite** temple near the outer canthi of the eye. **(See Fig. 61)** This is held for 30 seconds to 3 minutes. Use a very light touch and you may even feel the atlas reposition itself. It can also help to imagine energy being drawn from the fingers on the temporal bone to those touching the atlas.

4. Retest atlas to ensure correction has been made.

5. Even if only one side showed initially, go back to both lateral atlas points as correcting one side can disturb the opposite side.

Allergies and the Atlas

One way of testing for allergies including airborne and contact allergies is as follows:

1. Check atlas and correct as above if necessary.

2. Place suspected allergen on the navel and test an AIM whilst client contacts either process of the atlas. If the indicator unlocks, the substance is an allergen.

Atlas and Heel Tension

If you find that on every visit your client needs their atlas correcting, it's likely to be due to Achilles tendon tightness. There is a direct fascial connection between the motion of the atlas and heel tension on walking. The lateral atlas can be felt to move in response to a pumping motion of the heels. With the client prone, bend the knee and dorsiflex the feet (pushing on the ball of the foot so that the toes move down towards the couch). If there is unequal tension, stretch each Achilles tendon by first positioning the leg at a 45° angle and then pump the foot up and down (alternate plantar flexion – pointing the toes – and dorsiflexion) until both sides are freely moveable and of equal tension. (Ferreri) **(See Fig. 104 on page 185)**

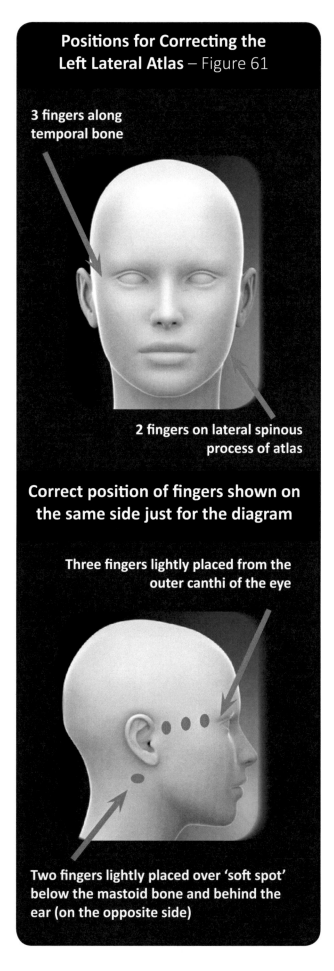

Positions for Correcting the Left Lateral Atlas – Figure 61

3 fingers along temporal bone

2 fingers on lateral spinous process of atlas

Correct position of fingers shown on the same side just for the diagram

Three fingers lightly placed from the outer canthi of the eye

Two fingers lightly placed over 'soft spot' below the mastoid bone and behind the ear (on the opposite side)

Moving Bones

Structural Finger Mode

Bones can be in the wrong place for ANY reason. Eating the wrong foods, for example, can cause the dura (covering of the spinal cord) to twist, thus stressing the spine and causing attached muscle to go into spasm. In clinic I've seen many cases of back problems where chiropractic/osteopathic adjustments just won't hold, yet these have been greatly relieved by addressing food intolerances. A period of prolonged stress can cause intrinsic muscles to contract and cause spinal misalignment. Also, spinal misalignments affect organs by impairing the nerve supply to both the organs and the blood vessels that supply them. **(See Table 17 overleaf)**

Find Out What the Person Does that Causes the Problem

Some causes of chronic problems:

- Old or cheap beds.

- The wrong pillows.

- Do they spend a lot of time stooped over a computer, reading, sewing etc.? Being in one position for long periods teaches the brain that this is a normal state. The muscles on the front of the body remain in a state of semi-contraction and the muscles on the back weaken, even when not in a stooped position.

- Are they stressed? Long periods of dis-stress can cause violent contraction of the rotator brevis muscles. This can cause a disc to bulge or rupture. Stress can cause long-term muscular bracing (dysponesis*) anywhere in the body.

    *****Dysponesis is defined as a reversible physiological state consisting of unnoticed, misdirected neurophysical reactions to various agents (environmental events, bodily sensations, emotions, and thoughts) and the repercussions of these reactions throughout the organism – Dorland's Medical Dictionary.**

Identifying the Muscles Involved

If you've attended a foundation course in kinesiology, then you will have a repertoire of muscle tests to use to find the problem.

Ask yourself the following questions:

- Which muscles would be in use when the pain comes on? What movement makes it hurt?

- Are there any origins or insertions in the vicinity of the pain? If so, are they involved in the lesion?

- Which muscles are likely to be too tight? Which muscles are actually painful when used?

- If there are tight muscles on one side of the body, then where are the corresponding weak ones on the opposite side of the body so that I can work on these too?

- What does my Foundation Kinesiology book tell me about which muscles are related to the obvious problem muscles that I am finding?

- Which muscles test as a modality/priority and need to be treated first?

Other Factors to Consider

Cranial faults (See page 170)

Gait patterns (See page 25)

Cloacals (See page 4)

Atlas (See page 137)

Fixations of the vertebrae (See page 146)

Sagittal suture tap (See page 232)

Dural torque (See page 149)

TMJ (See page 152)

Check out the chart to see if there might be any correlation between your client's symptoms/conditions and the spinal connection.
(See Table 17 overleaf)

Vertebra and Organ Involvement Connection – Table 17

Vertebra	Organ Involvement
C1	Blood supply to the head, the pituitary, the scalp, bones f the face, the brain inner and middle ear, the sympathetic nervous system
C2	Eyes, optic nerve, auditory nerve, sinuses, mastoid bone, tongue, forehead
C3	Cheeks, outer ear, facial bones, teeth, trigeminal nerve
C4	Nose, lips, mouth, eustachian tube
C5	Vocal cords, neck glands, pharynx
C6	Neck muscles, shoulders, tonsils
C7	Thyroid, bursa in the shoulders, elbows
T1	Forearms, hands, wrists, fingers, oesophagus, trachea
T2	Heart, heart valves, pericardium, coronary arteries
T3	Lungs, bronchial tubes, pleura, chest, breast, nipples
T4	Gall bladder, common bile duct
T5	Liver, blood, solar plexus
T6	Stomach
T7	Pancreas, islets of Langerhans, duodenum
T8	Diaphragm, spleen
T9	Adrenals
T10	Kidneys
T11	Kidneys, ureters
T12	Small intestines, fallopian tubes, lymph circulation
L1	Large intestine, inguinal rings
L2	Abdomen, appendix, upper leg, caecum, ileocaecal valve
L3	Sex organs, ovaries/testicles, uterus, bladder, knee
L4	Prostate gland, muscles of the lower back, sciatic nerve
L5	Lower legs, ankle, feet, toes, foot arches
Sacrum	Hips, buttocks
Coccyx	Anus, rectum

How to Find a Spinal Misalignment

1. The client lies prone or this could be done with them standing or sitting (you may get different results, which is very possible since they are in a different posture).

2. Find an AIM. If lying, then a hamstring can be used. If sitting or standing a deltoid works well.

3. Run two fingers quickly along the spine just along the side (about an inch away from the midline (not on top of the spinous processes in the centre of the back) and immediately test the IM. To show up a misaligned vertebra you may need to run your fingers first up the side of the spine, then test, and if nothing shows, run down each side until an IM unlocks (4 tests) **Fig. 62.** This gives you the direction and the side of the spine where you should run your fingers.

4. To narrow down which vertebra/vertebrae is the problem **(See Fig. 63 overleaf)**, run your fingers along just a quadrant of the indicated side of the spine in the appropriate direction i.e. cervical/upper thoracic area, lower thoracic/lumbar area and lumbar/sacrum area. The area that unlocks your IM is where the problem vertebra is (note that there can be more than one). You can then, using two fingers CL each vertebra in that sector to find the one/s you need to care for. Put a biro mark on the vertebrae that CL (or make a note of them) and address them in priority order.

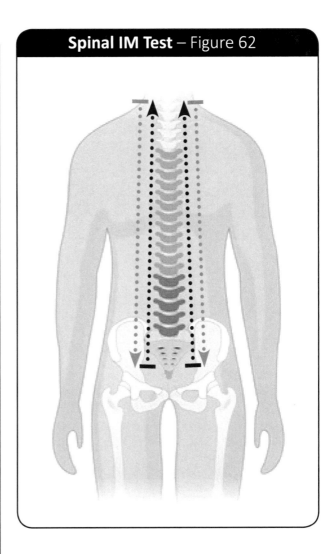

Spinal IM Test – Figure 62

Correcting a Spinal Misalignment

Three methods are described in this book:

1)   Inspiration assist

2)   Lovett Brothers

3)   Using Sound

Inspiration Assist

1. Contact the misaligned vertebra and test an AIM (unlock).

2. Making a correction during a phase of respiration aids with the adjustment so that no heavy digital pressure is needed. While still touching the vertebra ask your client to first breathe in as the IM is retested. If the IM now locks, the client needs to breathe in as the correction is being made. If breathing in does not change the IM, ask the client to breath out. If the IM now locks, expiration is the phase of respiration needed to assist the correction. If the misalignment is a priority the correction is usually made with inspiration.

3. Now challenge the vertebra to find the direction of correction by using a dynamic challenge (push the vertebra in a specific direction and release then test an AIM within 15 seconds, repeating for different directions of challenge). To do this use a thumb or 2 fingers and gentle pressure. The IM will unlock to show the specific direction of correction.

4. Balance the vertebra by gently applying digital pressure as the client breathes the phase of respiration you identified in Step 2. Release the pressure as they change breath. Repeat 5 or 6 times.

5. Retest as in step 1. If the IM now locks, check the other vertebrae misalignments you have noted and correct them in modality/priority order. Some may have corrected themselves.

6. Test each vertebra's Lovett brother (see page 144) and correct if appropriate.

Vertebrae of the Spine – Figure 63

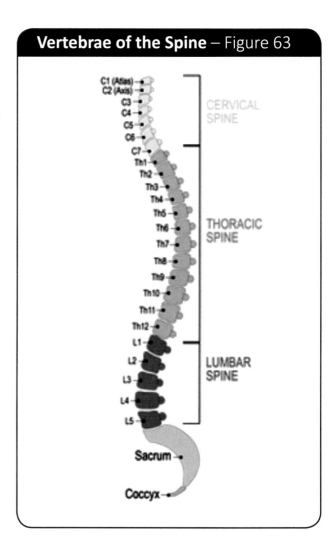

Moving a Vertebra Using its Lovett 'Brother'

The Lovett Brother relationship has been used by chiropractors, Bowen therapists and other body workers for decades.

Moving away from the mid-point of the spine between T5 and T6 in both directions toward the ends of the spine at C1 and L5. Each vertebra is shown to have a corresponding "Lovett Brother" indicator at the same vertebral position above/below the mid-point, where the movement or dysfunction of one is accompanied by movement or dysfunction of the other **(Fig. 64)**. For example, the cervical vertebral reflexes can be found in any posture but will be most prominent when in the position that clients experience their greatest amount of low back discomfort.

So, addressing the Lovett Brother relationship in a postural position is a good thing to do if possible.

"When there is a rotation in L5 there will always be a rotation in C1, its 'Lovett partner', even in the absence of symptoms of pain or lack of function at C1. Symptoms in the neck coming from the Atlas (C1) can conversely be caused by a dysfunction at L5. When one is out of neutral so will its partner. Often it is necessary to address the Lovett Partner as well to get a lasting or even successful correction. Anything that disrupts the mechanics of the sacrum and the coccyx can create adverse mechanical tension in the central nervous system leading to all sorts of musculoskeletal, neurological, visceral and hormonal problems that are difficult to resolve." (Walther, Lovett Reactor, 1988)

Lovett Brother Technique can be used as a stand-alone treatment for the spine, or it can be used in conjunction with other spinal adjustments.

Lovett Brother Reactor Examples – Figure 64

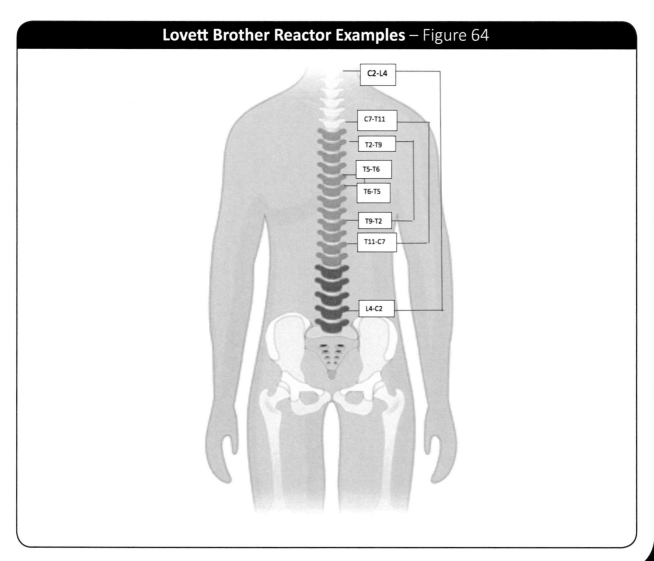

Procedure

1. Identify which vertebra/vertebrae need attention **(Fig. 62 on page 141)**.

2. Any vertebra that unlocks your IM is out of balance. If more than one, identify the modality and treat that one first.

3. CL the vertebra, the muscle should unlock, and put it into circuit retaining mode. The IM will now remain unlocked.

4. CL the Lovett Brother. If it is involved the IM will lock. **(Fig. 64 and Table 18)**

5. Tap the matching Lovett Brother on the spinous process while simultaneously touching the vertebra that you are treating.

6. Cancel the pause lock and retest the original vertebra and the IM should now lock. If it still unlocks repeat step 5 until clear.

7. Test any other vertebrae that you previously found and repeat steps 2 - 6.

Lovett Brother Vertebra Identifier – Table 18

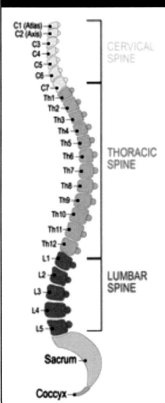

Skull & Cervical Vertebrae	Lovett Brother
Sphenoid	Coccyx
Occiput	Sacrum
C1	L5
C2	L4
C3	L3
C4	L2
C5	L1
C6	T12
C7	T11

Thoracic Vertebra	Lovett Brother
T1	T10
T2	T9
T3	T8
T4	T7
T5	T6
T6	T5
T7	T4
T8	T3
T9	T2
T10	T1
T11	C7
T12	C6

Lumbar & Sacrum Verebrae	Lovett Brother
L1	C5
L2	C4
L3	C3
L4	C2
L5	C1
Sacrum	Occiput
Coccyx	Sphenoid

Notice the pattern. If your chart isn't handy, just remember that T5 and T6 are brothers next to each other.

Correcting a Vertebra Using Sound

Structural Finger Mode

Sound is undoubtedly the highest form of healing one can use. I have found it extremely successful in coaxing a vertebra back into its correct place. Its painless and very safe to do.

The principle behind it is this is that vertebrae have holes (spinal foramen) that house the spinal cord and transverse foramen where nerves stemming from the spinal cord exit. Anything that is partially hollow will vibrate in response to certain frequencies. You can find examples of this on YouTube. The performer chinks the glass and listens to the resonating sound. They then sing loudly the exact same sound/frequency and 'voila', the glass shatters. So, whilst that is an extreme example, creating a particular frequency that resonates with the vertebra will cause it to react and adjust itself.

Creating a Sound

I use tuning forks, just an ordinary set in 'concert' pitch. There are places where you can buy amazing tuning forks, such as tuningforks.co.uk. If you'd rather not spend that much, you can get started by buying a cheap pitch pipe from Amazon or other online stores. You'll need a chromatic one which has the whole range of notes including sharps and flats. They are more awkward to use, and you might find it a bit strange initially, but it's worth trying first with one of these to see if you like the technique before spending the money on a more elaborate way of making a nice sound. Another option that works is a set of chromatic tuning forks that are available online.

1. Test an AIM and find the vertebrae imbalances. The IM will unlock.

2. After finding the modality vertebra, place it in circuit retaining mode (pause lock).

3. Place the set of tuning forks/pitch pipe on the body and retest. If the IM changes, i.e. locks, sound is an appropriate remedy.

4. Whilst testing your IM, touch each of the tuning forks or over each reed of the pitch pipe. The one that changes the IM is the one to use.

5. Touch very lightly at the side of the vertebra you're treating and simultaneously play the note that you have identified as the corresponding frequency. If you're using tuning forks, strike them to start off the vibration and place the tip on the vertebra itself making sure that you don't touch the forks themselves, which will cancel the vibrating sound.

6. After doing this, close pause lock and retest the vertebra. The IM should be locked.

7. Identify its Lovett Brother and correct if it two-points (unlock) (see page 144).

Case Study Using Sound to Adjust Vertebrae

A lady came to clinic with long standing back problems. She had been visiting the osteopath every 2 or 3 weeks because adjustments were not holding.

I did think that the problem might be something other than structural - maybe a nutrient deficiency, psychological conflict, emotional stress or perhaps food intolerances might be impeding her progress. Usually if clients have already had a lot of structural work done, it's worth first checking out other avenues first. My client however was quite adamant she didn't wish to take supplements. After evaluating muscles, TMJ and various kinesiology tests, I decided to test the vertebrae for subluxations and there were a few that needed addressing. I chose to use tuning forks to correct each vertebra. Treating them in priority order and completing the therapy by addressing the Lovett Brother was no doubt instrumental (I couldn't resist the pun!) in her progress but the lady improved so much over a few sessions that she only needed to see her osteopath every few months. Whenever she came, she would always insist that I would just use the sound to correct her spinal misalignment.

Fixations of the Vertebrae

Structural Finger Mode

Vertebral fixations occur when the attached intrinsic muscles become tight. Instead of moving independently, sometimes two or more vertebral segments lock together work as one unit. Unlike spinal misalignments, fixations will not TL or CL and will only respond to a challenge. Muscles that test weak bilaterally are an indication that vertebrae are fixated.

> **If Fixations show, check Dural Torque too. (See page 149)**

David Leaf DC says that vertebrae fixating is a way of the body protecting the spinal cord from torqueing.

Shining a light onto the glabella seems to stimulate centres in the brain that instruct the intrinsic muscles to relax. This simple technique from Bruce and Joan Dewe works very well.

> 1. Ask the client to look at a black cloth or a black piece of paper. If the IM unlocks, the client has a fixation.

> 2. Shine a small torch on the glabella (the spot between the eyebrows) for about 30 seconds or so. An intermittent light can be slightly more effective. A laser can be used, but make sure that the client keeps their eyes shut tightly to ensure the light does not get in the eyes.
>
> 3. Repeat step 1. The IM should now lock when the client looks at the black object.

When someone presents with fixations in my classes, any chiropractors, osteopaths or physiotherapists on the course are asked to assess the spine first. After this treatment has been carried out, they assess again. They tell me that there is definitely a palpable difference to the spine after treatment!

Spinal Reflexes

Bilateral muscle weaknesses require a mechanical correction (Deal). Dr Deal found it greatly beneficial to rub one finger in each groove either side of the vertebrae between the spinous and the transverse processes and he would do this for all of his patients. Later Dr John Thie did further research on this and was able to correlate which fixated vertebrae were associated with which bilaterally weak muscles. Spinal reflexes and their associated muscles can be found in the **Touch for Health manual**.

Ligament Stretch

Biochemical Finger Mode

Flexibility of ligaments can be impaired if there is a manganese deficiency. Hypoadrenia can also be a cause of weak ligaments.

> a. Stretch any joint (a finger joint works well for this test) and hold the stretch for 5 seconds, then test an AIM. If the IM unlocks your client's ligaments would benefit from manganese. 2mg daily for 1 month is recommended (Deal).
>
> b. If just briefly stretching a joint and then immediately testing an IM causes a change, this indicates adrenal insufficiency. For the nutritional programme for adrenal support, go to page 216.

Spinal Torque

Structural Finger Mode

Scoliosis is when the spine torques sideways into the shape of an 'S'. This is because the tiny intrinsic muscles that hold the vertebrae together get too tight on one side of the spinal column weakening the muscles on the opposite side **(See Fig. 65)**. A spinal torque is not necessarily obvious when observing someone's back unless there is a severe problem. Check for this in cases of low back and neck pain as well as thoracic pain.

'S' Shape Curve in Spine – Figure 65

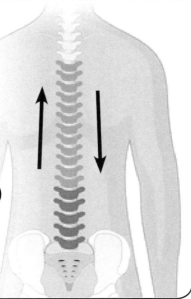

Convex

Concave

This protocol identifies the nutritional support needed for the involved muscles and uses Golgi tendon technique to strengthen the intrinsic muscles on the convex side of the spine. Tightening tiny little muscles that are weak on one side will release the tight intrinsic muscles on the opposite side thus taking the strain off the spine itself allowing it to return to the correct position.

1. The **client is prone for this test**. Place your palms in opposite directions on either side of the thoracic spine and push one hand towards the head (superiorly) and the other towards the feet (inferiorly). Then immediately test an AIM (a hamstring is ideal). **(See Figs. 66 & 67)**

Concave Curve on the Right – Figure 66

If pushing up on the left and down on the right unlocks the IM the client needs Zinc. (Check Ridler's Reflexes for zinc deficiency) see page 68.

Concave Curve on the Left – Figure 67

If pushing up on the right and down on the left unlocks the IM, the client needs manganese. (Check ligament Stretch Technique on page 146 and/or Ridler's Reflexes on page 68 for a manganese deficiency)

3. **Correct the convex side of the spine first** to tighten the weak intrinsic muscles **(Fig. 68 & 69 overleaf)**. Pressure is applied with the thumb, fingers or side of hand, on to the transverse processes of the concave side. The other thumb is placed on top of the spinous process above and **push the thumbs together**. Repeat this the length of the thoracic spine and up to the cervicals.

4. Go to the **concave side of the spine** where the aim is to weaken the tight intrinsic muscles. Place thumbs in same position as no 3 (on transverse process on the convex side and the spinous process above) but **pull the thumbs apart**, along the thoracic spine, to unlock the muscles.

5. Repeat step 1.

Concave on the Right – Correction
Figure 68

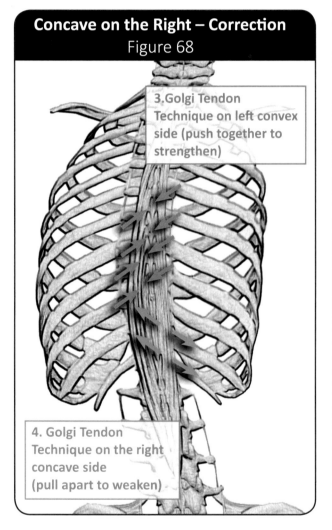

3.Golgi Tendon Technique on left convex side (push together to strengthen)

4. Golgi Tendon Technique on the right concave side (pull apart to weaken)

Concave on the Left – Correction
Figure 69

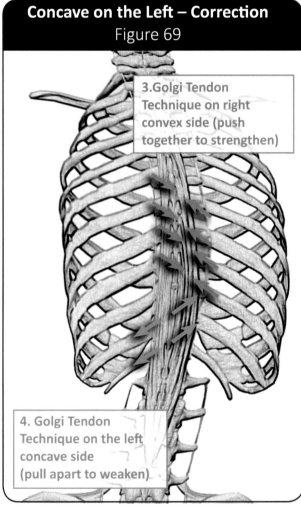

3.Golgi Tendon Technique on right convex side (push together to strengthen)

4. Golgi Tendon Technique on the left concave side (pull apart to weaken)

Dural Torque

Structural Finger Mode

The dura consists of three coverings (membranes) surrounding the brain and spinal cord, the dura mater (which is the tough outer covering), the pia mater and the arachnoid mater. They are also collectively called the meninges. The dura only attaches to a few places along the spinal column therefore if there are any fixations or any spinal misalignments, this can torque the dura. The dura attaches to the atlas, axis and C3 and is an integral to the skull. **(See Fig. 70)**

Function:

- Contains cerebrospinal fluid which protects the brain and spinal cord from impact.

- Protects the nervous tissue. Torqueing helps prevent a problem in the spinal area of the dura going further into affecting the meninges in the brain.

- Supports the brain inside the skull.

- Is an integral part of the cranio-sacral mechanism.

What can go wrong if the dura contracts over a long period of time?

- The sutures of the skull will jam.

- The upper cervical vertebrae fixate, particularly the atlas.

- The sacrum tilts.

- The body distorts into a symptomatic pattern.

- The body is on "Red Alert" permanently. This brings about:

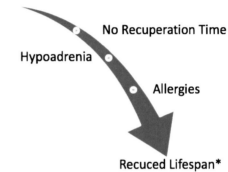

Energy Waste → No Recuperation Time → Hypoadrenia → Allergies → Recuced Lifespan*

Apparently studies show that people live longer if their dura is straight. I could not find where this research came from.

Cerebrospinal Fluid – Figure 70

Superior Sagittal Sinus

Arachnoid Villi

Subarachnoid Space

Skull

Ventricles of the Brain

Central Canal of the Spinal Cord

CSF Cerebrospinal Fluid

Spinal Cord

Factors that Affect the Dura

 Use this frequently. Correcting the dura can have a profound effect on the rest of the body

- Chronic Stress
- Allergic insults
- Gait patterning
- Scoliosis
- Cranial faults
- Upper cervical fixations
- Pelvic structural lesions

Dr Sheldon deal comments that correcting the dura is probably one of the most powerful techniques we have learned in kinesiology. Dural torque is a common condition where the body, because it's compensating, has a slight clockwise or anticlockwise twist in the dura. This creates dural tension. When the dura is stretched, such as bending or sitting, the torque becomes worse, much like a kink in a rubber band is worse when it's stretched. Symptoms can be stiffness and fatigue with a loss of range of motion. (Deal)

Assessing the Dura

Indications:

If the spinal cord is more than ½ " longer between standing up, lying and sitting.

- Unequal leg length
- Unequal strides when walking

Rationale

The aim of this technique is to take the body out of distortion which will in turn alerts the brain to take note and allow for this pattern to be readjusted. We use wedges called Dejarnette blocks – named after Major Bertrand Dejarnette, osteopath and chiropractor, who extensively used blocks in his treatment protocols which are collectively called Sacro Occipital Technique (SOT). His study during the 1920's brought about a system of adjusting patterns in the body, not just single body parts.

Dejarnette Blocks

These are available to buy in various materials, but they can also be made out of wood or polystyrene. The blocks need to roughly measure 21cm long x 13cm wide and 11cm deep at the thickest end. **(Fig. 27)**

Dejarnette Block – Figure 71

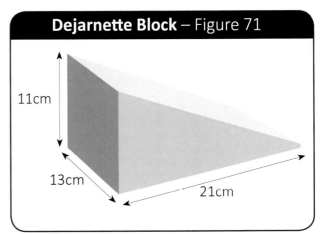

11cm

13cm

21cm

1. To test if the dura is stretching sufficiently the client lies prone. Use a sustained challenge by placing the heel of the hand on the sacrum and pushing down towards the feet **(See Fig. 72)** whilst testing an AIM (a hamstring is the most convenient). This stretches the dura thus exaggerating the lesion.

Test Position for Dural Torque – Fig. 72

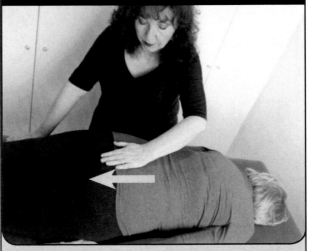

2. You may be able to observe a spinal torque as the person lies prone. One shoulder and hip may be slightly lifted off the couch. Place a wedge (Dejarnette block) under one hip and the opposite shoulder. The thin ends should be pointing diagonally towards the navel.

3. Test an AIM (hamstring) and test again as in step 1. The correct combination should negate the stretching test. Often, the blocks placed in the wrong combination will weaken any muscle in the clear, even without a dural torque challenge. So it's easy to establish the correct positions for the blocks.

Correcting Dural Torque – Figure 73

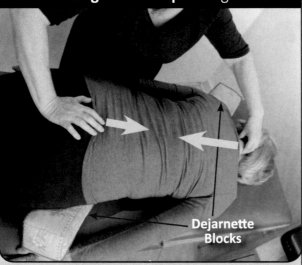

Dejarnette Blocks

4. Leave the blocks in position.

5. On inspiration, hold the coccyx with the palm of one hand and the neck (just below the occiput at C3) with the other hand. Push them towards each other (coccyx superiorly and C3 inferiorly) as if shortening the spinal column as the client breathes in **(Fig. 73)**. Repeat 6-10 times.

6. Remove the blocks and repeat step 1.

Check and correct any fixations or spinal misalignments.

Additional Tests and Corrections to Help Prevent Dural Torque (Deal)

It is also possible to test for dural torque when the client is supine (face up). This technique seems to focus on the upper part of the dura as it attaches to the atlas, C2 and C3 and occiput. One compensation that can contribute to tension in the dura is a hypertonic external pterygoid muscle (see section on the temporomandibular joint (TMJ) for more detail on page 152). This muscle is involved with the action of opening the mouth. Not every practitioner is comfortable with placing fingers in people's mouths, so this is an optional extra. In the following protocol you could place the result of step 3 into pause lock and go through the 4 key finger modes instead of carrying out step 4.

1. Have your client flex their neck so that their chin is on their chest. If an AIM unlocks, this also indicates a dural torque issue because the dura is being stretched.

2. Whilst your client is in this position push on the lateral side of the neck just behind the ear in a medial direction and retest the IM. One side will usually lock the IM again. It is possible that both sides will need addressing.

3. Assuming the client isn't switched, TLing the TMJ, on the same side as step 2, will also lock the IM. (see section on TMJ for more information on pages 152-158)

4. The external pterygoid is a difficult muscle to contact as it is a tiny muscle between the TMJ and the skull. Using a finger cot or disposable gloves, slide your index finger as far as it will go on the buccal (cheek) side of the upper jaw on the same side as the TL. Push down and up in 1/2 of a second. Retest. This is spindle cell technique in miniature!

5. Repeat step 1.

Mode for Dural Torque

Thumb pad is placed on lateral side of the proximal joint of index finger **(Fig 74)**.

Use this sub-mode if the structural finger mode shows and you want to narrow down whether the body needs dural torque carrying out in relationship to the problem online.

Dural Torque Finger Mode – (Fig 74)

Temporomandibular Joint Dysfunction

Structural Finger Mode

The TMJ is one of the most influential joints in the body. Identifying the position of the joint will lead you to observe that the jaw is the 'pelvis' of the head **(Fig. 75)**. Using the principal 'as above, so below', the TMJ can certainly affect the pelvis. If the pelvis is out of balance, this affects the vertebrae and pulls shoulders out of alignment. Whenever you are dealing with a back problem, always consider the influence of the TMJ. 50% of the sensory and motor brain cells are devoted to the TMJ area. These act as a computer telling the body what to do. Many people are affected with occlusal distress (dysfunctional bite). In studies it was found that in 86% of cases reviewed, the TMJ was compensatory in correcting all other lesions of the body. Therefore, it is prudent to perform injury recall on the TMJ at the beginning of a treatment to help to remove compensations, (see page 206).

TMJ Dysfunction can be Symptomatic or Asymptomatic

Symptoms may include a clicking jaw, irregular opening of the jaw, pain in jaw or bruxism (teeth grinding). There could be involvement in persistent headaches, tinnitus, earache, stress incontinence, infertility (women), chronic digestive disorders, chronic fatigue or any muscle weakness in the body. If there is hyperactivity between the brain and the TMJ this can contribute to dysponesis (low grade muscular bracing or habitual tension anywhere in the body).

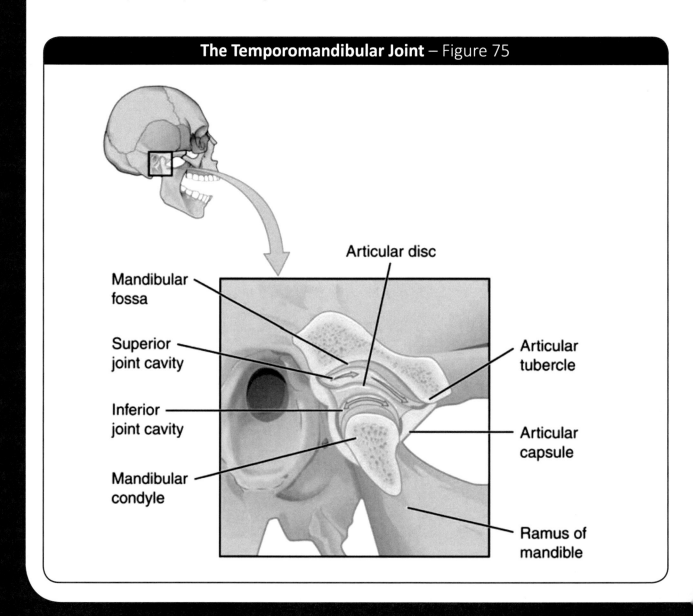

The Temporomandibular Joint – Figure 75

Articular disc

Mandibular fossa

Superior joint cavity

Inferior joint cavity

Mandibular condyle

Articular tubercle

Articular capsule

Ramus of mandible

If someone has experienced whiplash, check the TMJ. This is because the action of the head being thrust backwards then wrenched forwards on to the chest can crush the delicate ligaments around the joint. This can displace the articular disc, which is the cushion that sits between the TMJ and the skull. (Goddard, 1991)

When checking the TMJ, it is worth checking the following as these can also be part of the symptom picture:

- Walking gait
- Hyoid
- Dural torque
- Atlas
- Cranials
- Retrograde lymphatics

Ileocaecal Valve and TMJ

There is often a link between these two dysfunctions.

It is advantageous to prioritise between them if both conditions exist. Correcting the priority will often resolve the other.

How to Check for a TMJ Link with Any Lesion

Since the TMJ can be an underlying factor in many health problems, a short-cut test to check for a connection is two pointing to Small Intestine 5 just behind the wrist bone.

Other TMJ connections

If after retesting the TMJ after correction shows that more needs to be done, look for upper trapezius and/or walking gait problems. (See page 25)

Correcting the TMJ will often resolve weakness in the piriformis muscles.

Evaluation of TMJ

Muscles involved: Masseter, buccinator, medial and lateral pterygoids and temporalis. Their combined functions are complex as some of the muscles attached to the hyoid are also involved in moving the jaw. The described tests and corrections for each of these specific muscles are evaluating their prime movements.

Pressing with the fingers on the muscles around the temples and jaw will be tender or cause discomfort if a TMJ problem is present. If the client puts their little finger into each ear as far as they will comfortably go and then slam their teeth together and there is pressure felt on the fingers or they experience pain, the jaw is over-closing.

Obviously, the jaw does not like this sort of treatment. It often gets pushed right off the articulating disc at the back and the clicking that can be heard is the condyle clicking on and off the disc as the mouth is opened and closed **(See Fig.75)**. Look for signs of problems:

- **Inter- incisal opening (can the person open their mouth wide?).**

- **Clicks and pops.**

- **Rotation and translation (mandible moving forward).**

- **Is the lateral excursion (range of sideways movement) the same for both sides?**

- **Teeth should touch only lightly when swallowing.**

- **When saying "Mississippi sixty-six", the teeth should not clash.**

- **Compare the degree of pain on each side of TMJ when palpating the joint.**

- **Test tenderness of temporalis by palpating the temple. Tenderness means that the person clenches their teeth.**

- **Look for worn facets on the front teeth, shiny spots on fillings, fractured fillings or mobile teeth.**

TMJ Blanket Test

TL'ing the TMJs themselves does not always change an IM. This test even shows an existing problem when TL'ing the TMJ itself doesn't.

Testing an AIM, the client TLs their symphysis menti (tip of chin). An indicator change shows a TMJ problem. If the IM does not change, ask your client to move their jaw laterally, forward and backwards, and up and down and retest as the client contacts the symphysis menti again. This will reveal any hidden problems.

Proceed to the **SPECIFIC TEST** to locate the attached muscle causing the problem.

1. Test an AIM whilst the client TL's TMJ on one side. The indicator may not change until it is further stressed by opening the mouth wide, chewing on the same side or biting teeth together. A change in indicator on any or a combination of these actions indicates specific muscle hypertonicity. If just TL'ing the TMJ whilst the jaw is in a neutral position does unlock an IM, there may be a problem with the articulation of the joint itself.

If the indicator **unlocks** when TL'ing one side of the TMJ, the action of **opening, biting, chewing** that **locks** the indicator again is the muscle on the same side that needs caring for.

Correct the priority lesion

 The following corrections for the TMJ all involve any hypertonic muscles around the joint. Spindle cell technique is used in all cases.

Biting Together

MASSETER AND BUCCINATOR

The masseter **(Fig. 76)** runs almost vertically from the origin at the zygoma (cheek bone) and the insertion into the ramus of the jaw. It elevates the mandible to assist the jaw in closing. The buccinator 's fibres **(Fig. 77)** run horizontally with its origin in the mandible, the maxilla, the crest of the buccinator and the TMJ itself and forms part of the cheek. It compresses the cheek when masticating.

Note that when a TL to the TMJ changes on closing the mouth, **with pressure on the molars**, there is a problem with the temporalis on the same side (see temporalis for correction on page 155).

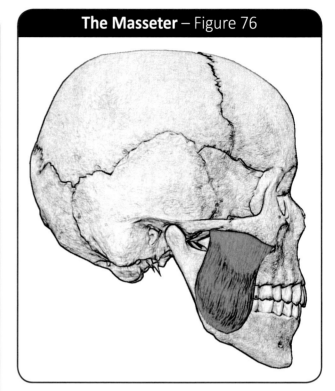

The Masseter – Figure 76

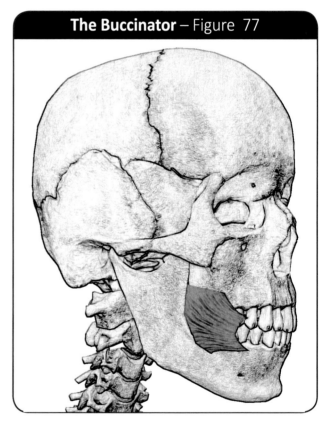

The Buccinator – Figure 77

The muscles cross over one another, so to treat both at the same time draw the skin on the cheek apart and then push the skin in a scissor-like movement vertically, then horizontally on these cheek muscles to reset the spindle cells. Retest TMJ **(See Fig. 78)**

Treating Spindle Cells of the Masseter and Buccinator – Figure 78

Chewing

TEMPORALIS MUSCLES

When a TL to the TMJ changes when the client chews with pressure on the molars, these muscles are likely to be the problem.

> Treat the same side as the TMJ TL. Pinch the belly of the temporalis muscle (situated on the skull at approximately 1" away from and around the ear) all the way around in a fan shape **(See Fig 79)**. Each pinching movement must be done in a rapid movement of around ½ second.

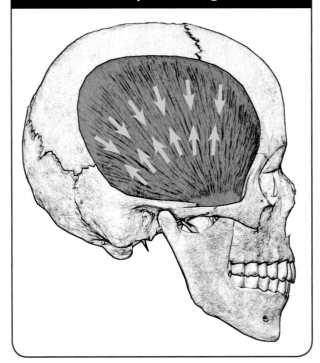

Spindle Cell Correction for the Temporalis – Figure 79

MEDIAL (INTERNAL) PTERYGOID

This muscle elevates the mandible and assists the jaw in protruding. It is actively involved with the chewing mechanism. Because the origin of this muscle attaches to the medial surface of the lateral pterygoid plate of the sphenoid **(See Fig. 80)**, any imbalance can affect the sphenoid bone (see cranial section on page 176) which, being the floor of the skull, plays a major part in the equilibrium of the cranium.

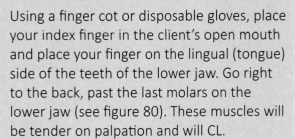

The specific test for the medial pterygoid is – client protrudes their mandible (jaw) whist TL'ing the TMJ . ✓

Using a finger cot or disposable gloves, place your index finger in the client's open mouth and place your finger on the lingual (tongue) side of the teeth of the lower jaw. Go right to the back, past the last molars on the lower jaw (see figure 80). These muscles will be tender on palpation and will CL.

Medial Pterygoid – Figure 80

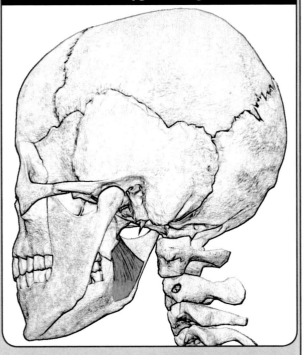

Make a fast sweep to stimulate the neuromuscular spindle cells. Push up and down in a brisk sweeping movement of around ½ second each. This will be very painful, so it needs to be done quickly and efficiently.

An alternative correction would be to place the lesion in circuit retaining mode and use finger modes to identify the correction.

Opening the Mouth

LATERAL (EXTERNAL) PTERYGOID

This is the first muscle to activate when the mouth opens. It is involved in protruding the mandible and also some lateral excursion (action of grinding teeth) **(See Fig 80)**

This muscle is involved when a TL to the TMJ changes the IM when mouth is wide open, or the client moves their jaw from side to side:

Using a finger cot or disposable gloves, slide your index finger as far as it will go on the buccal (cheek) side of the upper jaw on the same side as the TL. Push down and up briskly, each movement around ½ second. Retest. ✓

When the pterygoid muscles are hypertonic, this correction can be painful!

Lateral Pterygoid – Figure 81

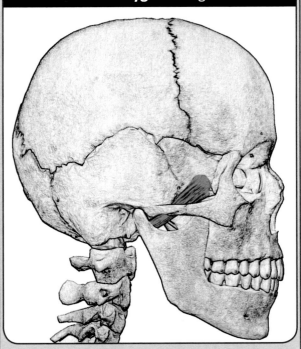

Again, it is possible to put the lesion into circuit retaining mode and use the finger modes to find the resolution.

HOMEWORK FOR CLIENTS
Instruct clients with TMJ dysfunction to massage their jaw area daily to help alleviate tension building up in the muscles.

Other Considerations

- If the symphysis menti test (tip of jaw) is positive but TL'ing the TMJs bring about no change to the IM when your client opens closes and chews, there could be a problem with:

  A. The ligaments in the joint itself. **Ligament Interlink** technique **see page 159** on the TMJ may be indicated.

  B. A jammed symphysis menti **see page 178** on cranial fault.

- To support TMJ function check **walking gait** and **hyoid**. **(See pages 25 & 9)**

- The **adductors** and **piriformis** muscles may be affected by TMJ dysfunction.

- There may be reactive muscle involvement **see page 164**:

  - Temporalis – Opposite quadratus lumborum
  - Masseter – Opposite gluteus medius
  - Medial Pterygoid – Opposite psoas
  - Lateral pterygoid – Opposite adductors

- If there are lateral or medial pterygoid issues, check for **cranial faults** (sphenoid on **page 170**).

- Check **dural torque on page 149**; the coccyx and the TMJ help to take up the slack in the dura if inappropriately loose.

- Supporting nutrition – Vitamin B5 (pantothenic acid) and iron.

TMJ protocol summary

General test

Client TL's symphysis menti. Indicator change shows a TMJ imbalance.

> #### *Specific test*
>
> 1. Client TL's TMJ on one side at a time. Indicator may or may not change.
> 2. Ask client to open mouth wide, close, chew on side that they are contacting (3 tests). Test an AIM for each test.
> 3. Indicator change signifies a problem. If more than one, prioritise.
> 4. Check the other side in the same way.

> #### *Correction – go to specific correction for:*
> 1. External (lateral) pterygoid for opening
> 2. Masseter & buccinator for closing
> 3. Temporalis and internal (medial) pterygoid for chewing
>
> If general test still shows after all corrections have been carried out, check:
> - **Jammed symphysis menti (cranial faults)**
> - **If the TMJ is painful, ligament interlink**
> - **ICV**
> - **Hyoid**
> - **Upper trapezius**
> - **Walking gait**

N.B. If corrections will not hold, send to a sympathetic dentist for further TMJ evaluation.

TMJ Case Study

Some years ago, I saw a young university student who was suffering from crippling headaches. They were so debilitating she was contemplating giving up her degree course because studying just made her headaches worse. Previously she had been everywhere for a diagnosis. A neurologist had told her that it was 'all in the mind', her doctor told her much the same.

Two things came to mind, firstly hypoglycaemia and secondly a TMJ problem. Addressing hypoglycaemia didn't seem to help although the kinesiology test was positive. Her TMJ tests proved negative. What was interesting was that when she put her head forward as if to read, TL'ing the symphysis menti revealed a TMJ dysfunction. Despite making all the necessary corrections in that position, her headaches were no better. It was clear when looking at her bite that she had an overbite which would mean that the discs on the mandible condyles would be displaced. She was advised to visit the orthodontist that I had recommended. However, she chose to go to her own dentist who made her a dental splint "just because she'd requested one". I didn't see her for some time but returned a few months later. She explained that the splint had made her worse than ever and so decided to go to the specialist I'd recommended. After seeing her he wrote a letter to me explaining that her bite problem was so complex he also needed to refer her to another specialist some distance away. I heard no more for a couple of years when I received a letter from her thanking me for finding out what was wrong. After extensive treatment she was now well. She was so grateful even though I didn't actually solve her problem personally. She said, "without you I would have never found the answer". She expressed how angry she was with the treatment she'd previously received including her own dentist who didn't spot her problem.

Correcting a TMJ using the techniques outlined might not have a lasting effect if there are more difficult underlying problems, but you can still be successful and point your clients to people who can help.

How to Check Dental Splints

Discourage maxilla splints if possible because it does not allow the cruciate suture see page 177 (comprised of the intermaxillary suture and the palato-maxillary sutures) to move with the cranio-sacral rhythm. Ask your client to talk to their dentist about a mandibular splint instead.

To Identify if Your Client Might Benefit from a Splint

To ascertain if a splint might be beneficial for your client if TMJ dysfunction persists.

1. Carry out a TMJ test in the usual manner without making any corrections. The blanket test TL'ing the symphysis menti will unlock an AIM.

2. Place an increasing number of pieces of thin cardboard between the molars. The bite may only need adjusting on one side and retest as in step 1 each time you make a change. The correct depth and combination will lock the IM, or, when the depth of the cardboard gets too high, the IM will unlock again.

Although this is a crude test, it will help to determine whether a visit to an orthodontist for a proper evaluation is needed.

Before Your Client Visits an Orthodontist

1. Balance the cranium (see section on cranial faults on pages 170 -182) at least three times prior to the orthodontist measuring for the splint, the last visit being as near to their appointment as possible. To reveal any hidden cranial faults:

2. Have the client bite down really hard with the incisors touching.

3. The client protrudes the mandible.

4. Have the client move the jaw laterally.

5. Recheck for cranial faults.

Checking that a Splint Corrects a TMJ Fault

With the splint inserted, client TL's the symphysis menti – the TMJ blanket test. If the IM is locked, the splint will be correcting the TMJ. If the TMJ blanket test unlocks an IM, their orthodontist may need to adjust the splint again. Often small changes occasionally need to be made to the splint over a length of time as the muscles and teeth adjust.

Ligament Interlink

Structural Finger Mode

George Goodheart noted the connection between opposite joints in a gait pattern after a client with severe rheumatoid arthritis told him that the pain in his inflamed knee was relieved when he flexed his opposite elbow.

Ligaments connect bones together. Tendons connect muscle to the bone. So, for this protocol we are working right into the joints.

Pain in the joints following ligament damage, caused by injury or arthritis, can be very persistent in spite of all related muscles being balanced. For these sore joints, ligament interlink is usually appropriate.

This technique is based on the interaction of joints in the gait mechanism. The nerve supply to the ligaments are connected in opposite quadrants: (Deal)

- **The shoulder relates to the hip on the opposite side**

- **The elbow relates to the knee on the opposite side**

- **The wrist relates to the ankle on the opposite side**

- **The thumb relates to the big toe on the opposite side**

- **The sacroiliac joint relates to the sternocostal articulations (where it joins the sternum) on the opposite side.**

- **The acetabulum (hip joint) relates to the opposite TMJ**

- **The side of any spinal vertebra relates to the opposite side of its Lovett Brother**

- **The xiphoid relates to the coccyx**

- **TMJ relates to the opposite TMJ**

The nutritional support for ligament interlink is vitamin B2 (riboflavin)

If the painful joint gives positive therapy localisation, this must be cleared first. Similarly, any positive therapy localisation in the related contralateral joint must be cleared.

1. Establish an AIM in a leg not involved in the test, e.g. Quadriceps.

2. Have the client TL the most painful area of their troublesome joint. The IM should stay locked. If it unlocks, treat the joint first.

3. Now have the client TL the related contralateral joint. If an AIM unlocks, treat the area first.

4. Have the client TL both the painful joint and the corresponding area of the contralateral joint (two-point). If the IM now unlocks, this is a case for ligament interlink technique to be performed.

5. Apply pressure with the fingertips, for 20-30 seconds, to the related contralateral area located in the test *while the client holds the hyoid towards the side of the correction (Fig.9 page 9)*. Find any painful areas in the contralateral joint – it will cause discomfort to the client in an area where they didn't know they had a problem! This will usually greatly reduce the degree of pain in the original joint.

6. Repeat step 4.

Nutrition for Ligaments

Biochemical Finger Mode

Nutrition is important for damaged ligaments and vitamin B2 (riboflavin) is the nutrition for ligament interlink technique.

Manganese Test:
Ligaments can lose their elasticity and manganese is an important mineral involved in ligament strength. The saying is "wobbly knees need manganese"!

Stretch any ligament around any joint, e.g. 'pull apart' a finger joint, for approx. 5 seconds. If this weakens an AIM, the person needs Manganese (2mg daily for one month is a recommended dose in this instance).

Retrograde lymphatics

Structural Finger Mode

The body's entire lymphatic system drains into the blood vascular system through the subclavian ducts, located under the left and right clavicles, emptying into the inferior vena cava. The right duct drains lymph from the head and the right arm and shoulder. The left duct drains lymph from the rest of the body. These lymphatic ducts are very vulnerable to being squeezed shut if the clavicles clamp down on them. This can occur if the pectoralis minor muscles are out of balance.

> **" This technique can work very well for insomnia. "**

When this happens, the lymph backs up in the system and a variety of conditions can ensue. The most common of these are bruxism (grinding the teeth), swelling anywhere in the body after lying down, frequent urging to urinate at night, reduced resistance to infection, eustachian tube problems, nose and throat problems, any conditions that occur during sleep, and childhood hyperactivity.

> **(!) Remember to look for this problem in the presence of any chronic recurring condition.**

Also, look for this problem in the presence of any chronic recurring condition such as joint problems, numbness and tingling in the extremities, and joint trauma that is slow to heal. (Walther D. S., 1988) An explicit indicator is that the person will habitually raise the arms over the head when lying down or sleeping.

When the retrograde lymphatic test is positive, it has been noted that there is consistently a pectoralis minor muscle involvement as it passes over the major lymph vessels. With a weak (hypotonic or under facilitated) pectoralis minor, the ribs are dropped down and the shoulder pulled back. The pectoralis minor connects the shoulder socket to the 3rd, 4th and 5th ribs. **(See Fig. 83)**

With an overtight (hypertonic or over facilitated) pectoralis minor, the shoulder girdle is pulled down and forwards which can impede lymphatic drainage.

> **(!) If a client has this problem, raising both legs together at 45 degrees will turn off every muscle in the body.**

There are a few ways of checking for and correcting retrograde lymphatics recorded in literature. This is the one that I use in clinic.

There are three tests that will confirm that the semilunar ducts are being impinged. Find the one that you are most comfortable with, or for a thorough evaluation, test all three.

1a. Use a PMC or an anterior deltoid as accurate indicator muscles. Ask your client to flex the hips and raise both their legs off the couch at an angle 45°. This is to induce extra pressure onto the subclavian ducts as more lymph travels towards the head. You may need to support their legs in this position for them as it is necessary to maintain this position for at least 15 seconds. Retest an AIM. If the IM now unlocks this shows a retrograde lymphatic impingement. (Any muscle in the body will unlock if there is an issue.) This test rarely shows right subclavian duct impingement. To cover head and neck lymphatic drainage issues, check anterograde lymphatics, page 162.

Pectoralis Minor Test – Figure 82

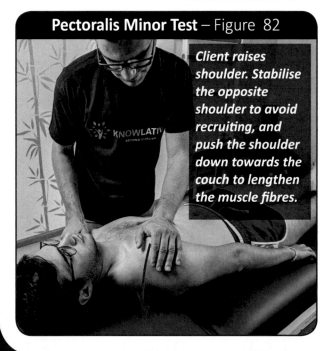

Client raises shoulder. Stabilise the opposite shoulder to avoid recruiting, and push the shoulder down towards the couch to lengthen the muscle fibres.

Ask your client, still with legs raised, to raise one arm above their head whilst you test an IM. Raising an arm above the head will release any impingement on the ducts on the same side. If the IM now locks, this is evidence that the pectoralis minor has an impact on the thoracic duct and needs addressing. Carry out the same procedure on the other side. If raising the arm does not change the unlocked state, there is no obvious impingement on that side.

1b. If the person cannot raise their legs, or as a confirmation test (all good kinesiologists have more than one way to assess a problem), test the pectoralis minor **(See Fig. 82)** (The outcome may be weak or hypertonic as both conditions will affect the thoracic ducts). If the test shows no weakness, test for hypertonicity by raising the shoulder off the couch and extending it posteriorly to rapidly stretch the pectorals muscles. The client could do this themselves by taking their arm behind their back and stretching their shoulder posteriorly. Immediately test the pectoralis minor again and if it now weakens the muscle is hypertonic.

1c. Place thumb on the coracoid process (insertion of the pectoralis minor), which is under the clavicle **(See Fig. 83)**. Place the fingers on the external surfaces of the 3rd, 4th and 5th ribs (the insertion). Let your client know what you are doing before you begin to test and correct! If your client is a woman, you may need to ask her to move her breast out of the way to do this.

Squeeze the thumb and fingers together and test an AIM. If it unlocks to this challenge, there is a constriction of the lymphatic duct on that side. It can show bilaterally, but it is most commonly found on the left side.

Origin and Insertion of the Pectoralis Minor – Figure 83

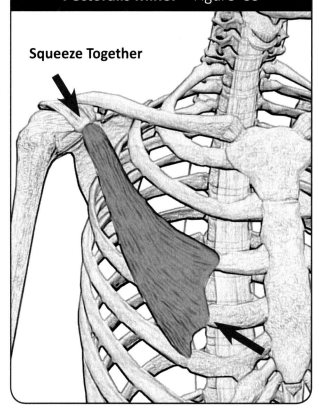

Squeeze Together

2. Have your hand contact the belly of the pectoralis minor. If your client is a woman, ask them to move their breast out of the way. The hand stays stationary. Simultaneously, with the other hand, firmly rub the neurolymphatic points for the fascia lata on the same side (situated on the lateral thigh from the hip to just below the knee). Keep rubbing these points as they need to be rubbed quite vigorously. (Deal) This procedure supplants the need to massage the pectoralis muscle itself.

3a. **If the pectoralis minor tested weak in the clear in step 1b**, go to the Golgi tendon organs at the origin and insertions of the pectoralis minor. **(Fig.83)** Press one thumb on the coracoid process and the other thumb in turn, on the origin at the 3rd, then 4th then 5th ribs. Keep the thumb on the coracoid process and push the other thumb towards it as if pushing the thumbs together. Repeat the procedure on the other side if necessary. The neurolymphatic reflex is situated a body inch above the xyphoid process of the sternum. Warn your client that it will be painful! (Walther D. S., 1988).

3b. **If the pectoralis minor tested hypertonic in step 1b**, test the middle and lower trapezius muscles (opposing muscles to the pectoralis minor) and correct if necessary as weakness of these often causes a hypertonic pectoralis minor. There could be a fixation at T12/L1 if the weakness is bilateral (See Fixations of the Vertebrae on page 146). To weaken the hypertonic pectoralis minor, pull apart the Golgi tendon apparatus (opposite of 3.1).

4. Retest step 1.

Other Considerations

The nutritional for retrograde lymphatic technique is vitamin *A, reishi and/or cordyceps* if corrections don't hold.

Check the pelvic muscles (see category corrections, on pages 183-192) as retrograde lymphatic imbalance will return quickly in the presence of a pelvic discrepancy.

Check for reactive muscles, see pages 164-167.

Instruct the client to be aware of their breathing as diaphragmatic breathing improves lymph flow.

After correction, benefit can also be obtained by raising the foot of the bed 1" for the first month and increasing the angle of the bed by 1" per month until the foot is 6" above the head. Do not go beyond 6".

Anterograde Lymphatics

This test is for any lymphatic congestion that specifically relates to the head area. Symptoms could include sinus congestion, runny nose, facial pain.

Any disturbance affecting the pectoralis minor could impede lymphatic drainage from the head and neck.

The test is to ask your client to drop the head forwards towards the chest. This test is used in a number of protocols such as checking for dural torque and may show if there are any neck lesions. The distinguishing factor for anterograde lymphatics is that dropping the head forward will two-point to the acupuncture point Kidney 27. **(See Fig.11 on page 14)**

Both Kidney 27 points are major neurological switches and master neurolymphatic reflexes for the whole of the lymphatic system. K27 on the right is the NL of the head and K27 on the left is the NL for the rest of the body. (Ferreri)

1. Ask the client to lean against a wall and drop their head forward and test an AIM.

OR

If the client is supine, ask them to bring their head towards their chin and test an AIM.

If the AIM unlocks, anterograde lymphatics could be involved because the neck muscles are compromised.

2. Put the test into circuit retaining mode (unlock).

3. CL each K27. If the IM now locks on either or both, there is an anterograde lymphatic involvement.

4. Contact each of the Beginning and End points on the face (See Page 221-223 on General Techniques). Note the one/s that locks the IM. The B & E point should be on the same side as the K27. If not, consider that the person may be switched.

5. Tap K27 together with the relevant B&E point (s).

6. Rub Lymph as step 2 of the Retrograde Lymphatic protocol on page 161.

Check for a retrograde lymphatic imbalance.

Shock Absorbers

Structural Finger Mode

Shock absorber problems in the arms can be tested and corrected in a similar fashion, as also can fingers and toes.

The body has a system of shock absorbers, which help to protect it from everyday shock to the body (e.g. from walking on hard surfaces). These are the ball and socket of the hips and shoulder and hinge joints in the knees, ankles, elbows etc. If the client is injured in any way, this technique may help to speed the healing process.

It's a process of elimination to find out which joint/s in the limb is a problem.

Warn the client of what is to come, so that they are ready.

1. Establish an accurate indicator muscle, e.g. Quadriceps. With the leg straight, strike the bottom of one heel with a firm blow (approx. 10lbs pressure) enough to make an impact through the ankle knee and hip. Immediately retest the IM. If it unlocks, then there is a shock absorber problem in the ankle, knee or hip on that side.

2. Bend the knee (to isolate the force just to the ankle joint) and again strike the bottom of the heel, as before. If this unlocks an IM, the problem is in the ankle.

3. With the knee straight, grasp the leg just below the knee (to isolate hip and knee) and 'jam' leg towards the hip joint. If the IM unlocks, there is a problem in knee and/or hip.

4. Bend the knee and grasp the thigh above the knee (to isolate the hip joint) and apply the force towards the hip. If the IM now unlocks this indicates a problem in the hip joint. If the IM remains locked, correction to the knee joint is required.

5. **Ankle** – Turn the foot in slightly, take a firm hold on the ankle joint and give a strong tug on foot and the calcaneus to release the ankle joint.

   Knee – Bend the leg so that the foot is flat on the table. Stabilise the foot by gently sitting on it. Grasp the leg behind the knee (in the popliteal crease) and tug the calf forwards to release the knee joint.

   Hip – Have the client hold the sides of the table, with leg straight and relaxed. Grasp the leg above the knee and tug the thigh sharply to release the hip joint.

Use the Alarm Points to Find Muscles Involved with a Lesion

Structural Finger Mode

From your foundation training you will know that each meridian shares its circuit with specific muscles.

This example shows how you can narrow down the field when looking for muscles that are involved with a lesion.

1. Using an AIM, enter the lesion into pause lock.

2. Activate the 4 key finger modes. The **structural finger mode** shows (locks the IM) and add this to the circuit.

3. Touch each alarm point (See Figs. 12 & 13 on pages 18-19 in section Electromagnetic Imbalances and Corrections). The alarm point that unlocks the IM gives you the group of muscles that are involved with the lesion, e.g. if the large intestine alarm point changes the IM then the muscle involved will be either the tensor fascia latae, hamstrings or quadratus lumborum. To find the specific muscle involved with the lesion, CL the belly, the origin or insertion of each muscle. Any that are involved will unlock the IM.

Reactive Muscles

This technique is important for intermittent pain, restricted range of movement, long-term postural problems and for structural problems that persist despite other corrections having been done. Enlarged muscles or very flabby muscles can be indications that reactive muscles are involved.

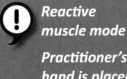

> ! *Reactive muscle mode*
>
> *Practitioner's hand is placed 2" above the client's head*

Muscles should work together, and the brain signals them to contract and relax according to the movement being carried out (agonists, antagonists, synergists). If the neurological signalling gets out of sync (neurological disorganisation) this can cause a faulty interplay between muscles that should otherwise be working together (reciprocal facilitation and inhibition). It is thought that trauma, or extreme contraction that is performed too rapidly, can cause the affected primary muscle's spindle cells to continually send an inappropriate message to the spinal cord causing elevated tonus.

This can then cause a subsequent inappropriate weakening in other muscles (reactive), which is detrimental. This means that other muscles that stabilise the affected joint or act as antagonists to the damaged muscle, will have inappropriate change of tonus (reactive muscles). This in turn can incorrectly inhibit the agonist and the body adapts to that pattern. The exact neurophysiology is unknown but the hypothesis is that the spindle cells or Golgi tendon apparatus in the primary (sometimes called the reactor muscle) is at an inappropriately high tension and sends strong signals to the central nervous system which, causes continued inhibition (weakening) of the muscles that react to it. Since treating the muscle's proprioceptors often corrects the problem, we understand this assumption to be correct.

> *Primary muscles (Reactor muscles) are over-energised and too strong. Elevated tonus causes a change of tonus in other muscles.*
>
> *Reactive muscles become inappropriately weak when the reactor is activated.*

Reactive muscles usually test strong in the clear so they can easily be missed when carrying out an assessment. They are often a problem for athletes who do repetitive fast movements. For an in-depth discussion of Reactive Muscles, see Robert Frost's excellent book 'Applied Kinesiology'. A primary/reactor muscle is usually hypertonic and may have typically received an injury. It's worth asking your client about such injuries as it will help you to locate the primary muscle. Primary-reactive problems can also be caused by continuing periods of muscle tension, commonly seen in the neck and shoulders.

Look out for reactive sets in the upper trapezius, anterior serratus, anterior deltoid, supraspinatus, deltoid, latissimus dorsi, posterior neck extensors and anterior neck flexors.

Suspect the possibility of reactive muscle involvement if a muscle, when strengthened, becomes weak again after certain activities. After strengthening muscles, ask your client to perform an activity that causes them problems, such as walking upstairs, bending over etc. If the muscle weakens again, consider that it could be caused by the action of a primary.

This protocol consists of a fact-finding mission to identify the primary and the reactive/s. Once found, the treatment is simple. It involves activating the neuromuscular spindle cells or Golgi tendon techniques to normalise the hypertonic primary and then immediately 'resetting' the reactives by firmly muscle testing them.

In 'reactive muscle' mode the alarm points will show you the reactor/primary muscles.

1. Establish an AIM. Activate the 'reactive muscle' mode by placing the flat palm of your hand 2 inches above the top of your client's head (Deal). If the IM unlocks, there is at least one set of primary/reactive muscles. Enter the mode into pause lock (**unlock**).

2. With an unlocked IM, contact each alarm point (see chart in section on Electromagnetic Imbalances and Corrections Figs 12 & 13 on pages 18-19 to find the primary). If more than one is found, prioritise between them (**locked**). You now know that the reactor is one of the group of muscles sharing the same circuit as the alarm point. *This is information only, so you don't need to enter this into circuit.*

3. The meridian has now been identified and it is necessary to determine which associated muscle is the primary muscle. To do this, CL the belly of each of the muscles associated with that meridian, e.g. a small intestine alarm point would indicate that either the quadriceps

or the abdominals were primary. Usually only one muscle will lock the IM.

4. Now you have found the primary, **pause lock can be cancelled**.

5. Test the primary itself (it will test very strongly) and enter this into pause-lock. The indicator muscle will remain strong (**lock**).

6. Muscle test any possible reactives **(See Table 19 overleaf)** or any muscles related to the area of pain are tested, the reactive muscles will now test weak (**unlock**).

7. Note these and cancel the lock.

8. Using spindle cell technique and/or Golgi tendon technique, turn off the primary muscle and immediately place it in pause-lock whilst it still tests weak.

9. Firmly muscle test all the muscles that were previously reactive to it and check that they are now in strength.

10. Cancel the lock and check that the reactor/primary muscle has returned to strength.

11. Re-check the reactive hand mode as in step 1. If the indicator unlocks, there are further reactive sets and all steps are then repeated.

Guidelines to Determine Reactive Muscles

Common reactivity patterns can occur between muscles:

- That share the same origin and/or insertion

- Whose fibres run parallel to each other

- And their partner muscle on the other side of the body

- Psoas – Diaphragm

- Quadriceps – Hamstrings

- Anterior Neck Flexors – Posterior Neck Extensors

- Upper Trapezius, one side of the body vs. the other

- The masseter muscle is considered to be the strongest primary muscle because it is the most dense and powerful, size for size, in the body. It strongly contracts when eating and contracts and clamps the jaw (the pelvis of the head) shut in fight or flight activity. Its reactive muscle is the opposite gluteus medius which is an important pelvic muscle. Therefore, when evaluating the TMJ the most accurate muscle to use to reveal dysfunction is the opposite gluteus medius. (Ferreri).

 When testing one side of the TMJ the most neurologically correct indicator muscle to use is the opposite gluteus medius (Ferreri).

Primary – Reactive Muscle Chart – Table 19	
Primary Muscle Requiring Sedation (Reactor)	**Possible Reactive Muscle**
Adductors	Tensor fascia latae, iliacus, piriformis, gluteus medius, gluteus maximus
Hamstrings	Sacrospinalis, quadriceps, popliteus, latissimus dorsi on contralateral side
Deltoids including anterior and posterior divisions	Deltoids, rhomboids, pectoralis major and minor, latissimus dorsi, subscapularis
Gluteus Medius	Masseter (opposite side), contralateral rectus abdominis, adductors,
Gluteus Maximus	Sacrospinalis, pectoralis major clavicular, iliacus, rectus femoris, sartorius, piriformis, adductors, tensor fascia lata
Hyoid (Stylo and Omohyoid)	Opposite psoas
Infraspinatus	Anterior deltoid, pectoralis majors, the infraspinatus itself
Iliacus	Adductors, diaphragm, gluteus maximus, contralateral neck flexors
Latissimus Dorsi	Upper trapezius, contralateral hamstrings, supraspinatus, deltoids, levator scapulae
Masseter	Opposite gluteus medius
Pectoralis Major Clavicular	Teres major and minor, Latissimus dorsi, middle trapezius, posterior deltoid, rhomboids, supraspinatus, gluteus maximus
Pectoralis Major Sterna	Supraspinatus, upper and lower trapezius, posterior deltoid, anterior serratus, rhomboids
Pectoralis Minor	Anterior serratus, supraspinatus, deltoids, trapezius, rhomboids

Peroneus Longus	Tensor fascia lata, anterior and posterior tibials, anterior neck flexors, gluteus medius, tensor fascia lata, adductors, hamstrings, gastrocnemius, quadriceps, hamstrings
Popliteus	Gastrocnemius, quadriceps, hamstrings, upper trapezius, rectus abdominis, q contralateral gluteus medius sacrospinalis, rectus femoris, sartorius, quadratus lumborum
Pterygoid (Lateral)	Opposite adductor
Rectus Femoris	Gastrocnemius, rectus abdominis, hamstrings, sartorius, gluteus maximus, adductors
Rhomboids	Deltoid, anterior serratus, supraspinatus, latissimus dorsi, pectoralis major and minor, trapezius
Sacrospinalis	Rectus abdominis, gluteus maximus, hamstrings
Sartorius	Quadriceps, gluteus medius and maximus, adductors, tensor fascia lata, tibialis, peroneus
Neck Flexors (SCM)	Neck extensors, upper trapezius, pectoralis major clavicular, opposite sternocleidomastoid (SCM)
Subscapularis	Teres minor, infraspinatus, deltoids, supraspinatus
Supraspinatus	Rhomboids, pectoralis minor, teres major and minor, latissimus dorsi
Temporalis	Opposite quadratus lumborum
Tensor Fascia Lata	Adductors, peroneus, hamstrings, gluteus maximus
Teres Major	Pectoralis majors, anterior deltoid, teres minor, infraspinatus
Teres Minor	Subscapularis, latissimus dorsi, deltoid, supraspinatus
Trapezius – Lower	Pectoralis majors and minor, levator scapula, upper trapezius
Trapezius – Middle	Pectoralis majors and minor
Trapezius – Upper	Latissimus dorsi, biceps, subscapularis, contralateral upper trapezius, neck flexors (SCM)

Correcting the Sacrum

Structural Finger Mode

The pelvis moves when we breathe and the sacrum tilts slightly. The apex anteriorly and the base of the sacrum moves posteriorly. The reverse happens when we breathe out.

This technique is suitable for use with low back pain symptoms. It is classed as a structural fix for the hamstrings. The tension of the hamstrings helps to stabilise the pelvis. If the hamstrings test weak bilaterally there will be a sacral fixation which in turn could contribute towards sacroiliac dysfunction.

1. The client is prone, and test both hamstrings.

   a. There is a *Sacral Inspiration Fault* If they both test weak in the clear and the muscles test strong as the client breathes in deeply.

   b. There is a *Sacral Expiration Fault* if the hamstrings test strong in the clear but weaken as the client deeply breathes out.

2. A sacral misalignment will TL unless it is fixated. Ask your client to place their hands together (as if praying) and contact the sacrum. Retest the hamstrings. If the IM changes, this is confirmation that the sacrum requires correcting.

3. A bilaterally weak hamstring test indicates the presence of a Universal Cranial Fault (See Page 174 on Cranial Faults). Test and correct this if it is a modality/priority.

4. The correction is:

   a. If you have established a *Sacral Inspiration Fault* in step 1a, place the palm of your hand over the sacral apex (where the sacrum joins with the coccyx), fingers pointing towards the head, and apply pressure anteriorly (down towards the front of the body) and gently push the sacrum superiorly (towards the head) as your client takes a slow, deep in-breath. The pressure is released as they slowly breathe out. Repeat 5 or 6 times.

   b. If you have established a *Sacral Expiration* Fault in step 1b, the same correction applies as in 4a, but the sacrum is pushed during slow expiration and released on slow inspiration. Repeat 5 or 6 times.

5. Repeat step 1 or step 2

This protocol may be repeated from time to time with benefit, especially if the person has a sedentary job.

Exercise for the Sacrum and Low Back Problems

1. Ask your client to sit on the floor with their knees up towards their chest. They clasp their hands below the knees and pull them gently towards their chest. Ask them to rock backwards and forwards 6 to 8 times on the sacrum. *Stand behind the person to steady them as it is easy to overbalance and topple backwards*

2. This exercise stretches the lower back. Your client lies on a flat surface and holds the back of their thighs to pull their knees up towards their chest as far as is comfortable without pain, until they feel a stretch. This position is held for **at least 15** seconds. The position is relaxed and then repeated. It should become easier for the knees to reach the chest as the muscles gradually release.

3. Instruct your client to rub their inner and outer thighs. These are the NL's for the hamstrings, abdominals and tensor fascia lata muscles.

Sacral and 5th Lumbar Fixation

When walking the iliacus and piriformis muscles switch off on the side of the leg that goes forward. This allows the sacrum to move backwards. In a lot of individuals with back problems, the piriformis muscles are commonly hypertonic. Because these muscles are not switching off, the sacrum and 5th lumbar become fixated and cannot move when walking.

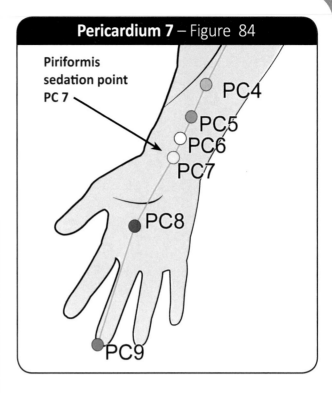

Pericardium 7 – Figure 84

1. Test the piriformis on both sides. If they test strong, check that contacting the piriformis sedation point on the same side of the muscle you're testing will switch the piriformis off **(Fig. 84)**. If the sedation point fails to unlock, the muscle is over-facilitated, and the sacrum is fixated and not moving correctly.

2. Correct by either:

   a. Carrying out a dynamic (rebound) challenge on the sacrum (it will not TL or CL) and correct by pushing the sacrum in the direction that changes the IM using inspiration assist.

   b. Ask your client to look at a black cloth or black paper. If the IM unlocks there is a fixation; shine a light at the glabella to correct (see under Fixations of the Vertebrae page 146).

Cranial Faults

The skull is made up of separate bones joined together with sutures. A suture is a type of fibrous joint that is only found in the skull. The bones are bound together by Sharpey's fibres (fibres of collagen that connect periosteum to bone). These fibres allow for a tiny amount of movement of the sutures, which contributes to the compliance and flexibility of the skull. The bones of the skull, the intraosseous lesions, the temporal sphenoid line, and the sphenoid together with the base of the occiput, move with respiration. As the sacrum also moves with respiration, both skull and sacrum cause cerebrospinal fluid (CSF) to be pumped and moved throughout the brain and spinal cord. The cranium and sacrum also have their own pulses which are unrelated to respiratory rhythms.

Studies, carried out on people with cranial faults, revealed that 99% were low on zinc. (Note that zinc is best taken at the end of a meal for better assimilation.)

> *After correcting cranial faults, check for pelvic faults, particularly Category I and II. (See pages 184-190)*
>
> *Conversely, if you have corrected pelvic faults don't forget to check for cranial faults too.*

Every single sacral lesion will have a cranial lesion, but not every cranial lesion will have a sacral involvement. When CSF distribution throughout the body is sluggish, the body will try to remedy this by raising blood pressure to compensate. Therefore, idiopathic high blood pressure is often improved by treating jaw, cranium, and sacral dysfunction.

Cranial imbalances can impact on any part of the body and vice versa. This is because the dura, the tough flexible covering around the brain and the spinal cord, can torque (see Dural Torque on page 149) causing a jamming of the cranial sutures. A twisting of the trunk can put torsion into the dura which in turn causes cranial sutures to jam.

What Causes Cranial Faults to Occur?
Factors include:

- Birth trauma such as forceps delivery or caesarean.

- Tight neck muscles are a major cause of some cranial faults (a number of neck muscles have their origins attached to the skull). If the muscles pull tight, the sutures can jam causing cranial bones to be immobilised.

- Whiplash injury.

- Head injuries or falls.

- Excessively holding the breath.

- Jaw problems.

- Back problems.

- Zinc deficiency.

> **!** *It is important to check for cranial faults if your client is not improving. They may be a factor leading to their poor recovery.*

Cranial Fault Indicators

- Persistent headaches.

- Persistent sinus problems.

- Asymmetrical features.

- Muscle strength changes when breathing in or out.

Other Involved Imbalances

If other possible factors alongside cranial imbalances are not resolved, your treatment is unlikely to hold. Therefore, it pays to check the following and correct if necessary, in modality/priority order.

Dural Torque *Page 149*	Sacrum and Pelvic Categories – *Page 183*
Spondylogenic Reflex – *Page 54*	Neck muscles, Levator Scapulae, Upper Trapezius
TMJ *Page 152*	Gait mechanisms *Pages 4 & 25*
Injury Recall Technique – *Page 205*	Psychological Conflict *Page 41*
Heavy Metal Toxicity *Page 192*	Spinal Misalignment *Page 142*

Procedure to Test for the Presence of Cranial Faults

> If the client, when using imagery weakens a previously strong muscle, they will have cranial faults. The implications are that people who use visualisation techniques (athletes, cancer sufferers etc.) can be weakened whilst using visualisation methods for intensifying performance and healing. Thus, these methods would be futile to such persons if they have one or more cranial faults.
>
> To find out whether visualisation weakens your client, it is best to ask them to envision something that is not emotive. So, identify an AIM and ask them to visualise the performance of that muscle test being a good strong muscle. If a previously strong IM now unlocks, they will have one or more cranial faults.

Short-cut corrections

There are many separate procedures to test and correct individual cranial faults. Being more specific, they can give a clearer picture and a longer lasting result. However, the short cuts below will also work.

Use any One of These Methods

> **1a.** The cranium can be minutely moved by causing the blood vessels in the brain to become dilated thus increasing the size of brain tissue. This is achieved by asking the client to breathe in and out of a paper bag that is tightly closed around the nose and mouth to exclude all air. This increases blood CO_2. Ask them to continue doing this until they feel slightly dizzy. Nutritionally rewarding with zinc whilst this is being done can further ensure that the treatment will hold. Place zinc on the body whilst the client does this – this allows the brain to link zinc to any cranial faults – and then supplement with zinc thereafter.
>
> **OR**

> **1b.** When performing any balance, simultaneously treating the neuro-vascular and neurolymphatic points may help to correct any cranial faults as well as saving time.
>
> **OR**

> **1c.** Have your client contact GV20 situated midline towards the rear of the top of the skull. The tester simultaneously rubs the neuro-lymphatic points for the sternocleidomastoid muscle (anterior neck flexors) at St 13 (just below the clavicle in line with the nipple) while touching the neuro-vascular point on the ramus of the jaw (on the same side) using the other hand.

Specific Cranial Corrections

It is always best to correct individual cranial faults. Many of these are presented in Walther's Applied Kinesiology Synopsis. The most common cranial faults that you are likely to see are in connection with the inferior occiput, the sphenoid and the TMJ.

Cranial faults will TL, but the best method of identification is a challenge. This is because there might be other non-cranially linked factors picked up such as an active stress receptor or an infected sinus for example. However, there is confusion in some of the literature since it is not always stated whether the challenge should be a sustained or dynamic. The method of challenge described here is a dynamic (rebound) challenge, which means that the correction is made in the same direction that the challenge was found. (Walther)

The corrections are made using respiration to assist. In most cases this will be on inspiration as we would only correct cranial faults that are a modality or priority. The pressure should be gentle and continuous throughout the phase of respiration. Strong forces should be avoided as this only causes the body to resist (Walther). You may feel a change occur in the 'springiness' of the cranium as you make the correction. Initially it may feel solid and un-yielding but as you continue you may feel the quality change.

Wear disposable gloves or finger cots for any corrections that involve going into the mouth.

Contraindications

It is inadvisable to use any of the specific cranial corrections on anyone who has suffered from a recent skull fracture, a recent cerebral haemorrhage, a recent stroke or has a known cerebral aneurysm.

Methods to Find and Correct Unspecified Cranial Faults

There are many possible cranial faults, and no doubt some have yet to be discovered. As already mentioned, challenging for the various faults is the preferred method, but sometimes it's difficult to find the fault even though the indicators are there. If that is the case, do not despair! Try one of the following that may narrow down your search.

a. Pinch an area of the scalp and test an AIM. If the indicator unlocks, this could indicate a cranial fault in that area of the skull.

OR

b. Find a weak muscle and rub over a section of the scalp. If the weak muscle strengthens, again there could be a cranial fault in that area.

c. After finding a possible fault using method a. or b., place the area in circuit retaining mode and find the correction using the four key finger modes.

OR

d. Find the cranial fault as in a. or b. Have your client TL the fault and perform Injury Recall see page 205. Retest to check the fault has been resolved.

Sphenobasilar Compression Cranial Fault

The sphenoid is a complex bat-shaped bone that forms the base of the skull. It is critical because it articulates with many other cranial bones (frontal, temporal, parietal and the basilar part of the occiput). Attached to it are the lateral pterygoid muscles involved with moving the jaw.

If this fault is present and tests as a modality or priority, it can clear up to 80% of other cranial faults and is worth checking for routinely.

It may be present due to the following circumstances:

A blow to the frontal bone	When all of your client's muscles test either weak or hypertonic
Caesarean birth	Metabolic disturbances
An underlying factor in chronic conditions difficult to treat	Zinc deficiency

Fixation

The sutures of the sphenoid and the base of the occiput (basilar) should flex and extend with respiration. This procedure unjams the suture line between the two.

1. The test for this fault is a challenge. Ask your client to place a hand each side of their ribs and squeeze them together. Use either the gluteus medius or quadriceps as your AIM.

2. If the IM unlocks you need to rule out other reasons why this area might challenge. If inspiration or expiration changes the IM (**lock**) then this confirms that there is a sphenobasilar suture is compressed and tells you which phase of inspiration to use in the correction.

3. To make the correction, on both sides of the skull, place your thumbs on the greater wings of the sphenoid and your fingers on the mastoid part of the occiput. **(Fig. 85)**

4. With gentle pressure rotate the two bones in an anterior direction as your client breathes in and dorsiflexes their feet (pull towards head). **(Fig. 85)** It has been suggested that this stretches the dura (which attaches at the inside of the occiput) and increases CSF flow.

5. Then rotate in the opposite direction in a posterior direction as your client changes their pattern of respiration and relaxes the feet.

6. Repeat steps 4 & 5 ten times.

7. Repeat step 1

8. The Lovett Brother to the occiput is the sacrum, therefore check for a Category I pelvic fault (see section page 184 on pelvic faults)

9. Check and correct the lateral pterygoids on page 156. Attached to the sphenoid, these muscles are involved in clamping the jaw shut. Some people permanently clamp their jaw shut due to tension, so this should be considered as if hypertonic they can cause the sphenobasilar suture to fixate.

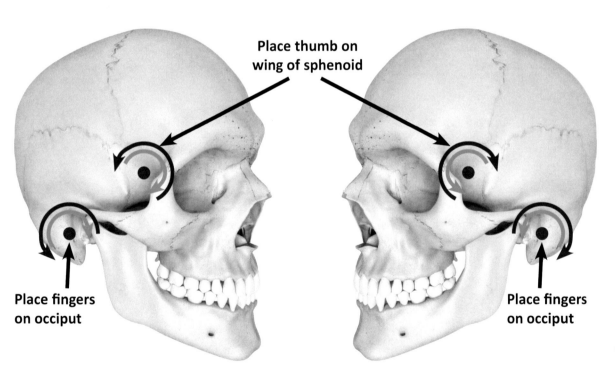

Sphenobasilar Correction Points – Figure 85

Place thumb on wing of sphenoid

Place fingers on occiput

Place fingers on occiput

Step 3 Treat both sides simultaneously. Digital rotation in direction of green arrows, client inhales and dorsiflexes feet. Digital rotation in direction of purple arrows, client exhales relaxes feet.

Inferior Occiput

1. Use a hamstring as an AIM as your client needs to be prone.

2. Ask your client to place a hand on each side of the occiput. If the IM changes, then TL each side separately. If neither side shows but TL'ing both sides does, then there is a universal cranial fault (see opposite).

3. Carry out a dynamic challenge on the side of the occiput that TL's, by torqueing it both clockwise and anticlockwise. A positive challenge is the direction that changes the indicator muscle from **locked** to **unlocked**. **(Fig. 86)**

4. Torque the occiput on inspiration in the same direction that challenged in step 3.

5. Repeat step 2.

6. The Lovett Brother to the occiput is the sacrum, therefore check for a Category I pelvic fault (see section on pelvic faults on page 184)

Inferior Occiput Test – Figure 86

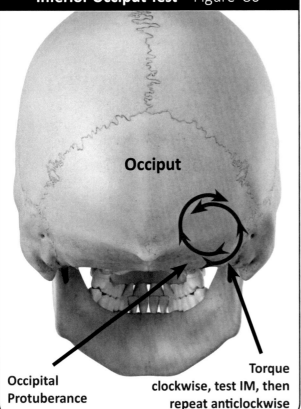

Occiput

Occipital Protuberance

Torque clockwise, test IM, then repeat anticlockwise

Universal Cranial/Occiput Fault

As with the inferior occiput fault, this cranial fault is also linked to a sacral lesion (with every sacral lesion there is always a cranial lesion). If your client has a chronic ionisation imbalance (see page 15 for Electromagnetic Imbalances), it may be due to a universal cranial fault.

Universal Cranial Fault – Steps 3 & 4
Figure 87

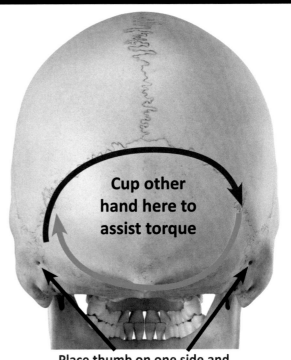

Cup other hand here to assist torque

Place thumb on one side and middle finger on other side of the atlantooccipital junction to torque the occiput

1. Ensure that breathing in does not weaken your client, so first ask them to breathe in through their nose and test an AIM. There should be no IM change to this challenge.

2. Now challenge by asking them to breathe in through one nostril whilst they block off the other. Test an AIM. If single nostril breathing unlocks the IM, there is a Universal Occiput imbalance.

3. Your client now lies prone with their feet extended off of the bottom of the couch. Find a suitable AIM – usually a hamstring. Continue by carrying out a dynamic challenge to the **whole occipital bone** by torqueing it in one direction, then the other. **(See Fig. 87)** for hand positions.

4. Whichever direction responds to the dynamic challenge (unlocks an AIM), is the direction of correction. Torque the occiput on inspiration using a firm pressure. Your client dorsiflexes their feet during the in-breath. ✓

Sagittal Suture Cranial Fault

This is an important suture to test and correct at the end of a treatment before your client leaves the couch.

Sagittal Suture – Figure 88

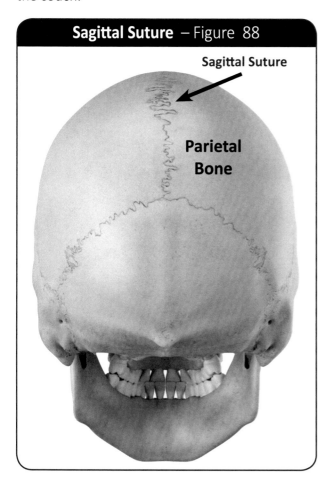

Sagittal Suture

Parietal Bone

> ❗ *If the abdominal muscles are under-facilitated, as soon as your client leaves your table and walk out of your office, the imbalances that you've so carefully corrected can all return!*

People with a jammed sagittal suture **(Fig. 88)** will have a tendency towards narcolepsy or may feel sleepy during the daytime, regardless of how much sleep they get.

A jammed sagittal suture is linked with weak abdominals, so this correction can be used as a self-help technique to strengthen these core muscles if they persistently test weak.

Ensure that any structural or centring corrections will hold by routinely testing at the end of a treatment session for a jammed sagittal suture. The nutritional reward for the sagittal suture is magnesium.

Sagittal Suture Correction – Figure 89

> ❗ *Jamming together the sagittal suture temporarily at night-time can help sleep disorders. On waking, it should be pulled apart again.*

George Goodheart found that spreading the sagittal suture after any type of correction helps the treatment to hold when the client leaves the table. For more detailed instructions see page 232 on General Imbalances and Corrections.

1. Challenge the sagittal suture by 'pulling' the parietal bones apart and then quickly testing an AIM dynamic challenge.
If it unlocks:

2. Pull apart the parietal bones 5-6 times on your client's in breath (inspiration assist). **(See Fig. 89)** ✔

3. Retest as No. 1.

Temporo-sphenoid Line Fault (Pineal Gland Fault)

(Structural correction for the pineal gland)

Look for this in cases of head injury, traumatic birth, persistent headaches or learning difficulties. The person with this fault may not like sleeping in the dark and have problems with night driving.

This fault causes the mandibular joint to be squeezed together. By spreading the lower jaw, this will automatically affect and release the position of the sphenoid bone.

1. Challenge the sphenoid bone by squeezing together the greater wings. This is done by simultaneously pressing medially and bilaterally, both sides of the hairline, just about level with the eyebrows **(See Fig. 90)** and testing an AIM. This is a sustained challenge. ❓

2. On inspiration, spread the ramus of the jaw by placing your fingers inside both sides of the lower jaw on the lingual (tongue) side of the premolars and pulling the mandible, (not the teeth!) laterally. **(See Fig. 91)** ✔

3. Repeat step 1.

Correction of Pineal Gland Fault
Figure 91

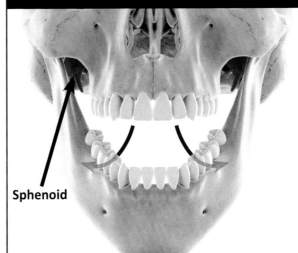

Sphenoid

Step 2. Hook fingers into mandible and pull outwards on inspiration to release wings of sphenoid

Test for Pineal Gland Fault – (Fig 90)

Greater Wings of Sphenoid. Squeeze together both sides

Parietal   Frontal   Frontal   Parietal

Sphenoid   Sphenoid

Temporal   Temporal

Temporo-mandibular Joint   Temporo-mandibular Joint

Ramus of Jaw   Ramus of Jaw

Step 1. Using an dynamic challenge, squeeze together both wings of the sphenoid

Jammed Intermaxillary and Palatomaxillary Sutures

Formerly known as the Cruciate Suture (Fig. 92)

Look for this in cases of headaches or persistent sinus trouble (jammed sutures inhibit sinus drainage).

Inferior View of the Skull
Figure 92

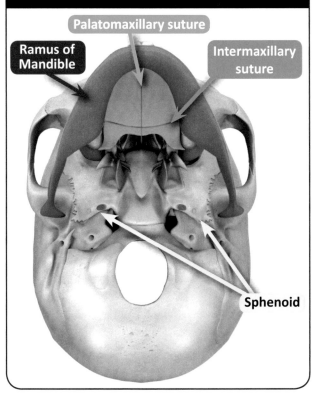

Palatomaxillary suture

Ramus of Mandible

Intermaxillary suture

Sphenoid

1. Squeeze the maxillary bones below the zygoma (cheek bones) and test an AIM **(Fig. 93)**. If it unlocks:

2. Go to the roof of the mouth, on the lingual side of the pre-molars, placing your fingers on the maxilla, not the teeth, bilaterally **(Fig. 94)**. Spread the cruciate suture by pulling the mandible in a lateral direction. Do this several times, fairly firmly on inspiration.

Test Positions for Jammed Intermaxillary and Palatomaxillary Sutures – Figure 93

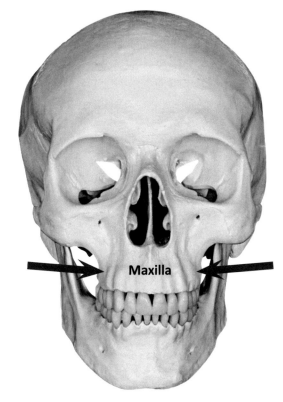

Maxilla

Step 1. Test: Squeeze together

Spreading the Maxilla – Figure 94

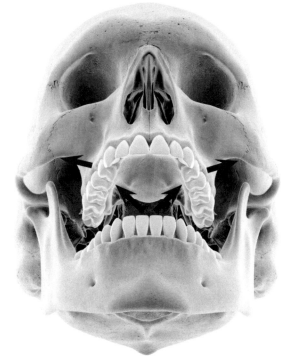

Step 2. Correction: Release suture by spreading the maxilla

Cranial Fault for Learning Disabilities

This fault is so-named because it is frequently present in people who have this problem.

1. Ask your client to place one index finger on each side of the hard palate and press gently. One finger should be each side of the intermaxillary suture – the right index finger on the right side, the left index finger on the left side – and the hands and arms must not touch.. Test an AIM. If it unlocks:

2. Place your thumb on the centre of the hard palate (if this fault is present you may find it to be very domed in shape, as opposed to arched). With your other hand, contact the top of the head (vertex) and simultaneously press down inferiorly (towards the feet) whilst pushing superiorly with the thumb (towards the vertex) **(Fig. 95)** Use inspiration assist and a medium pressure for 4 or 5 times. It is helpful if the client assists by extending their feet towards their head on inspiration (stretches the dura and increases the movement of cerebrospinal fluid).

NB. Check for a jammed sagittal suture both before and after making the correction.

Learning Disabilities Cranial Fault Correction – Figure 95

Press vertex of skull inferiorly towards the hard palate

Press thumb superiorly towards the vertex

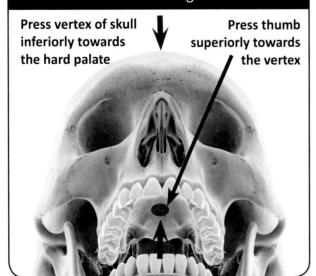

Jammed Symphysis Menti

When the sphenoid is compressed, the mandible jams squeezing the symphysis menti. These faults may well occur simultaneously. Look for this fault in people who talk a lot, feel tired, head trauma, headaches or sleep problems.

Jammed Symphysis Menti – Figure 96

Step 2. Hook fingers onto mandible behind the incisors and pull laterally

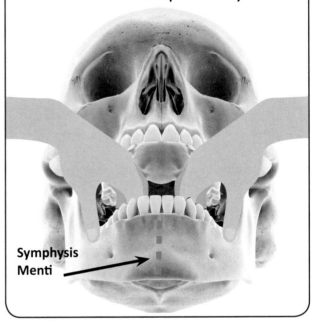

Symphysis Menti

1. The client TL's the symphysis menti (the same test as the blanket TMJ test). If the IM changes, there is either a TMJ fault present or a jammed symphysis menti. To differentiate, when the TMJ fault is a jammed symphysis menti, a previously strong pectoralis major sternal muscle will weaken when it is tested when your client lifts their opposite hip off the table. This is unique to this fault.

2. Place your fingers on the lingual side below the lower incisors and pull gently in an outward direction (laterally). **(Fig. 96)**

3. Repeat step 1.

Glabella Cranial Fault

This cranial fault may be involved with breathing patterns as the glabella is located close the nasal passages. This fault is also associated with hypertension as a drop in diastolic blood pressure between 10-20 mm Hg has been observed after correction (Walther).

1. Your client lies supine and TL's the glabella above the bridge of the nose with one hand, and the occipital protuberance with the other. If an AIM unlocks to this dynamic challenge:

2. Place a thumb, or the heel of one hand, on the glabella and the other hand on the back of the head over the occiput area **(Fig. 97)**. Press them together towards each other on inspiration four or five times. The client can extend their feet towards the head (dorsiflexion) on inspiration.

3. Keeping your hands in the same position as step 2, and still contacting the occipital protuberance, place your middle, ring and little finger on the spinous processes of the 2nd, 3rd and 4th vertebrae. Apply pressure in an inferior direction towards the feet, 4 or 5 times on inspiration while compressing the glabella and occiput as in step 2, stretching the vertebrae away from the occiput **(Fig. 98)**

4. Retest step 1.

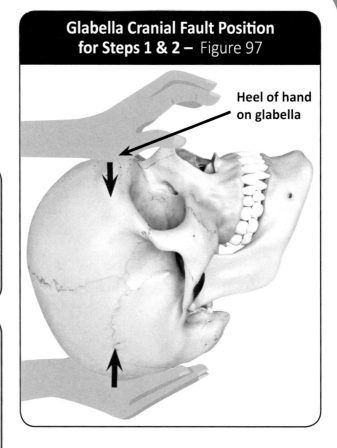

Glabella Cranial Fault Position for Steps 1 & 2 – Figure 97

Heel of hand on glabella

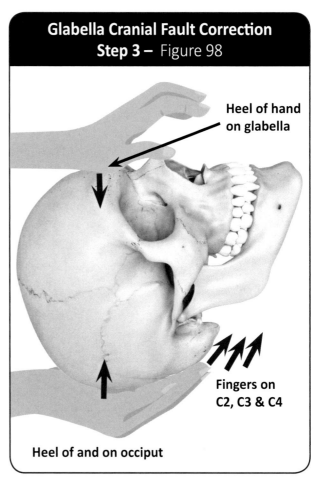

Glabella Cranial Fault Correction Step 3 – Figure 98

Heel of hand on glabella

Fingers on C2, C3 & C4

Heel of and on occiput

Pituitary Gland Structural Fault

(Structural correction for the pituitary)

The pituitary is situated at the base of the brain and snugly sits in the sella turcica – a bony pocket in the centre of the sphenoid bone, which forms part of the floor of the skull. A number of cranial bones join together in one area at the bridge of the nose. These are the frontal bone which also forms part of the orbit of the eye socket, the nasal bone, the lachrymal bone, and the maxilla. Part of dura (falx cerebri) attaches from the frontal bone and extends to the cerebellum dividing the hemispheres of the brain. If this area jams, sphenoid restriction occurs and pituitary function could subsequently be affected.

Symptoms can be tiredness, blood sugar imbalance, yawning, or frequent urination.

As with all cranial faults, check the need for zinc. The Australian Bush Flower Essence Yellow Cowslip Orchid may help the treatment to hold.

1. Challenge the bridge of the nose by pinching it together. Test an AIM. If it unlocks to this dynamic challenge:

2. Hook fingers into orbit of the eye (frontal bone) with one hand and hold the occiput with the other hand **(Fig. 99)**. Simultaneously pull in a superior direction on inspiration 4 or 5 times. The client assists by extending their feet towards the head on inspiration.

3. Repeat step 1.

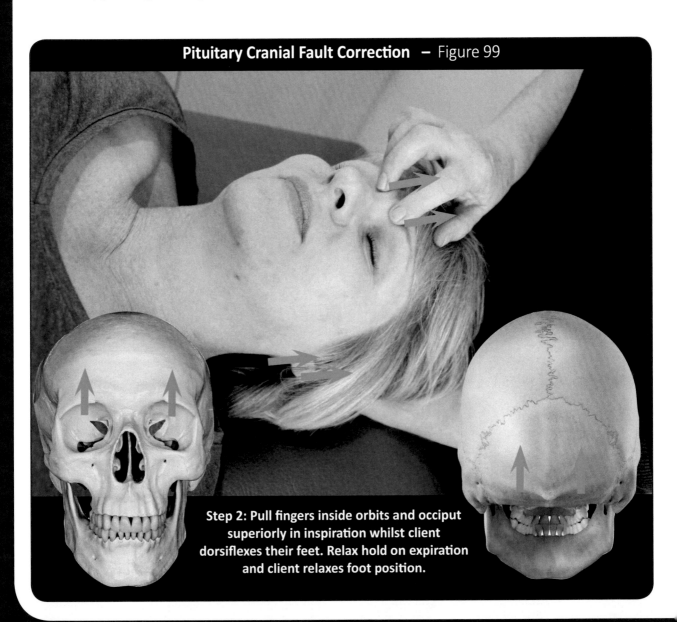

Pituitary Cranial Fault Correction – Figure 99

Step 2: Pull fingers inside orbits and occiput superiorly in inspiration whilst client dorsiflexes their feet. Relax hold on expiration and client relaxes foot position.

Temporal Bulge Cranial Fault

When this fault is present, there can be a bulge which manifests as a convexity on the affected side and a concavity on the opposite side. There could be a category II pelvic fault after this fault has been addressed see page 189. The correction is carried out with a half-inspiration assist.

The pectoralis major clavicular muscles (PMC) will test weak bilaterally when this fault is present.

1. Test the PMC muscles individually and correct if necessary.

2. Test both PMCs bilaterally and simultaneously. If they now unlock, but return to strength, when your client takes in **half** of a full breath, this indicates a temporal bulge cranial fault is present. The best way to describe to your client how to half inhale is to ask them to exhale, then breathe in just about half of their lung capacity. It might be necessary to ask your client to try slightly different phases of inspiration in order to strengthen the muscle test (half-inspiration) and this is the phase used during the correction.

Temporal Bulge Cranial Fault
Steps 3 and 4 – Figure 100

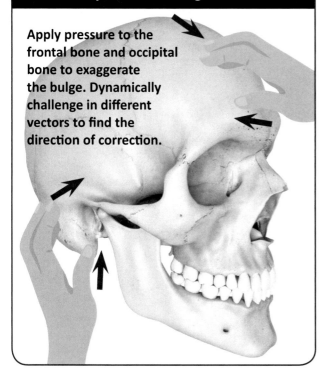

Apply pressure to the frontal bone and occipital bone to exaggerate the bulge. Dynamically challenge in different vectors to find the direction of correction.

3. Dynamically challenge the temporal bulge by exaggerating the lesion. This is done by applying pressure to the frontal bone and the occiput, in effect, squeezing the temporal bulge further. Try testing different vectors until you find the direction that unlocks the AIM. **(Fig. 100)**

4. Correct in the same vector that you found in step 3. The two-handed direction of pressure is carried out as the client half inhales (the phase of inspiration you found in step 2).

Parietal Descent

First test and correct the temporal bulge cranial fault.

This is a half-breath respiration assist correction similar to the temporal bulge challenge and correction. This time, the phase of respiration is a half expiration assist.

1. Place your fingers along the parietal bones just above the temporoparietal suture. The dynamic challenge is to lift both parietal bones and then test an AIM. **(See Fig. 101 overleaf)**

2. Enter into circuit retaining mode (unlock).

3. To identify the exact phase of respiration, ask your client to breathe in and then breathe out halfway (similar to temporal bulge but expiration this time). The phase of expiration that **locks** the IM is the phase to be used during correction.

4. The correction is to lift the parietal bones as the person takes their half exhalation and then release on their next phase of inspiration. Your client dorsiflexes their feet as the parietal bones are raised. This is repeated about 10 times. Take care not to jam the sagittal suture by placing your thumbs either side and separating it as you lift the parietals.

5. Repeat step 1

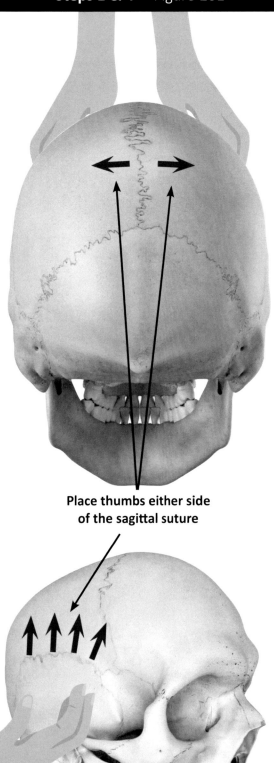

Parietal Descent Cranial Fault
Steps 1 & 4 – Figure 101

Place thumbs either side
of the sagittal suture

Lift both parietal
bones with fingers

Pelvic Categories

With this technique, you can find and balance different dysfunctions of the sacroiliac joint. Any distortion affects the flow of cerebrospinal fluid as the sacral pump becomes inefficient.

The pelvic category system was developed by Major Bertrand DeJarnette in his system called Sacro-Occipital Technique (SOT). DeJarnette blocks (See Fig. 71 on page 150) are used to help to correct pelvis dysfunction by:

- Correcting the rotation of the pelvis.
- Relaxing the spine's musculature.
- Calms proprioceptors.
- Affects dural tension and traction on spinal nerves.
- Corrects a dural torque and any minor dural constrictions.

Pelvic dysfunctions are divided into three categories.

 Remember that any pelvic category adjustment will not hold unless specific muscles attaching to the pelvis are rectified as well. These muscles stabilise the pelvis and are the underlying cause of pelvic torsion. To save a lot of time and effort, before checking for category faults, it is prudent to test and correct all the involved muscles first and correct any muscle imbalance in modality or priority order.

Categories I and II are dysfunctions between the innominate bones (the hip bones formed from the fusion of the ileum, ischium, and pubis) and the sacrum, and between the sacrum and the coccyx. For anatomical positions **(See Fig. 102 overleaf)**

Category III addresses dysfunction between the whole pelvis in relation to the 5th lumbar vertebra but can involve the whole lumbar spine (L1-L5).

See Fig. 103 overleaf for illustration of pelvic category faults.

Order of Correction

During my research I have found that there are differing opinions as to the best order of correction. In my own practice I use the principles of Neural Organization Technique (N.O.T) developed by the late Dr Carl A. Ferreri. He stresses some particularly important factors involving neurological priority.

- **As above, so below;** Address and correct the atlas first (if a modality). The atlas should be freely moveable in order to balance the head on the neck. See page 138 section on the Lateral Atlas and Heel Tension, showing the atlas link to the whole fascia. The Lovett Brother of C1 is L5 and the Lovett Brother to the sacrum is the occiput. Both 'ends' need addressing for lasting pelvic realignment. (see page 144)

- A reminder that **every sacral lesion has a cranial fault involvement**, therefore check for cranial faults before and any residual cranial faults after fixing the categories. (See pages 170-182)

- Test for **reactive muscle groups**. (See page 164)

A client may show as having all 3 categories and in AK they are corrected in reverse order – category III first, category II, then category I, which is sometimes automatically corrected by addressing II and III.

In AK Category I is found first and always corrected last (if other category pelvic faults are present).

It is possible for a client to need only a category III adjustment, but this is rare.

It is possible to have just a category I pelvic imbalance.

But it's not possible to have a category II pelvic fault without having a category I.

Dr Ferreri advocates that the client lies prone and after an atlas correction, category I is tested and corrected first.

 Why not make yourself a checklist of all the muscles involved with category pelvic faults? For anyone with back problems, check them first before starting this procedure.

Anatomy of the Pelvis – Figure 102

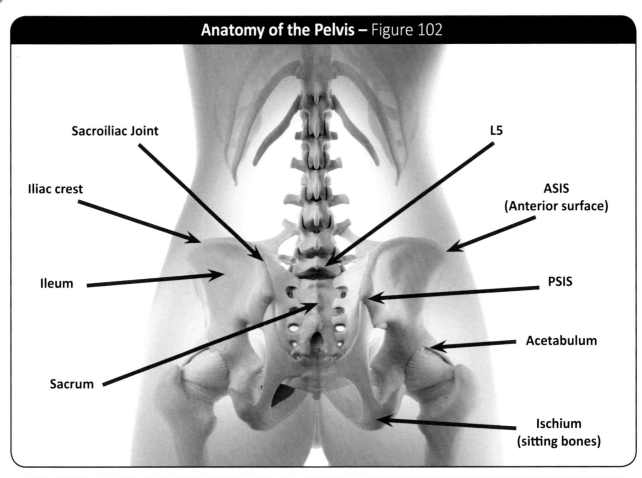

Sacroiliac Joint

Iliac crest

Ileum

Sacrum

L5

ASIS
(Anterior surface)

PSIS

Acetabulum

Ischium
(sitting bones)

Pelvic Categories – Figure 103

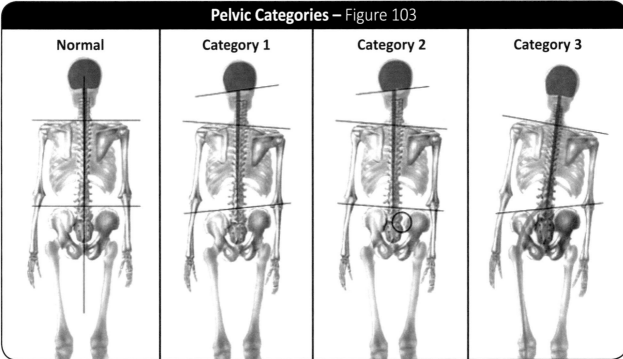

Normal

Category 1

Category 2

Category 3

Category I

The category I pelvic fault is a torsion of the pelvis itself. The sacroiliac joint is not misaligned in this case **(Fig. 103)**, but one hip moves forward and the other backwards (rotates). There is a specific dural torque. Because the dura is attached to C3, with this type of twist the dura will pull C3 out of alignment causing neck problems. The dura is also rigidly attached into the skull through the foramen magnum in the occiput. Both ends of the dura are involved which makes it of primary importance therefore Ferreri considered it to take neurological priority over other categories and should be cleared first. It is a non-weightbearing pelvic fault, so your client lies prone. The piriformis and the gluteus maximus contract when traumatised and fixate the sacrum in an attempt to keep the pelvis stable, the piriformis underneath tightens (anterior) the sacrum and the gluteus maximus, on the outside (posterior) of the sacrum, reacts to this and also tightens causing a sacral fixation on the affected side.

A common complaint of this pelvic category is pain and limited motion on turning the head (dural torque involvement). This will usually be more marked on one side. Secondary to the pelvic torsion, there is often torsion of the shoulder girdle and the head tilts in response to the pelvic rotation.

The typical pain location on palpation is at the inferior medial aspect of the posterior superior iliac spine (PSIS) on the side of the pelvis that tests positive. Tenderness is increased by pulling posteriorly on the ilium, and relieved by pulling it forward. This is probably better evaluated while your client is standing.

---

1. Your client lies prone. Correct the atlas by pumping the Achilles tendons (see Lateral Atlas on page 138) Correcting the atlas will often reveal a weak hamstring/s that did not previously show. **(Fig. 104)**

Pumping the Achilles Tendon
Figure 104

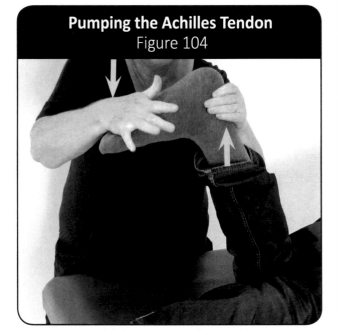

2. If one hamstring now tests weak in the clear:

    a. Using an AIM, CL the transverse process of C3 (See Fig. 63 on page 142). It will CL on the same side as the weak hamstring. This should be adjusted first by rubbing the lamina of C3 or use any of the corrections outlined in section on Addressing Spinal Misalignments (or any other methods you may use in your practice) see pages 139-148.

    b. If both hamstrings test weak, check and correct sphenobasilar and occiput cranial faults (see section on Cranial Faults on page 172).

3. Test the following muscles with the client standing and correct if necessary. If you find this difficult for the client (or you!), try putting the client into pause lock when they are in a standing position. Whilst holding pause lock, the client then moves to the couch. You are then testing the muscles' function in a 'standing position':

    a. Piriformis (often weak on one side and hypertonic on the other)

    b. Gluteus medius

    c. Sacrospinalis

    d. Quadratus lumborum

    e. Gluteus maximus

    f. Abdominal obliques (have a major lever effect on the iliac crest). An easy way to assess these is – T12 (origin) will two-point to the pubic bone (insertion) on the same side

4. Use the hamstrings as an AIM (They will now test strong in the clear). The client simultaneously TL's with their left hand on the left SI joint and the right hand on the right SI joint. **(See Fig. 105 overleaf)** If there is no IM change, ask your client to TL with the opposite side of their hands in case there is an ionisation imbalance is causing TL problems (see Section on Electromagnetic Imbalances see page 15).

TL'ing Sacroiliac Joint Step 2 – Figure 105

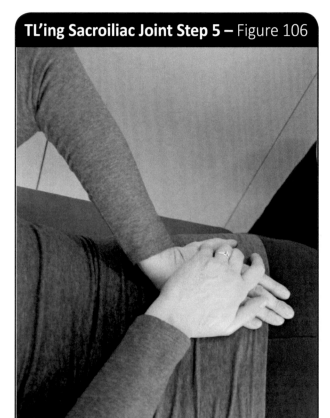

If there is no more category I involvement showing at this time, proceed to test for category II. (?) Sometimes category I will only show when the person is standing or walking.

5. If this TL causes an indicator change, then perform another TL, this time with **client's hands one on top of the other over one sacroiliac joint**, then the other (double TL) **Fig. 106**. The side that cause the IM change gives you the side that is torqued into dysfunction (the same side as the weak hamstring in step 2).

6. To relieve the pelvic torsion, have (✓) the client lying prone. On the side of the SI joint that double TL'd in step 5, place a **DeJarnette block under the ASIS** (this is the anterior protrusion of the ilium) so that it pushes the ilium posteriorly. A second block is placed contralaterally **under the acetabulum** on the posterior ischium side. The thin end of the wedges point towards each other. **(See Fig. 107)**

TL'ing Sacroiliac Joint Step 5 – Figure 106

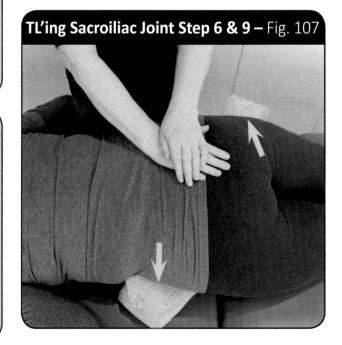

7. With blocks properly placed (✓) pointing towards one another, check with TL the PSIS found at step 5. There should no longer be positive indicator change. The client's **body weight lying on the blocks** will adequately make the correction.

TL'ing Sacroiliac Joint Step 6 & 9 – Fig. 107

8. **Releasing the tension of the gluteus maximus and piriformis**; with your elbow firmly rub the trigger point in the belly of the gluteus maximus on the same side found in step 5 (the ASIS block side). Warn your client first as it will be painful!

9. A light pumping-type action repeated approximately ten times over the SI joint on the side of the blocked acetabulum can be added on to facilitate and speed the correction **(Fig. 107)**.

10. Whilst the client is still prone, ask them to contact their **hand over their navel, and with the other hand rub both K27's then the coccyx (GV1)** This neurologically resets the distribution and processing information from the left to right and top to bottom of the body.

11. Remove blocks and repeat step 5. There should no longer be a positive TL.

12. Re-test the same muscles tested at step 3 as several muscle dysfunction patterns are often associated with, and probably the cause of, category I pelvic faults None of these muscles should test weak. If any still do, correct the muscles with specific corrections: Neurolymphatics, neurovasculars, origin/insertion, tonification/sedation points, and so on.

13. Often with a category I pelvic dysfunction there is disturbance in cranial primary respiratory function. Evaluate the **cranium, particularly the sphenobasilar cranial fault and the TMJ**.

14. Finish by testing and correcting **the gait** if necessary.

Reference (Knowlative) (Ferreri)

Notes & References:

David Walther - Applied Kinesiology - Synopsis - 2nd edition 1988-2000, pages 115-116,

see also:

Bruce & Joan Dewe - International College of Professional Kinesiology Practice, Practitioner Database, Section C, 1999-2000, pages 30,

David Leaf - Flowchart Manual - Italian edition 1998, page 174-175.

Category II

A category II pelvic dysfunction is misalignment of the sacrum and the innominate (hip bones). Ligaments in the pelvis stretch and the sacroiliac joint separates and can slip to one side. Misalignment can cause nerve root compression and subsequently pain. The shoulder girdle and neck can become distorted as with category I as can the balance of other weight bearing joints such as knees, ankles and foot arches. When present it changes the position of the lower jaw, which is the 'pelvis' of the head. This is due to the change in the curvature of the neck and spasm of the muscles attached to the mandible.

Category II is identified by positive therapy localization over the sacroiliac joint. Therapy localization is usually done with the client supine because this adds some weight on the pelvis.

It's worth testing for a category II pelvic fault when your client tells you that the pain starts when in certain positions such as being in the car, standing or walking for a long time, getting up from sitting down etc. **It's really valuable to ask your client to get into the position that causes the pain, enter that posture/movement into circuit retaining mode and THEN check again for category II.**

There are two major types of category II pelvic dysfunction; the posterior ilium and posterior ischium. They have different muscle involvements and areas of tenderness that differentiate them from each other and from a category I.

1. Client is supine. Using an AIM (usually gluteus medius). Your client TL's each the sacroiliac joint, one at the time, right hand on right joint and left hand on left joint (test both palms up and palms down if ionisation hasn't been checked). **If neither TL causes an IM change then there is no Pelvic Category II so proceed to check Category III.**

Otherwise:

2. Push on the anterior superior iliac spine (ASIS) (Fig. 102 on page 184) on the involved side to make the Ilium move

posteriorly. If this movement causes an indicator change, then the category II pelvic dysfunction is a **posterior ilium**.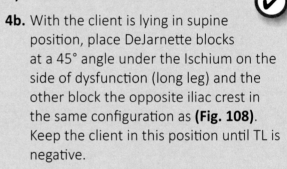

If this movement does not cause an indicator change,

3. Check for a **posterior ischium** dysfunction. To do this, pull anteriorly on the posterior superior iliac spine (PSIS) **(Fig. 102)** on the involved side/side that TL'd that will in turn tip the ischium posteriorly. If this movement causes an indicator change, then the category II pelvic dysfunction is a posterior ischium.

a) Posterior Ilium

The posterior ilium is nearly always associated with dysfunction of the sartorius and/or gracilis muscles on the side of involvement. They give anterior support to the pelvis. Sometimes the muscles will not test weak in the clear – but a weakness will be found by therapy localising the neurolymphatic points or other factors involved with the muscle. They may also only test weak in a weight-bearing position. There will be tenderness at the origin and insertion of the gracilis and/or sartorius and along most of the muscle's length. The leg on the side of the posterior ilium will appear short due to the pelvic torsion. An anatomically short leg is rare.

a) Posterior Ilium

4a. With the client is lying supine, place DeJarnette blocks under the iliac crest of the side of dysfunction (short leg) and the other block at a 45° angle at the base of the buttock, under the opposite ischium. **(Fig. 108)**

5a. Keep the client in this position until TL is negative.

6a. Test, with the client standing and correct if necessary:
   a. Sartorius
   b. Gracilis
   c. Latissimus Dorsi

7a. Repeat step 1

b) Posterior Ischium

The posterior ischium is not as common as the posterior ilium. It is usually secondary to weak hamstring or gluteus maximus muscles and these have probably been corrected if Category I has been addressed. If the hamstrings are not weak in the clear, then test them with the person standing. The leg will be long on the side of the posterior ischium in the absence of congenital anomalies. There will be tenderness at the origin of the hamstrings on the ischial tuberosity ('sitting bone'), and there may be tenderness at any points of hamstring insertion. The anterior and posterior 1st rib head attachments will usually be tender because of shoulder torsion.

b) Posterior Ischium

4b. With the client is lying in supine position, place DeJarnette blocks at a 45° angle under the Ischium on the side of dysfunction (long leg) and the other block the opposite iliac crest in the same configuration as **(Fig. 108)**. Keep the client in this position until TL is negative.

5b. Test, with the client standing and correct if necessary:
   a. Hamstrings
   b. Gluteus maximus
   c. Adductors

6b. Palpate the 1st anterior and posterior rib attachments on the side of dysfunction to check if it is still painful.

7b. Repeat step 1

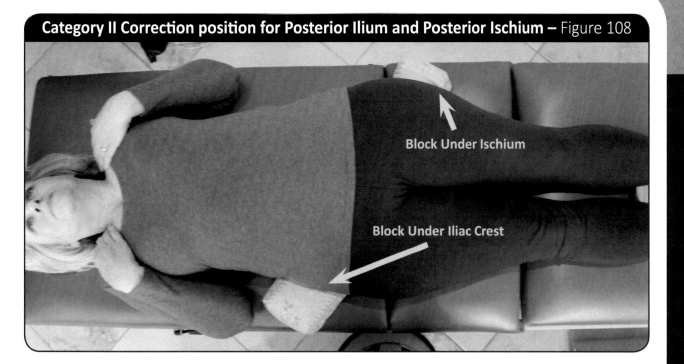

Category II Correction position for Posterior Ilium and Posterior Ischium – Figure 108

Block Under Ischium

Block Under Iliac Crest

Category II Symphysis Pubis

(Also known as Pseudo Category II)

Researched by George Goodheart, this common fault may occur even if other category II pelvic faults are not showing. Think about testing for this if your client has the following symptoms:

- Neck and / or shoulder and arm pain

- Cervical paraspinal muscle pain

- Thoracic paraspinal muscle pain

- Gluteal pain

- A low back problem

With this fault:

- The symphysis pubis on the side of the lesion will TL – if both sides TL check which side is priority.

- One or both of the sartorius muscles will test weak. The origin of the sartorius muscle is on the anterior superior iliac spine (ASIS) and just below it. The sartorius will be weak on the same side as the symphysis pubis TL. The sartorius muscle helps to stabilise the pelvis so if it is weak the ilium is allowed to tilt backwards.

- The client could complain of medial thigh pain on opposite side, particularly at night and not in the day.

- Due to pelvic distortion, the leg opposite to the lesion will be shorter.

- The cervical spine will be sore on the same side around the area of C3.

---

1. Your client is supine. Test both sartorius muscles. (Make sure the knee is held down and the ankle is resting just above the opposite knee).

2. Ask your client to TL the symphysis pubis on each side.

3. Correct the weak sartorius using NL's, NV's or address using the 4 key finger modes. This will help stabilise the ilium before the blocking.

4. Whichever side the sartorius and the symphysis pubis tested positive, place a block under the PSIS on the same side and one under the opposite ischium so that the thin end of the wedges point towards one another. This will encourage the pelvis to move forward.

5. Ask your client to hold the blocks in place. Lift a leg, bend it at the knee and hold securely at the distal end of the upper leg; gently rotate the femur in a circular motion taking it gently through its whole range of movement 3-4 times. Repeat with the other leg. ✔

6. Repeat steps 1 & 2.

Pelvic Category III

In a category III pelvic fault is a dysfunction of the lumbar spine with an intact pelvis. The whole pelvis will either be tilted forwards or backwards causing subluxations of the lumbar vertebrae. Symptoms from a category III pelvic fault can be local or elsewhere and often there is severe sciatica. A category III may exist in conjunction with a lumbar disc involvement, facet syndrome, or other conditions that involve the lumbosacral spine. There will be an increased lordosis (inward curvature) of the lower spine as the pelvis tilts forward. The pain may be in the low back and eases with movement and comes back with standing. There can also be cervical problems because of sternocleidomastoid weakness, or digestive problems as a result of vagus nerve involvement (see page 131). The category III pelvic fault influences hip rotation because of muscle imbalances. To check for this, grasp your client's ankles and turn the legs inwards. There will be much greater internal rotation on one side. This can be rechecked once the procedure has been carried out.

Clients with this problem can tend to lean to ease their leg pain either towards or away from the side of pain or they may want to lean forward.

1. The abdominals and gluteus maximus (for posterior pelvic support) are often bilaterally weak which causes the opposing sacrospinalis and quadratus lumborum muscles to be hypertonic. Check these first (i.e. abdominals and gluteus maximus) and correct if necessary. When testing the gluteus maximus ensure that the client ❓

bends their leg so that their foot is as near as they can get to their buttock (if it's difficult the quadriceps will be hypertonic). Check and correct if necessary other muscles associated with Category III: ❓

- Adductors (posterior pelvic support)
- Hamstrings (posterior pelvic support)
- Quadratus lumborum
- Psoas and Iliacus
- Latissimus dorsi
- Neck muscles

2. Your client lies prone. A challenge is necessary to evaluate for category III because the pelvis is intact therefore the SI joint will not TL. Contact the anterior portion of the ischium and lift it posteriorly while the L5 spinous process is pressed toward the side of ischial contact. This in effect squeezes the pelvis on to L5. Then immediately carry out a muscle test using a hamstring as an AIM. **(Fig. 109)** Repeat the dynamic challenge on the other side. Only one combination of ischium spinous process challenge will be positive and note this.

Pelvic Category III Test Step 2
Figure 109

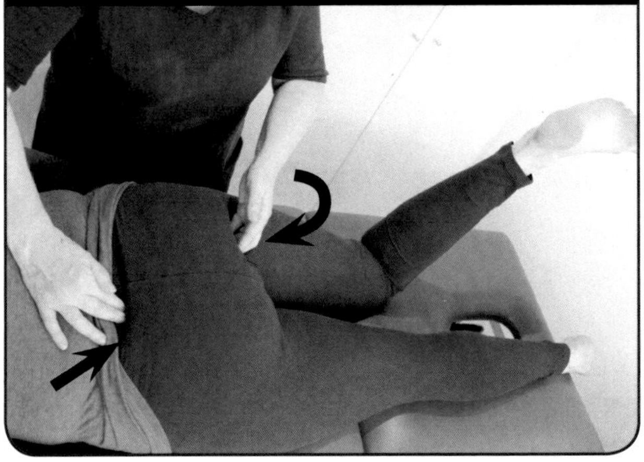

3. Check for any subluxations to L2,3,4 and 5 (see section on Correcting a Spinal Misalignment on page 142). Correcting this alone will often resolve a category III pelvic imbalance. Correct using inspiration assist. ✔

4. Correct the sacrum (see section on Correcting the Sacrum on page 168).

5. Retest step 2 and if a category III pelvic fault still shows, continue on to step 6.

6. Place one block 90° to the spine under the ASIS on the side of the positive challenge. **(See Fig. 110)**

7. Place a second block 90° to the spine opposite on the non-involved side anywhere. Move this block until you find the position that gives maximum relief until the pain is eliminated or is diminished and feels comfortable.

8. Leave the blocks in place for a time to allow the pelvis to adjust itself.

9. Repeat step 2

Pelvic Category III Correction Steps 6-8
Figure 110

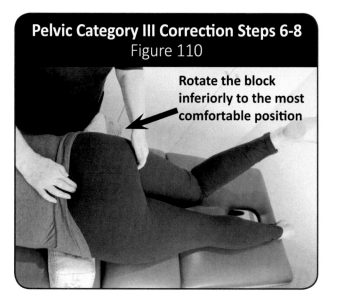

Rotate the block inferiorly to the most comfortable position

Pelvic Categories Quick Reference

Category 1

1. Client prone. Correct atlas by pumping Achilles tendons.

2. Check hamstrings.

   If just one is weak in the clear

   a. CL C3 on same side as hamstring. Adjust.

   If both hamstrings test weak,

   b. Check and correct sphenobasilar and occiput cranial faults.

3. Test with client standing and correct if necessary:

   a. Piriformis
   b. Gluteus medius
   c. Sacrospinalis
   d. Quadratus lumborum
   e. Gluteus maximus
   f. Abdominal obliques

4. Using hamstrings as an AIM client TLs both SI joint.

5. If IM unlocks, double TL each side the side of IM change is side of torsion.

6. Place block under the ASIS on the side of weak SI joint found in step 5. The second block is placed under the opposite acetabulum. Tapered ends towards each other.

7. With blocks in place recheck step 5.

8. Elbow in belly of gluteus maximus on same side as found in step 5.

9. Gentle thrusts over SI joint on the side of the blocked acetabulum.

10. Client holds navel and rubs K27's and GV1.

11. Remove blocks and recheck step 5.

12. Recheck muscles in step 3 and correct if necessary.

13. Evaluate TMJ and sphenobasilar cranial fault.

14. Test and correct gait if necessary.

Category II

1. Client supine, client TL's SI joint one at a time. If neither shows go to Category III.

2. Push on ASIS on side of positive TL. If IM changes it is a posterior ilium correction.

   If this movement doesn't cause and IM change.

3. Pull anteriorly the PSIS on side of positive TL. If IM unlocks it is a posterior ischium correction.

a) Posterior Ilium

4a. Place block at 45° under the iliac crest on the side of dysfunction and another at 45° under the base of buttock, tapered ends pointing towards each other. Leave for a few minutes.

5a. Test with client standing and correct if necessary:

   a. Sartorius
   b. Gracilis
   c. Latissimus Dorsi

b) Posterior Ischium

4b. Place block at 45° under base of buttock on the side of dysfunction and another at 45° under the Iliac crest, tapered ends pointing towards each other. Leave for a few minutes.

5b. Test with client standing and correct if necessary:

   a. Hamstrings
   b. Gluteus maximus
   c. Adductors

Category II Symphysis Pubis

1. Test both sartorius muscles.
2. TL each side of symphysis pubis.
3. Correct weak sartorius.

4. Place block under ASIS on the side of weak sartorius and symphysis pubis TL.
5. With client still on blocks, rotate each femur through its full range of motion.

Pelvic Category III

1. Check gluteus maximus and abdominal muscles. Correct if necessary, along with:

   - Adductors (posterior pelvic support)
   - Hamstrings (posterior pelvic support)
   - Piriformis
   - Quadratus lumborum
   - Tensor fascia lata
   - Psoas and Iliacus
   - Latissimus dorsi
   - Neck Muscles

2. Lift one side of ischium and squeeze L5 towards the lifted ischium and then test an IM. Repeat on the other side.

3. Check for spinal misalignment of L2,3,4 and 5 and correct if necessary (with inspiration assist).
4. Correct the sacrum.
5. Place block 90° to spine under the ASIS on the side of the positive challenge.
6. Place the second block at 90° to the spine on the opposite side. Move block until L5 pain subsides.
7. Leave blocks in place to adjust.
8. Remove blocks and repeat step 2.

Uterine Lift and Functional Short Leg

Structural Finger Mode

This technique can correct two problems in one. It is probably best avoided if it is known that the client has fibroids.

a. A tilted pelvis will cause one leg to be set higher than the other. A functional short leg is where the leg bones do not vary in size but appear to be shorter because of pelvic distortion. This is opposed to a rare anatomical short leg where the legs themselves differ in length. Weak abdominal floor muscles (the pelvic diaphragm) and a drop in position of the abdominal organs (ptosis) causes pressure on the pelvic organs. This can alter the pelvis and cause a functional short leg. This procedure resolves a functional short leg every time. You may have clients who have a recurring functional short leg even after treating the pelvis and lower back. It may be that this is the underlying problem. (Deal)

b. Correcting a uterine ptosis is excellent for preventing problems later in life such as haemorrhoids, bladder repairs, prolapsed uterus, etc. Uterine ptosis contributes to PMS and menstrual pain. If this technique is performed just prior to a period it can be of tremendous benefit. Think of this technique if your client suffers from bladder weakness as the uterus can press on the bladder reducing its capacity. *Let us not forget that this technique is not just for women; for the same reasons it can also relieve prostate problems too!*

1. It's always useful to have visual proof that a procedure has corrected something so check the leg length first. There are various methods; the one I use is grasping the client's ankles holding your thumbs immediately above the medial malleolus (ankle bone). Pull the client's legs towards you with a gentle tug and give them a little shake to release any tension in the hips. Immediately place the client's legs together and note the position of your thumbs. If they are not aligned, this shows up a functional short leg (if they have an anatomical short leg the following treatment will not correct the leg length).

2. Your client may need to empty their bladder before carrying out this test. Use a sustained/static challenge, and with your fingers push into the centre of the uterus halfway between the symphysis pubis and the navel area and inferiorly towards the symphysis pubis. You are exaggerating a potential ptosis. If an AIM unlocks then this technique is appropriate.

3. The correction is lifting the viscera. Have the client bend their knees and, if they are able, stretch their arms above their head. On inspiration push the heel of your hand just superior to the pubic bone and into the viscera (posteriorly) thus lifting the uterus/viscera towards the client's head (superiorly). Release the pressure on expiration. **(See Fig. 111 overleaf)** Repeat this about 10 times.

4. Retest step 2

5. Measure the leg length as in step 1 which should now be level. In my experience this technique invariably causes the hips to level. However, if there is no change in leg length, either your client has an anatomical short leg, or they require further pelvic assessment.

   This issue is associated with jaw problems because the jaw is the pelvis of the head. Therefore, TMJ assessment is also recommended. The homeopathic remedy sepia may be useful as ongoing support. Test for this before administering the correction.

Case Study

One of my clients came to clinic complaining of a prolapsed uterus which was severe enough to require medical intervention. She had six children, which had taken its toll and her uterus would prolapse quite badly at times (procidentia). She was not keen on an operation and asked if I could help. Using this technique dramatically reduced the effects of the prolapse which was so stressful to her. She was also advised to eat extra fibre in order to ensure that her bowels were never overly full as a full colon can easily press onto the uterus causing it to drop. Her husband was instructed on how to carry out this technique occasionally at home. She would return to the clinic periodically for further treatment and she found she was able to cope very well with her problem and avoided the operation.

Abdominal Floor Correction

To test and improve the strength of the abdominal floor muscles and the adductors, the client is supine with both knees bent approximately 45° with their feet flat on the table. Place your hands on the inside of the knees and forcefully pull them apart whilst your client forcefully holds their legs together. If they are unable to do this, continue this activity as many times as needed (with rests in between if necessary) until the muscles get progressively stronger and they can hold their legs together against your pressure. (Ferreri)

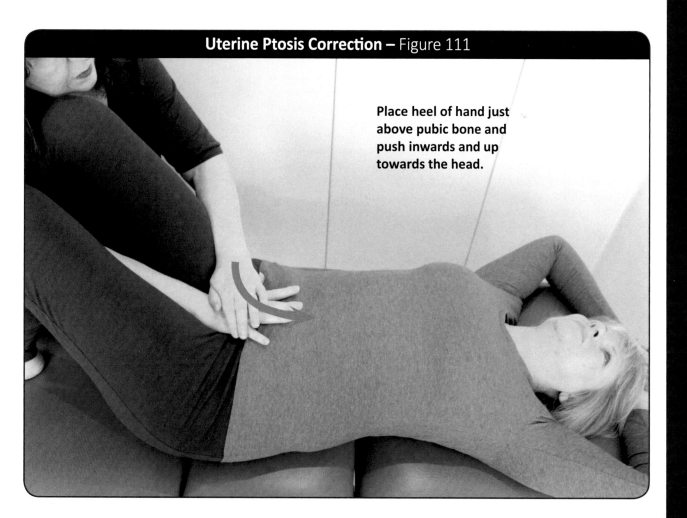

Uterine Ptosis Correction – Figure 111

Place heel of hand just above pubic bone and push inwards and up towards the head.

Cystitis Technique

Structural

It's not unusual for women (and occasionally men) to suffer from bladder irritation and yet the lab tests show that there is no bacterial infection present. If the bladder has been under trauma for some time from, for example a previous infection, it can still continue to spasm giving the sufferer the same sensation of fullness as when they had an infection. The following technique will quickly bring relief to most cystitis sufferers.

This technique is also invaluable for women who suffer from vaginismus or have difficulty in achieving an orgasm.

The bladder comprises of smooth muscle – not striated like skeletal muscle. However, it still seems to respond to this type of neuromuscular spindle cell technique which 'resets' signalling from the brain telling the bladder that it's full.

This procedure will often bring immediate relief.

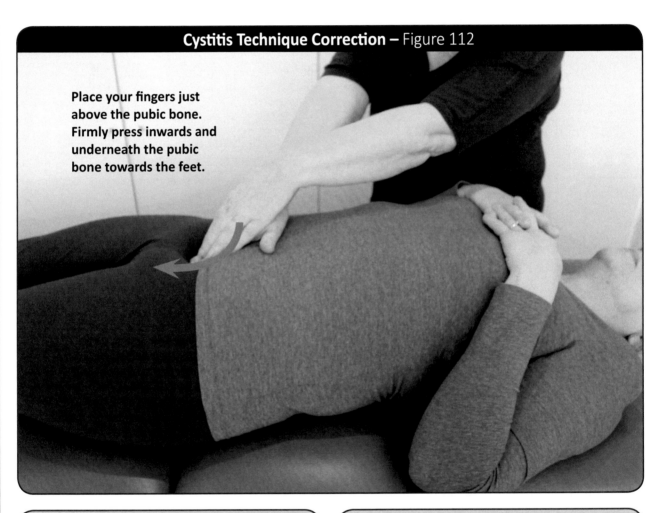

Cystitis Technique Correction – Figure 112

Place your fingers just above the pubic bone. Firmly press inwards and underneath the pubic bone towards the feet.

1. Your client may need to empty their bladder before you carry out this procedure. Place your fingers firmly under the pubic bone and test an AIM. If the muscle unlocks and when priority/ modality is added (locks), the technique is appropriate.

2. Using both hands push the fingers firmly underneath the pubic bone towards the feet and hold for 30 seconds to 2 minutes. You may feel the tension in that area releasing. It is sometimes necessary to change the vector of the fingers slightly. **(See Fig. 112)**

3. Retest as in no. 1.

More on Muscles

When a structural problem won't hold or you are stuck, these gems can help you through and aid you to 'think out of the box'.

Surrogate Muscles

This one is weird, but it does work!

Some muscles are anatomically impossible to get to. Examples of these are the psoas, subscapularis, the piriformis, and the pelvic floor muscles, and rectal muscles. You might even think about backing out from treating the pterygoids with spindle cell technique and decide to use a surrogate muscle instead (chicken!).

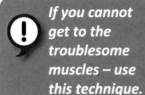 *If you cannot get to the troublesome muscles – use this technique.*

Just as it is possible to test one person as a surrogate for another, it is also possible to test one muscle as a surrogate for another. As with surrogate testing, we can hold the intention and tell the brain that we are going to substitute one muscle for another. It goes like this:

1. Choose muscle that is easy to get to as your surrogate. I tend to use the quadriceps. This muscle should be strong in the clear.

2. Then verbalise the following, or similar, "this muscle is now the surrogate for ....". If there is an issue with the muscle that you are surrogating the quadriceps will then unlock. At the same time visualising the location and the structure of the muscle you are surrogating reinforces the procedure.

3. Still using the quadriceps muscle carry out the appropriate structural corrections, such as fascial release (massaging the muscle and 'ironing out' any muscle kinks), and/or spindle cell or Golgi tendon apparatus techniques.

4. Retest the quadriceps which should now test strong.

5. Now reset the quadriceps muscle by verbalising "this muscle is now the quadriceps".

Aerobic and Anaerobic Testing

Sometimes muscles only fatigue under certain conditions. We can test a person's ailing muscle while they are lying on the couch, and yet a problem does not show. This could be because the muscle only fatigues after running, exercising, walking upstairs etc. Dr Goodheart discovered this when he was treating U.S. athletes during the Olympics. When an athlete competing in the skiing slalom, complained of acute knee pain that came on only when he was halfway down the course, Goodheart was puzzled that none of the muscles associated with the knee tested weak. When he simulated movement by testing the muscle several times, then the weakness then showed. He also discovered that there was a difference in the nutritional support for that muscle depending on whether the problem occurred when testing the muscle aerobically or anaerobically. (Deal)

1. If there is no obvious weakness in the suspected muscle:

   a. Test the muscle aerobically by testing in ten times in ten seconds.

   b. Test the muscle anaerobically, test it twenty times in ten seconds.

2. He found that when muscles fatigued under these circumstances the following nutrition helped.

   a. If the muscle weakens on aerobic testing it will respond to **iron** supplementation. Check by placing an iron supplement on the body and retest step 1a.

   b. If the muscle weakens on anaerobic testing it will respond to **pantothenic acid (B5)**. Check by placing the supplement on the body and retesting step 1b.

If the nutrients in step 2 do not help, an alternative for both muscle tests is **black currant seed oil** or another type of **omega 6 essential fatty acid**.

Interestingly it has been demonstrated that if

food or a beverage containing more than 3% sugar is consumed before exercise, this inhibits aerobic activity. Therefore, it is inadvisable to consume anything sugary before exercising or training.

Fix it in Motion

This is particularly useful for repetitive strain injuries. It is also an excellent method to ensure that the treatment holds.

A muscle may strengthen but then fail to remain strong on continual usage. It is possible that the activity of the muscle may reactivate the imbalance that caused it to weaken in the first place.

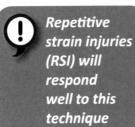

Repetitive strain injuries (RSI) will respond well to this technique

1. The muscle often tests strong in the clear. If it tests weak, make a correction.

2. Ask your client to activate the prime mover through its whole range of movement several times then retest. If the muscle now weakens:

3. Apply the correction while your client takes the muscle repeatedly through its range of motion.

4. Repeat step 2. Consider that reactive muscle patterns may be involved (see section on Reactive Muscles on page 164).

Sustained Testing

It is quite possible that a troublesome muscle will test strong when it is first tested but may only become a problem after continual use. E.g. when going up a flight of stairs, the quadriceps may feel weak to a person.

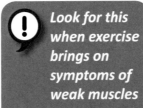

Look for this when exercise brings on symptoms of weak muscles

1. The muscle will likely test strong in the clear. Test the muscle repeatedly until the weakness eventually shows.

2. Instead of rubbing the associated neurolymphatic reflex, **hold** it for about 30 seconds.

3. Retest the muscle repeatedly. The muscle test should now remain strong after repeated testing.

Bilateral Piriformis May Indicate a Jaw Problem

If the piriformis tests weak bilaterally, this may indicate the need for a jaw correction.

1. Ask the person to touch the symphysis menti (tip of chin) whilst the piriformis muscles are retested.

2. If doing so strengthens the previously weak muscle, there is a jaw connection.

3. Massage the length of the jawbone both above it and below it. Give particular attention to tender or tight areas. (See section on TMJ for a thorough examination and treatment on pages 152-157).

4. Retest the piriformis muscles, which should now test strong.

Bilateral Psoas May Indicate a Neck/Occiput Problem

If the psoas tests weak bilaterally, this can be due to an occipital lesion.

1. Test both previously weak psoas muscles whilst your client TLs the back of the head by simultaneously placing a hand on each side of the occiput. If the psoas strengthens to this TL there is an occiput connection.

2. Massage firmly at the base of the skull then apply a gentle stretch in a superior direction whilst cupping the forehead with one hand and holding the index and middle fingers on each side of the cervical spine underneath the occiput. ✔

3. The psoas muscles should now test strong in the clear. Additionally, it is wise to check the anterior and posterior neck muscles, the upper trapezius, levator scapulae and the latissimus dorsi.

4. Retest step 1 and if the problem doesn't correct, consider checking the individual cranial faults (see section on Cranial Faults on page 174).

Bilateral Gluteus Maximus

The gluteus maximus is an important muscle stabilising the pelvis. In the case of a bilateral gluteus maximus there will also be a C3 misalignment which should be addressed (see section on Spinal Misalignment on page 142).

A bilateral gluteus maximus can be common in men with benign prostate hypertrophy. The herb saw palmetto is a nutritional assist for these muscles which may facilitate correction and help resolve back problems. Also check for a bilateral gluteus maximus weakness in women with PCOS (polycystic ovary syndrome) again with saw palmetto as a nutritional assist for the correction.

General Techniques, Imbalances and Corrections

Here you'll find tests and corrections that cannot be classified. Their scope is broad and stand-alone, or they may fall into several categories. You'll also find some high gain techniques to aid your investigations and handy quick reference charts containing suggested procedures to go to for common health issues.

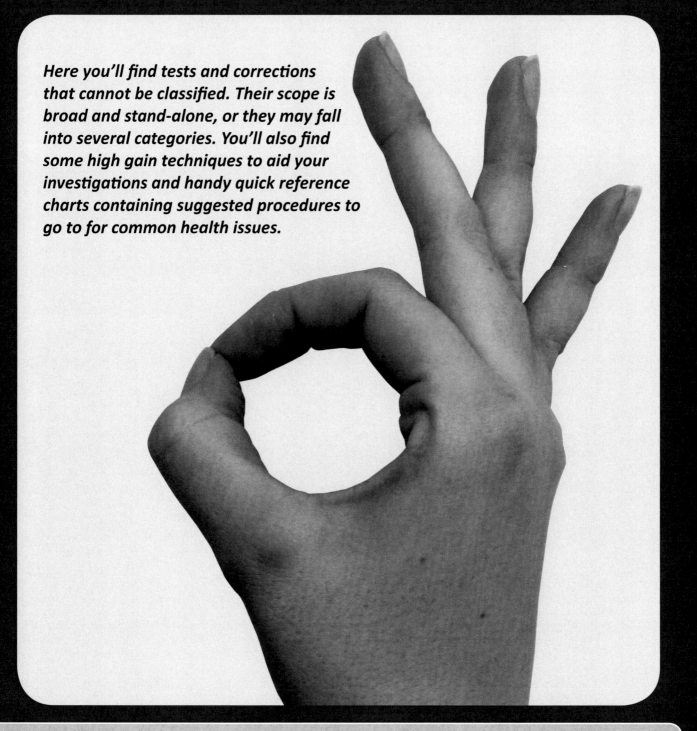

Table of contents

Pre-stressing

High-gain Technique

Some people are so strong or so unresponsive that they will test as if hardly anything is out of balance, even though the evidence is abundant that there is in fact something wrong.

To uncover problems in these people – even problems that will not show in the presence of a pinch test, it is necessary to "pre-stress" their system.

This is achieved by tapping on each of the following acupuncture points **in Figure 113**:

CV9   (1" above the umbilicus)

CV24   (on mid chin just below the lower lip)

GV26   (on upper lip at midline)

Tap each of these 5-6 times with the suspected lesion in circuit.
No specific order is necessary.

When you have finished tapping, retest the client for whatever the original test was. The client should now show to any hidden imbalances.

> **NOTE: This is very useful to show problems that occur spasmodically and are not particularly giving trouble at the time of the test, e.g. a calf pain that only occurs after running for a period of time.**

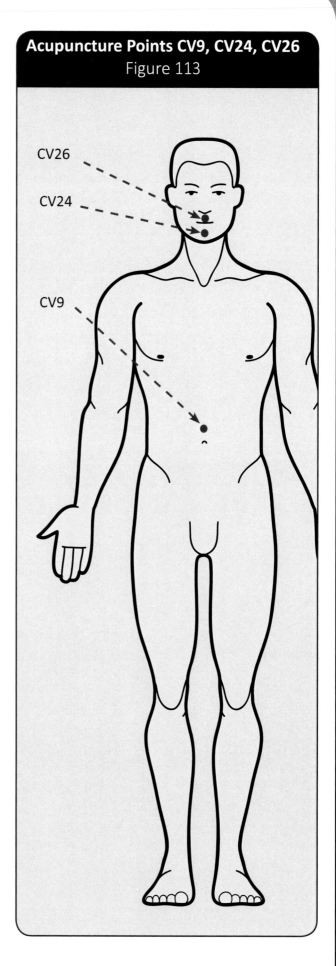

Acupuncture Points CV9, CV24, CV26
Figure 113

CV26
CV24
CV9

Pulse Synchronisation

Technique to Reduce Compensations

In the introduction, I advised you not to be alarmed if you found that you had different result, with the same client, from a fellow practitioner – yes, it happens to all of us! Building a rapport with your client is a positive way of ensuring that your results are accurate. Dr Terry Franks, an associate of Dr George Goodheart, the founder of Applied Kinesiology, wrote a paper about this concept.

He considered that even clients who we might not feel a connection with, have the same life force running through them as we do. So, if we feel a disdain for someone, we are really feeling disdain for a part of ourselves too. Dr Franks felt that if we have a better appreciation for our fellow human being, if there is anything that we can do to get more in touch with our clients, this will greatly improve our objective of doing the best we can for them. (Deal)

To create a bond between two people and bind them together, ancient ritual would mix the blood together from the two individuals. Clearly this is not a practice we would care to do in clinic! However, Dr Franks devised another way. His concept is that the pulse is actually the blood moving like a wave through our body and another person can feel this – i.e. taking a pulse. He felt that synchronising our own pulse with the client's is a way of syncing our life force with theirs without spilling any blood. Then the definitive opportunity to bring about healing can take place.

How Do We Know That Synchronising Pulses Makes a Difference?

Try this as an experiment; find around half a dozen tests, that show as being positive, with your client. Note them, but **don't** correct anything yet.

> 1. Find the radial pulse (any pulse will work but this is the most convenient) on your own left wrist*. ✓
>
> 2. Then place the fingers of your left hand on the radial pulse of your client's left wrist – continuing to hold your own pulse.
>
> 3. Initially, they will not be beating at the same rate, but hold both pulses until at least one beat syncs with yours. This can really help to take away confusion, tension and frustration in both parties.
>
> 4. Once synchronization has been achieved, re-test the imbalances you found earlier. What has changed? It's most likely that quite a number of them corrected themselves because they were compensations that could easily be remedied. The imbalances that didn't correct using pulse synchronization will be anything that the body needs actual work on whether they are compensations or not.
>
> * *Either hand can be used, but it appears that the left hand works better*

Pulse synchronisation has been shown to help in the following situations:

- When seeing a client for the first time this technique will put both at ease, in tune and help build a rapport.

- Helps place the client and practitioner on the same wavelength.

- Helps intuition – knowing where to go next in the session.

- It's really quick to do so it is worth doing at the start of every session.

- It clears out some compensations at the very start.

- Pulse synchronization also benefits the tester too as both will benefit from any corrections made.

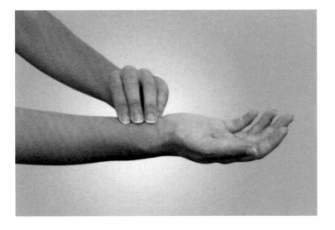

Injury Recall Technique (IRT)

No specific finger mode

A Quick Stand-Alone Technique to Use with Everybody!

Rationale

This technique originated from a podiatrist and has been adopted as a kinesiology protocol because of its incredible effect of increasing flexibility in all joints of the body. IRT (Injury Recall Technique) is a gentle procedure used following a recent or old injury or trauma. IRT restores muscle balance to pre-injury status, often dramatically relieving pain and restoring range of motion.

The late Robert Crotty, DPM, made the first observations of what we now call IRT. His protege and colleague, Gordon Bronston, DPM, made additional contributions to what they called the "Muscle Chain Response." In the late 1980's, Walter Schmitt DC, added manual muscle testing and applied kinesiology assessment procedures to the original observations and more fully described the "Muscle Chain Response" in terms of modern neurological concepts.

> **" There are few things that injuriously affect the body that do not cause the body to react by flexing the toes and jamming the mortice joint which then locks in a memory that something has happened "**

Every time a trauma is inflicted to the body whether it is for example a physical blow, surgery or a tooth extraction, primitive reflexes are activated. The reflex that makes us curl into a ball when there is a threat of trauma is an example of this. Reflexes are instinctive acts of our bodies. We carry them in our DNA, since their main function is to allow us to adapt to the surrounding environment that we interact with. When there is trauma all our joints are compounded in this posture and, even though we may not physically adopt this attitude when traumatised, the reflex is still activated. The memory of these trauma remain in tissue despite the original injury having long healed and every joint becomes that little less mobile as a result. In other words, the neurological pathways don't necessarily turn off and the hypothalamus may still be getting abnormal signals from the thalamus long after the pain has gone. We find that people who have experienced a lot of trauma to their body tend to have a much more limited range of movement in their joints.

The brain and spinal cord are receptor driven. 90% of the input to the cerebral cortex is as a result of receptors being stimulated. The largest number of receptors per inch of tissue is in the neck and the ankle. If the body is designed to receive stimulation, then the most natural method of healing is to stimulate these receptors.

Dr Crotty discovered that if there is still tissue memory in an injury in the body, stimulating these receptors would deactivate the memory that was locking the primitive reflex action of the trauma into the body. (Schmitt, n.d.)

You may wish to measure the person's flexibility before you carry out injury recall. To do this, you can use the hip as an example. Ask the person's permission to abduct (take out to the side) the leg as far as it will comfortably go and mark the range. If a person has difficulty raising their arm, see how much they can abduct it then check it again when you've carried out IRT. The difference can be amazing! The more injuries that have been addressed the more improvement will be seen in their flexibility. This is visual evidence that every joint in the body including the vertebrae has been released.

Activating the Landau reflex by extending the neck will reveal any trauma left by old injury sites situated on the head and torso. Compressing the ankle joint (mortice joint) will reveal any trauma left anywhere on the body.

Draw a simple chart of a body, front and back and ask the person to mark with a cross all their old injury sites. Include bad bruises, whiplash injuries, fractures, tooth extractions, vaccination sites, sprains and any surgical procedures.

Mammograms, root canal treatment and sprained ankles are particularly difficult for the body to handle.

1. Jam the mortice joint **Fig. 114** by quickly compressing the heel on each foot towards the head and then test a strong indicator muscle. You could use an anterior deltoid or the quadriceps. Make sure that this does not unlock your indicator muscle. If it does, it is not possible to carry out injury recall until you resolve the ankle lesion.

2. Ask the person to TL the site of an old injury. If the injury is old and healed, it will not cause the indicator muscle to unlock. This is normal. If it does cause the indicator muscle to unlock, the injury has not completely healed and may need to be addressed first; IRT may still be checked after carrying out the appropriate correction. Now sharply compress the heel on the same side of the body as the injury is situated. If the injury is in the centre, then compress both heels, one at a time. If injury recall is an appropriate treatment, the IM will now unlock.

3. The treatment is to separate the mortice joint whilst the person is still contacting the injury site with their hand/s. Dr Bronson confirms that just separating the mortice joint works for all areas of the body without the need to flex the head for injuries above C7 as is taught in a number of protocols. Place just one hand over the talus and tug in a plantar direction (towards soles of feet) to separate the mortice joint.

4. With the person still touching the old injury site, repeat step 3 for each injury. Sharply compressing the mortice joint of the ankle should no longer unlock your indicator muscle if the memory of the old injury has been diffused.

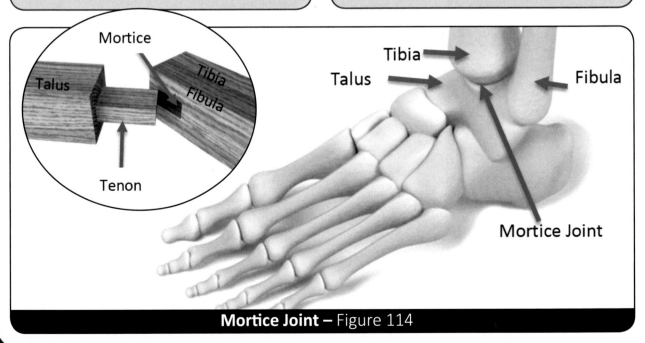

Mortice Joint – Figure 114

Continue the procedure until all old injury sites have been treated in this manner. If you measured the person's flexibility before treatment, now carry out the same procedure – abducting the leg or the arm. In most cases there is a significant improvement in flexibility. ✔

> **❝ Injury recall technique has enormous implications in other areas of healing techniques (Dr. Sheldon Deal). ❞**

I have described so far how IRT was found, how it is carried out, and its association with old injuries. Since its inception researchers have discovered that this simple technique can be used in many other circumstances, sometimes negating the need to carry out more complex procedures. Here are some examples:

Scanning the Whole Body for Old Injuries Requiring IRT

People don't necessarily remember all the injuries they have ever had.

1. Jam one talus by sharply compressing the heel and place into pause lock, then do the same on the other foot. By entering these tests into pause lock, they subsequently act as a 'filter'. *This filter will not in itself change an IM* but now only old injuries then require IRT will CL. When any part of the body is touched, only injury recall sites will show.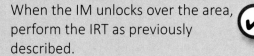

2. When the IM unlocks over the area, perform the IRT as previously described. ✔

> ❗ *When anything is entered into pause lock, the client no longer needs to TL as the practitioner can now CL for related points, which will help to speed up the process.*

IRT on TMJ Clears Compensations

This technique, performed at the start of a session, can be used instead of Pulse Synchronization. Pulse Synchronization is the best technique to 'get onto the same wavelength' as your client, but this protocol probably clears more compensations.

> ❗ *The TMJ is open to constant physical and emotional insults, so IRT will show frequently in relation to the TMJ.*

1. Ask your client to contact both temporomandibular joints simultaneously and test an AIM. The IM should remain locked. If it unlocks, a TMJ correction needs to be done before proceeding further, see page 152.

2. Carry out IRT on the TMJ in the usual way. ✔

Spindle Cells

If a weak muscle does not respond to neuromuscular spindle cell technique (taught in a foundation kinesiology course), then IRT is needed for the muscle.

1. Ask your client to TL the belly of the weak muscle. The IM will unlock.

2. With your client still touching as in step 1, if jamming the heel (talus) locks the IM, IRT is needed.

3. Perform IRT by separating the mortice joint as described previously. ✔

4. Retest the weak muscle, which should now test strong.

NB. *Use IRT in this way for muscle pain. This removes the need for strain counter-strain techniques.*

Emotional Technique Using IRT

Dr Deal says that this technique, although quick to do, seems to be as good as more lengthy techniques used for diffusing emotional stress as long as it is a modality/priority. The client does not necessarily have to verbalise their problem, they can just think about it if they prefer. Entering the thought into pause lock will mean they no longer need to keep focused.

1. Test an AIM whilst your client thinks about the issue and enter into circuit retaining mode. The IM will be in an unlocked state.

2. Contact the alarm points looking for any that lock the IM again, see pages 18-19..

3. Have your client TL the alarm point whilst you carry out IRT.

4. Cancel the lock and have your client think of the issue. The IM should now stay locked.

Testing the Endocrine System

The endocrine system consists of ductless glands, which have no direct anatomical links. They communicate through chemical messengers called hormones. These are chemicals that send messages around the body to signal various tasks such as determining the rate of growth, metabolism, responding to stressors and regulating blood sugar levels.

There is so much we could say about the endocrine system. The aim of this section is to give you an overview. Studying this subject in more detail will give you even greater insight.

The glands comprising the endocrine system are:

Pineal, hypothalamus, pituitary, thyroid, parathyroids, thymus, adrenals, islets of Langerhans (pancreas), ovaries, testes,

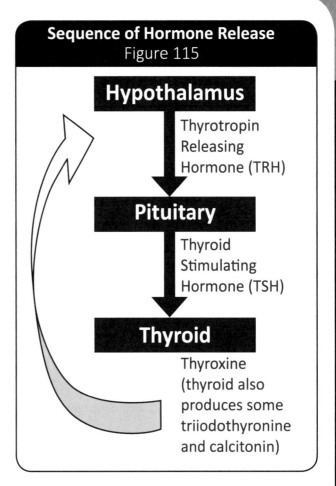

Sequence of Hormone Release
Figure 115

Hypothalamus

Thyrotropin Releasing Hormone (TRH)

Pituitary

Thyroid Stimulating Hormone (TSH)

Thyroid

Thyroxine (thyroid also produces some triiodothyronine and calcitonin)

Stress and the Endocrine System

The endocrine system may become out of balance due to many factors e.g.

Emotional:	Finances, family/work/relationship problems, low self-esteem
Mental:	Noise, prolonged stress
Physical:	Injury, surgery, excessive exercising
Chemical:	Poor nutrition, food sensitivities, drugs, pollution
Thermal:	Excessive heat/cold
Electrical:	Electromagnetic stress, geopathic stress etc.

Excessive and prolonged stress can cause these glands to be compromised due to their attempt to compensate for the heavy workload. The body cannot keep up with these demands ad infinitum and the endocrine system suffers as a result and becomes out of balance.

Although removing mental stresses and working with the gland provides relief for the body, additional nutritional support is of utmost importance in achieving optimum balance.

As the endocrine system is so interrelated, *one often needs to establish the gland that is causal.* **(See example in Fig.115)**

Studying the endocrine system in anatomy and physiology will enable you to establish what those relationships are, and the signs and symptoms that can be manifested by the client as a result of imbalances. There is also much that is yet to be discovered about the intricate web-like interactions between these glands and although there may be some connections that we do not understand, kinesiology will reveal the body's priorities.

Pause lock and two pointing can be used to help to determine which is causal, and the priority mode as to which one is ready to be treated.

Physiology of Endocrine Glands

Pituitary

The Pituitary gland lies below the hypothalamus in the cranium. The two work together using a negative feedback system. The hypothalamus monitors levels of certain hormones in the blood and, when they are low, produces an appropriate hormone (a releasing factor), which stimulates the anterior lobe of the pituitary to release its corresponding hormone. The latter, in turn, stimulates the target gland to produce its own hormone. The following example shows what happens when thyroid hormone levels are low in the blood.

The pituitary releases TSH under the stimulus of TRH from the hypothalamus. TSH then stimulates the thyroid to produce its hormones. The level of thyroid hormone increases in the blood and, when adequate, inhibits the secretion of thyroid releasing hormone by the hypothalamus. **(See Fig. 115)**

The pituitary produces hormones, which influence growth, metabolism, sexual development, milk production in new mothers, contraction of the uterus during childbirth, urine output (so regulating water levels in the body), levels of blood sugar and response to stress. Check pituitary in cases of:

Over/underweight	A TMJ or cranial fault
Excessive/low urination	Hypoglycaemia
Birth trauma	Infertility
Prolonged/excessive stress	People who yo-yo between feeling great and feeling ill.
A client that won't 'stay fixed'	Menstrual problems (also perimenopause)

Thyroid

The thyroid is a butterfly-shaped gland in the front of the throat at the level of C5/T1 and anterior to the larynx and trachea.

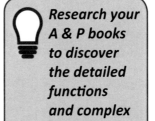
Research your A & P books to discover the detailed functions and complex links between these glands

The thyroid secretes thyroxine (T4) and triiodothyronine (T3) when the pituitary produces TSH. It also secretes calcitonin, which helps to regulate calcium distribution. The gland regulates cell metabolism and is instrumental in monitoring the consumption of oxygen and therefore the output of carbon dioxide. Dysfunction of the thyroid at birth can cause mental and physical growth to be retarded (cretinism).

Thyroid Imbalances

Hyperthyroidism occurs when the thyroid is overactive, causing rapid metabolism, high pulse rate, palpitations, inability to sleep, loss of weight, and a state of nervous irritability. Cardiac output is increased, causing a strain on the heart in prolonged situations. If the adrenals are exhausted, the thyroid will try and compensate by adjusting the metabolism. The thyroid and adrenals 'dance together'.

Hypothyroidism is a condition in which the secretion of thyroid hormone is too low. The metabolism slows down, weight gain occurs, energy is low, and movement is lethargic.

Signs and Symptoms of Hypothyroidism

Sherridan Stock, writing in Nutritional Therapy Today, lists the following as possible signs and symptoms of hypothyroidism.

Cardiovascular: Slow pulse (less than 65/min), palpitations, low blood pressure, high blood pressure (diastolic), poor circulation (especially in hands and feet).

Gastrointestinal: Poor appetite, dysphagia, poor digestion (low acid and pancreatic enzymes, decreased gall-bladder motility), gas, decreased peristalsis, constipation, pancreatitis.

Hair: Lifeless hair, coarse hair, loss of curl, premature greyness, excessive hair fall (especially in autumn), sparse eyebrows (especially outer third).

Metabolic: Diabetes, hypoglycaemia, hypercholesterolaemia, hyperuricaemia, anaemia, vitamin A deficiency (especially night blindness), calcium deficiency, and/or vitamin B12 deficiency (may result in pernicious anaemia).

Mind and Emotions: Nervousness, listlessness, mental sluggishness, lack of sparkle, fuzzy thinking, poor memory, poor concentration, easily distracted, emotional instability, irritability, bad temper, abnormal response to petty annoyances, hostility, chip on the shoulder attitude, introversion, dislike of confrontations, lying, suspiciousness, paranoia, dislike of being watched, dislike of crowds, sudden changes in personality, psychosis, depression.

Musculoskeletal: Muscle cramps (especially at night), myalgia, miscellaneous body pains, persistent low back pain, arthritis, joint stiffness (especially after immobility), osteoporosis, painful or sensitive costal cartilage, carpal tunnel syndrome, ligament and tendon laxity.

Nails: Weak nails, brittle nails, soft nails, thickened nails, lifeless nails, ridged nails, slow-growing nails.

Sex and Reproduction: Reduced libido, amenorrhoea, oligomenorrhoea, irregular menstruation, dysmenorrhoea, menorrhagia, endometriosis, infertility (both sexes), repeated miscarriage.

Skin: Cold skin, dry skin, thickened skin, puffy skin (especially of face and extremities), waxy skin, scaly skin, chapped skin, cracked skin (hands, feet), pale skin, diminished sweating, blackheads, whiteheads, acne, boils, eczema, psoriasis, ichthyosis, infections e.g. herpes.

Temperature Control: Low basal temperature, feels the cold, feels better in summer, feels better in hot climates, feels better as day progresses, feels better after exercise, symptoms worsen in autumn and spring when thyroid is re-regulating.

Thymus

The thymus gland is also part of the lymphatic system and lies in the upper thorax behind the sternum. It weighs about 10gm at birth and reaches its maximum size at puberty, after which it shrinks back to around the birth weight by middle age.

The thymus is linked to self-esteem and thymus energy is usually found to be low when the person is under emotional stress (fear, depression, anxiety, sadness, insecurity, anger, guilt etc.)

It produces the hormone thymosin, which stimulates maturation of T cells which provide protection against antigens.

T-lymphocytes are very low indeed in AIDS clients thus making them fall prey to every-day bacteria that our systems would be immune to.

Check thymus in cases of:

Low self-esteem	Frequent fatigue
Prolonged emotional stress	Degenerative Disease
Frequent infections	Exposure to X-rays, CT scans etc.
Swollen lymph glands (retrograde lymphatics may need attention)	The infraspinatus (See Figures 116 & 117 on page 216 -217) may be weak.

Hypothalamus

This gland is the master gland. Some clients have the symptoms of hypoadrenia, hypoglycaemia etc. but nothing shows in the usual tests, it can often be due to a hypothalamus imbalance. It produces many hormones that give instructions to regulate the pituitary and other organs.

> **" If the brain is the pharmacy, then the hypothalamus is the pharmacist. "**

Consider a hypothalamus imbalance in cases of:

Excess hunger or anorexia	Excessive/no urination
Body temperature problems	Heavy metal toxicity
Rage, fear, depression, excessive irritability/apathy	Excessive weight problems
Multiple unexplained symptoms	High/low blood pressure

There could also be a TMJ or cranial fault present.

There is a direct link from the receptors in the skin that respond to feather light touch to the hypothalamus. In clinical neurology, the thalamus is the principle relay station for sensory impulses that reach the cerebral cortex from the spinal cord. It allows crude appreciation of some sensations such as pressure and pain. Dr Michael Allen was checking someone who complained of draughts on the feet. He blew on the feet to simulate a draught and tested an I.M. that then weakened. He then identified that these nerve endings measuring light touch sensation sent signals up the spinal thalamic tract with 73% of the fibres involved going directly to the reticular formation where the hypothalamus is located in. This reasoning is used to determine the test for the hypothalamus. (Deal)

Pineal

Indications for a pineal imbalance are:

A temporo-sphenoid cranial fault	Headaches
Client will test weak in the dark.	Jet lag or on shifts
Clients will often complain of not being refreshed by sleep	Insomnia
Will feel depressed (particularly during the winter months when the days are shorter). This could also possibly be accompanied by a low sex drive.	Thyroid/adrenal insufficiency Confusion/poor mental ability Fluoride toxicity (causes calcification)

Parathyroids

There are four parathyroid glands, situated on the posterior lobes of the thyroid – two each side.

They regulate the calcium level in the blood in tandem with calcitonin from the thyroid. When the blood level of calcium falls, they secrete parathormone (PTH). That stimulates the rate of calcium absorption from the small intestine and reabsorption from the kidneys. If these are unable to respond with sufficient quantities, PTH stimulates reabsorption of calcium from the bones. The effect of calcitonin is opposite to that of PTH.

Check parathyroids in cases of:

Weak or brittle bones	Tingling, numbness of limbs or face
Poor quality of teeth and gums	Surgical excision of any part of the thyroid
Poor clotting of blood	Twitching or muscle spasms
Chronic severe insomnia	Severe psychological problems

Adrenals

The adrenals, situated above each kidney, is composed of two parts, the cortex (outer part) and medulla (inner part). They secrete adrenaline, noradrenaline, aldosterone and corticosteroids. They also are responsible for producing some androgens (sex hormones), maintenance of blood sugar levels, sodium/potassium levels, and carbohydrate metabolism.

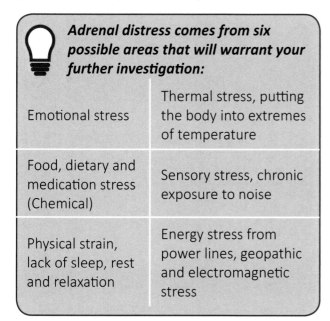

Adrenal distress comes from six possible areas that will warrant your further investigation:

Emotional stress	Thermal stress, putting the body into extremes of temperature
Food, dietary and medication stress (Chemical)	Sensory stress, chronic exposure to noise
Physical strain, lack of sleep, rest and relaxation	Energy stress from power lines, geopathic and electromagnetic stress

With today's hectic pace of life, it is a rare individual who is not stretched beyond reasonable limits on a regular basis. The fight/flight response is built into us to cope with sudden emergencies. Continuous excessive stresses wear down the ability of the individual to deal with it and the endocrine system becomes "tired". The person becomes nervy, irritable and unable to cope, concentrate, or manage life on an even keel without wide mood swings. They fall prey to everything that is "going around".

Check adrenals in cases of:

Prolonged stress	Digestive problems	Arthritis
Overwork/lack of rest	Dysfunction of other endocrine glands	Muscle weakness, low back pain
Chronic fatigue/ME	Menstrual problems	Candidiasis
Sudden weariness	Hypoglycaemia	Allergies

Some Possible Signs and Symptoms of Adrenal Stress or Hypoadrenia

Digestive problems	Chronic fatigue	Loss of energy
ME	Candida	Parasites
Low back problems	Hypoglycaemia	PMS
Skin problems	Mood swings	Headaches
Haemorrhoids	Varicose veins	Arthritis
Allergies	Clammy hands- "stress becomes distress".	

The person is sensitive to noise and light. Daylight is very balancing to these people. Plastic lenses are better than glass for letting in light to the eyes, and full spectrum light bulbs can be helpful.

Adrenal stress, and subsequently fatigue, frequently go hand in hand with hypoglycaemia, the low blood sugar syndrome, so it is a good idea to test for hypoglycaemia if adrenal fatigue is a problem. It is also advisable to check for the ICV syndrome, a disturbed atlas, and whether the person needs HCl and/or digestive enzymes. Since all health problems are lifestyle problems, you will need to be a detective and work out what they are doing that's chronic, i.e. look for long term problems caused by long-term lifestyle habits/patterns etc.

Hans Selye, MD, PhD (1907 - 1982), the "Father of Stress", was a Hungarian endocrinologist and the first to give a scientific explanation for biological "stress". Selye categorised adrenal stress in three stages, each of which will develop from the previous one if not checked and corrected. **(See Table 20 overleaf)**

Stage 1 - Simple

Stage 2 - Executive/ Resistance Stage

Stage 3 - Reversed Adrenal Syndrome

> *"Every stress leaves an indelible scar, and the organism pays for its survival, after a stressful situation, by becoming a little older."* - Hans Selye, MD, PhD

Procedures for Assessing and Correcting the Endocrine System

Testing Procedures

These are all CL points and can be contacted by both client or tester

An indicator change would show that an imbalance is present.

Using an AIM, check each gland as follows:

For a short summary of all endocrine checks **See Table 21 overleaf**.

Pituitary:

Client touches the glabella just above the bridge of the nose OR when the RIGHT leg is raised, it will switch off any previously strong muscle in the body.

Thyroid:

CL with tips of 2 fingers on one side and one thumb on the other side over the wings of the thyroid gland. This is halfway between the hyoid and the supra-sternal notch. This is probably best done by the client themselves!

Parathyroid:

Have the client contact the parathyroids (just above the lobes of the thyroid, pressing inwards to comfort limit) with a thumb and two fingertips.

Thymus:

Client places 2 fingertips on the angle between the manubrium and the body of the sternum. OR test the infraspinatus muscle. **(See Fig. 117 on page 217)**

Hypothalamus:

Test an AIM whilst blowing directly onto the person's skin or brushing the skin extremely lightly OR have them TL GV20. (The IM should NOT change with respiration, as this is a test for cranial faults)

Pineal:

Test an AIM when client is in the dark. OR when the LEFT leg is raised, it will weaken any previously strong muscle in the body OR have them contact GV1 at the tip of the coccyx.

Adrenals:

See Table 20 below for tests:

3 Stages of Adrenal Stress: – Table 20

Stage 1 – Simple

Sartorius/gracilis/soleus and/or gastrocnemius test weak in the clear.

Stage 2 – Executive Syndrome/ Resistance Stage

A strong sartorius weakens when the client CLs the PSIS bilaterally (lying supine) by putting the hands under the upper part of the buttocks. If the first test doesn't show an imbalance, check with client's palms both up and down over the PSIS.

Adrenal stress can de-stabilise the pelvis because the sartorius and gracilis (adrenal-associated muscles) are involved in anteriorly giving support to the pelvis. This weakness often doesn't show up until a related area is TL'd. This is probably due to the fact that the adrenals have adapted to the continuous stress during this stage.

Stage 3 – Reversed Adrenal Syndrome

A weak sartorius (or other related muscle) strengthens when white sugar is placed on the tongue or held against the jaw. Additionally, with sugar in the circuit, strong muscles may not weaken and may become hypertonic.

Blood pressure drops when client moves from lying or sitting down to standing up. Pupil size fluctuates when a bright light is shone into the eye for about 30 seconds.

How to Treat Endocrine Imbalances

All glands benefit from a vitamin and mineral programme such as those listed under 'Adrenal Syndrome'.

The following list offers a few additional suggestions and is by no means definitive. You would use nutritional support in any event – it is always indicated; however, you can put the imbalance into pause lock and find the correction. **Using finger modes, the treatment could be from any realm.**

Pituitary Gland

Trace minerals, magnesium, agnus castus, ginger, lapacho, kelp, irish moss, barberry, nettle.

 Key point: Whilst we treat the endocrine system with nutrition, the correction needed could be structural, emotional or electro-magnetic.

Structural correction: Pituitary cranial fault.

Thyroid Gland

Kelp or dulce, magnesium, vitamin A. (underactive), black walnut, siberian ginseng, nettle, evening primrose oil, liquorice (not if blood pressure high), various suppliers' remedies for underactive thyroid conditions.

200mcg selenium, 15mg zinc, 5mg copper, fucus (bladderwrack/bladderwort) can aid the conversion of T4 into T3.

Prunella (thyroid nodules and enlargement), lemon balm (reduces T4), bugle weed (reduces T4). In cases of overactive thyroid there is often toxicity or possibly a viral infection. Look for liver cleansing remedies, or specific remedies from suppliers for overactive thyroid.

Structural corrections: Have the client put their head back (neck extension) and tilt (not turn) it to one side to reveal more clearly the thyroid area either side of the 'Adam's apple'. To increase blood flow to the thyroid, tap this area for about 30 seconds whilst your client hums to vibrate the adjacent larynx. Tilt the head towards the opposite side and repeat the process on the other side of the

thyroid gland. This can be given as 'homework'. (Deal)

The teres minor may need correcting and there may be a subluxation or a fixation at C5, C6, C7 or T1, see page 146.

Parathyroid Glands

Magnesium / calcium citrate, mineral complex, vitamin D.

Structural correction: NL points for the levator scapula.

Thymus Gland

Herbal remedies for the immune system zinc, selenium. Vitamin A helps to reduce shrinkage.

Structural correction: Infraspinatus **(See Fig. 117 on page 217)**

Hypothalamus

Anti-inflammatory herbal combinations such as boswellia, essential fatty acids, agnus castus, B1, B12. Putting a drop of frankincense oil on the roof of the mouth 2 or 3 times a day may be helpful (also useful in cases of brain tumours).

Structural correction: Tap the junction of the sacrum and coccyx.

Pineal Gland

Chlorella, spirulina, moringa, milk thistle, chaga mushrooms.

Structural correction: Sphenoid cranial fault correction, a bilateral TMJ fault is an indicator of pineal gland dysfunction, see pages 176 & 156.

Adrenal Gland Syndrome

Stage 1 – Simple: correct muscle weakness utilising all indicated methods, as in TFH book. Test a high dose B complex and recommend a minimum of three grams of vitamin C, some of which should be taken at night.

Stage 2 – Executive Syndrome: hold posterior fontanel and simultaneously rub the NLs two inches above and one inch out from the umbilicus. Your client will also need nutritional support (see daily nutritional programme overleaf).

Stage 3 – Reversed Adrenal Syndrome: Use NV & NL as for Executive Syndrome. Encourage the person to reduce stressors in their lifestyle including learning to say 'no'. Follow the daily nutritional programme for at least a month.

Individuals in Stage 2 or 3 usually feel out of control of their lives. They need to find ways to 'play' by making quality time or relaxing pursuits and perhaps managing their time better.

Assertiveness courses may be appropriate for some. Stress is detrimental when we feel we have lost control over our lives or when we have expectations that do not, and never can, become a reality.

Daily Nutrition Programme for Adrenal Fatigue

Herbs/herbal combinations: liquorice (not if hypertensive), eleuthero (siberian ginseng), panax ginseng, ashwagandha (withania), rooibos tea, rhodiola.

Vitamin C   **– 3 grams**

Vitamin B complex

Vitamin B3   **– 1.5 grams (Niacinamide is very "grounding" when under stress)**

Vitamin B5

Chromium

Magnesium

Herbal formulae for adrenal support

Note: Research has shown that the sartorius is associated with the adrenal medulla, which produces epinephrine (adrenaline), and the gracilis is associated with the adrenal cortex, which produces corticosteroids.

In Applied Kinesiology the adrenal muscles can be associated with the CX or Pericardium meridian so it may be wise to check the alarm points for both the Triple Heater and the CX/Pericardium to see which is appropriate.

Test for Adrenal Fatigue and Corrections That Don't Last

! *Look out for this if the client is suffering from backache, joint pain, muscle pain, adrenal fatigue may be the cause.*

To check for this, use an AIM unrelated to the problem. Stretch a joint and retest. If it blows the indicator, but it strengthens when testing with adrenal substances or adrenal herbs in circuit, adrenal fatigue is involved. If relevant, this will show when any joint in the body is stretched.

Infraspinatus (Structural Correction for Thymus)

MERIDIAN: Triple Warmer

GLAND ASSOCIATION: Thymus

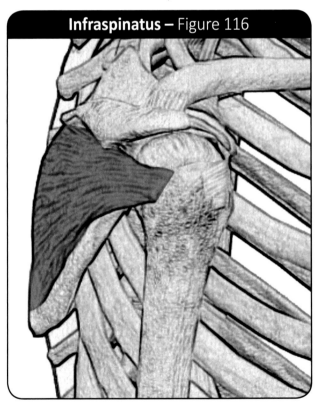

Infraspinatus – Figure 116

ORIGIN: Middle two-thirds of the medial edge of the scapula, below the spine of the scapula and above the teres major and teres minor.

INSERTION: Greater tuberosity of the humerus and the capsule of the shoulder joint. **(See Fig. 116)**

TEST: Arm held out to the side, elbow level with shoulder, forearm raised so that wrist is higher than shoulder, with right angle at elbow, palm facing forward. Stabilise elbow and apply pressure above wrist to rotate forearm downwards. (Almost reverse of test for subscapularis)

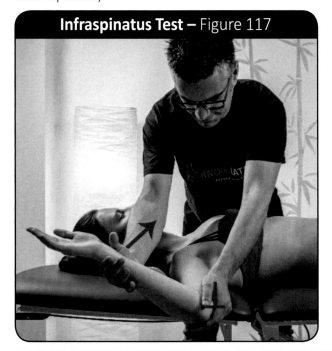

Infraspinatus Test – Figure 117

NEUROLYMPHATIC POINTS:

Front: Between ribs 5-6 on right hand side, near sternum.

Back: Beside the spine at the level of T12-L 1, on both sides.

NEUROVASCULAR POINTS:

Over the thymus gland at the angle of Louis on the sternum, and at the temples (as for teres minor).

NUTRITION:

Thymus/thyroid tissue extract, kelp, vitamins C, B3, B5, herbal compounds for thymus/thyroid.

ACUPRESSURE HOLDING POINTS:

To strengthen: FIRST: GB41 and TH3 SECOND: BL66 and TH2. To weaken: FIRST: ST36 and TH10 SECOND: BL66 and TH2 (see foundation manuals).

If the infraspinatus is hypertonic, tap the thymus and re-test. If the muscle now weakens, it indicates that there may be an infection.

Summary of Endocrine Checks – Table 21	
Adrenal Syndrome	***Stage 1:*** Sartorius tests weak in the clear. ***Stage 2:*** Sartorius only tests weak when placing hands on the PSIS. ***Stage 3:*** Sartorius is weak in the clear and strengthens when sugar placed in the circuit.
	An imbalance is present if an AIM unlocks on the following tests:
Pituitary	Two fingers are placed on the glabella or client raising the right leg will unlock any muscle.
Thyroid	Place two fingers and one thumb either side of the thyroid and just below the Adam's apple and above the sternal notch.
Parathyroids	Have the client contact the parathyroids (just above the lobes of the thyroid, pressing inwards to comfort limit) with a thumb and two fingertips.
Thymus	Two fingers are placed on the sternum at the manubrium.
Hypothalamus	Blow on client's skin and quickly test an AIM or CL GV20.
Pineal	Client raising the left leg will unlock any strong muscle. Test SIM whilst client is in a darkened room. Or use the 'pineal dysfunction' test vial. Or CL GV1. There will be a temporo-sphenoid cranial fault.

Past Trauma Resolution

Covers all Categories

This technique is sometimes known as Age Recession.

Symptoms or illnesses do not happen spontaneously, unless caused by an accident of some kind or overwhelming exposure to a toxic substance or pathogen. Sometimes it can take years of numerous stresses such as periods of poor nutrition, emotional trauma or environmental insults e.g. exposure to chemicals or electromagnetic fields. From as early as conception to the present day the sum of all these stressors can eventually manifest as a health problem.

> **!** *Past trauma resolution is not the same as injury recall technique. Clearing old injuries will dramatically help the healing process but this protocol resolves other aspects of mind-body memory.*

Past trauma resolution is useful when our client presents with a health issue where we may have done all we could to address any imbalances, without achieving sustained improvement.

- Using this technique, the mind-body is alerted to past traumas that have not fully been recognised as having healed – even with traumas that may have either been too subtle, or occurred too long ago, to be noticed.

- A client may forget but the body is still aware of the trauma.

With the client's health issue corrected in the consultation but still 'online', the process involves counting back the client's age from present day to conception. When the IM unlocks this indicates that there is some kind of trauma affecting the issue at the age identified. Despite the fact that the trauma no longer exists, it is an obstacle to the client's recovery and needs to be addressed so that the mind-body can let the trauma go.

Just a theory but I understand it to be that the subconscious is continuously recording everything about our internal and external environment. This record is what we're tapping into when we do age recession.

> **Analogy:** *You've missed your parent's wedding anniversary and even forgot to send them a card, so instead, you send a different kind of card that says, "sorry, I forgot". It's not the same as an anniversary card, but your parents are just as happy because they have been acknowledged, even though it's belated. Past Trauma Resolution is like a "Sorry, I forgot" card.*

Age Recession Mode: A thumb is laid into a clenched fist and placed over the client's navel. If the IM changes, there are past traumas that need resolving, relating to the lesion you have in circuit. (See Fig. 118)

Age Recession Mode – Figure 118

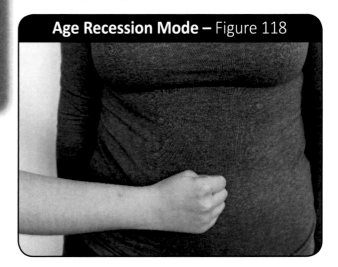

Protocol

1. The lesion needs to be cleared in the present first e.g. in the case of a persistent ICV problem carry out the protocol so that the IM is now locked when challenging the valve.

2. Note: This step is optional; when challenging or CL'ing the lesion, place the age recession mode over the navel. If the IM changes, this technique is appropriate. If the IM does not change then past trauma resolution is not relevant and not involved with the lesion.

3. Check the client's age in the present day and note the day and time of the test. This is because it's important to always bring the client back to the present day and time to finish.

4. Test the lesion and place into pause lock. Note that the IM will be locked to begin with as the lesion has been corrected in the 'now'. Then verbally challenge the client against previous ages, testing as you go.

   Example, the client is 51 yrs. old "We are looking for any traumas related to (the lesion) from:

   the present day to 50 and test IM

   From age 50-40 – test

   From age 40-30 – test

   From age 30-20 – test

   From age 20-10 – test

   From age 10 to birth – test

   From birth to conception – test

   The muscle will unlock to one of these challenges. Then to narrow down the year, verbalise each age within that 10-year period. One age will unlock the IM and once reached the **IM will remain unlocked.**

   > **!** *Key point: The body does not necessarily want the past trauma resolution to be done in chronological order. Honour the body's wisdom and address the time frame that the mind-body shows you first.*

5. Activate the four key finger modes. To avoid any confusion at the correction stage, just make a note of it but don't put into pause lock.

6. It seems that the correction itself doesn't have to be complicated. The mind-body will accept almost anything under that realm just to 'tell' the body that it's finally been addressed and it's okay to let go. So, go for the simple things first. (See following examples)

7. Once the correction has been carried out the IM should now lock as the mind-body

has accepted that all is now well. Note that if it still unlocks there is something else that needs addressing for that age, so activate the finger modes again.

8. Still testing the IM, verbally challenge as in step 4, but this time, starting with the age you are currently 'in'. It is very important to reverse the process to get back to the present time, present day.

9. Repeat step 4 until the IM does not unlock to any time frame or check the 'age recession' mode again in step 2.

Structural Mode Corrections

This finger mode may show if the client has, for example had a fall at a previous age, been doing a job requiring poor posture or maybe it could even be birth trauma such as forceps delivery. The client may be able to recall an event, but this isn't always the case. Check for the simplest first! The techniques below are described in the section on structure.

- **Fixations of the vertebrae**
- **Atlas correction**
- **TMJ**
- **Cranial faults** – The shortcut correction of breathing in and out of a paper bag should suffice.

Biochemical Mode Corrections

This needs to comprise of something that you can give to your client during the session as a nutritional reward. Bearing in mind the client might have had a period where their nutrition was not at its best, for example a picky eater as a child, bottle fed, or perhaps a time of poverty. What we are doing here is addressing this past trauma with some physical food so that the mind-body no longer perceives nutritional insufficiency as a threat. Give the remedy to your client whilst they are in the mode. There is no need to supplement the nutrient as it may not be relevant in the present day.

Good general remedies might include:

- **Spirulina (full of nutrients and protein).**

- **If you have them, Tissue Salts are very good for this.**

- **An amino acid complex for protein deficiency.**

- **Zinc (most people are short at some point).**

Emotional Mode Corrections

Once again, this needn't be complicated. The client may know what the event was that particular year, but on the other hand they may have no idea. The best way to resolve any issues, known or unknown, is to administer a flower formula vibrational essence, even Bach's Rescue Remedy maybe all that it takes to lock the indicator muscle and resolve the emotional imbalance that presented that particular year.

Electromagnetic Mode Corrections

Likely to be a centring mechanism, gait, hyoid, cloacal reflexes etc. I like to check the chakra mode here, as chakra imbalances can be hugely affected by trauma.

Summary

1. Correct the lesion in the present day first. The IM should then be locked on CL/challenge.

2. Verbalise the lesion and then, starting at present day count the years backwards to conception. The priority year that has a past trauma will unlock the IM.

3. The IM will stay unlocked, you don't have to pause lock it. Go through the finger modes to find the one that locks IM.

4. Take the mode off so that your IM is back to an unlocked state.

5. Search for the realm's relevant correction – locked IM.

6. Administer the correction.

7. Retest. IM should now be locked.

8. Whilst testing and IM repeat step 4 in reverse bringing the client up to present day and time.

9. Repeat protocol until all ages are clear.

Beginning and End (B & E) Points

This holographic technique effectively treats the body and the head at the same time. It encourages the brain to produce neurotransmitters. Neurotransmitters are the chemicals of communication within the nervous system and between nerves and structures throughout the body. Their effects include alteration of mood, stimulation of digestion and muscular movement.

The analgesic effects of acupuncture on the central nervous system has been studied and correlate with neurochemical changes in the central nervous system. Dr Goodheart found that in certain circumstances tapping the beginning or ending of the yang meridians (all situated on the head) often caused dramatic changes in body temperature, oral pH, vitamin C levels, and glucose levels within 2 or 3 minutes. He considered that the yang meridians are actively involved with temperature regulation of the pituitary gland via the blood flow around it (Walther). The hypothalamus-pituitary axis regulates various functions of body chemistry and tapping B & E points have been shown to be clinically effective in improving chemical regulation.

Michael Lebowitz and Walter Schmitt called these points hypothalamic set points. The medical definition of a set point is – the target value of the controlled variable that is maintained by an automatic control system, e.g, the point at which body temperature is modulated by the hypothalamic thermostat.

They based this on the principle that different organs have a set point with the hypothalamus, being the master controller. If the hypothalamus is stressed above and beyond normal levels, this would eventually cause symptoms and disease. Everyone of course has a limit before a system fails, which varies considerably from person to person. For example, studies have shown that liver function test values amongst 'healthy' adults can vary as much as 7-fold. We know that each blood test shows 'normal levels' as a set parameter but a test only shows a snapshot of what a person's blood levels looks like at moment the blood was taken. However, normal levels vary from person to person and can be affected moment to moment by numerous factors. Lebowitz and Schmitt used hypoglycaemia as a good example in their research because the results after tapping the B & E points on blood glucose levels was measurable.

For example, some people exhibit symptoms of drowsiness, irritability, or lack of concentration, after consuming 10g of sugar whereas others might have to eat 100g before they have any symptoms because their 'set point' is higher.

Fuse Analogy

Dr Sheldon Deal in one of his lectures explained the concept of hypothalamic set points in terms of an electrical fuse. In this analogy he explained that some people have higher fuses than others when it comes to their reaction to changes such as in blood sugar levels. Whatever size the fuse is, that is the 'set point'. So, if we could change the fuse from a 5 amp to a larger 13 amp, then they could consume more sugar before their fuse blows. So, the size of a person's 'fuse', or tolerance level, determines at what point they experience symptoms. Tapping the B & E points potentially sets the 'fuse' to a safe level, so this technique is very safe to use. It works really well in increasing tolerance to internal or environmental changes.

Since the original work of Goodheart, Lebowitz and Schmitt, these yang meridian points have been included in various treatment protocols and Dr Schmitt has done research in identifying which yang acupuncture points are associated with which neurotransmitter **(See Fig. 119 overleaf)**. Christopher Astill-Smith D.O. did further work and identified that the beginning and ends of the yin meridians, all situated on the body, relate to neurotransmitter excesses (Table 23 on page 225). However, the yang B & E points on the face are the ones used for corrections.

B & E points are useful in the following situations and you will notice that they are involved in various corrections described in this manual:

- Treatments that don't hold (the 'fuse' blows easily because it is not big enough) and where corrections have to be repeated, e.g. recurrent ICV or TMJ problems.

- Where we want the client to have a higher tolerance level to a particular stress that blows their system e.g. the amount of sugar one takes without it affecting their health, or a reaction to an environmental allergen such as pollen.

- Tapping the B & E points can be a treatment in its own right in some protocols, stimulating neurotransmitter production in relationship to the imbalance is circuit.

- Dr Schmitt and Christopher Astill-Smith researched this and devised a table showing the associated neurotransmitters and the nutrients needed to synergise and metabolise them. **(See Tables 22 & 23)**

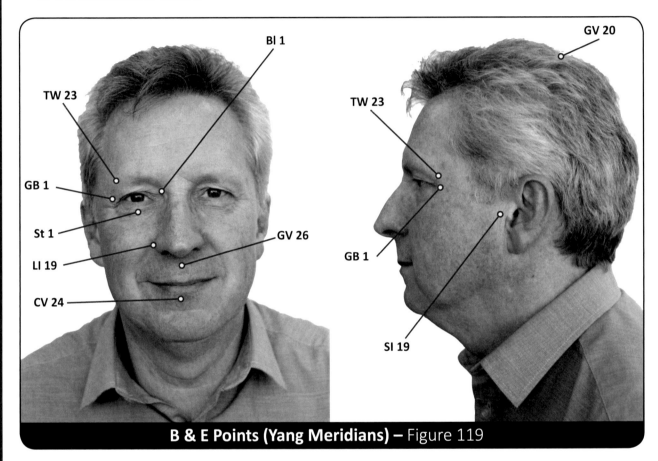

B & E Points (Yang Meridians) – Figure 119

'Changing the Fuse' with B & E Points

This technique is especially useful when you have carried out an adjustment thoroughly and yet when your client returns, the 'fuse' has blown again, and the correction hasn't lasted. The concept is that the hypothalamus controls the set points therefore tapping them at the same time that the correction point is contacted (treating the head at the same time as the body) resets the correction with a larger 'fuse' thus increasing tolerance levels. **NB the fuse is to help the correction hold, it is not a fuse for the imbalance itself.**

1. Correct the recurrent problem in the usual way, i.e. NL point, blood chemistry points, cloacals, etc. Check that all indicators are now locked on CL'ing.

2. Ask your client to TL the problem area or, if not a specific point, the neurolymphatic or alarm point associated with the complaint or organ. e.g. over the ICV area, the muscles of the jaw, a subluxated vertebra, a NL point or a NV point, meridian. The IM should be locked

> **When treating a point or organ that has a yin meridian involvement, treat it's paired yang meridian.**

3. While client maintains TL, CL each of the B & E points **(See Fig. 119)** on the face and find the one/s that two-point (unlocked). The point will be on the same side as the correction being TL'd. If you find a B & E point shows on the opposite side to the correction point, check that the person isn't switched. Prioritise if more than one point shows. At this juncture, you have the option to see if a nutrient listed in **Table 22** supports the correction (it may not always be relevant). This will lock the IM.

4. With **both hands over each other (double TL)**, your client contacts the area of the body or body point.

5. Simultaneously tap the involved B & E point at the rate of 3-4 per second 75-100 times.

6. Repeat step 2. The point should now have been reset and check, and correct if necessary, any other B & E points that showed in step 3.

Additional Pointers

When treating:

Low Blood sugar – often the thymus is involved.

Sleep patterns – the neurolymphatic point for the quadriceps.

Arrhythmia – the subscapularis (heart yin meridian) can often be involved. It may not always test as weak in the clear and may appear normal, but its NL, NV, or alarm point may two-point to small intestine 19 (its paired yang meridian). This technique can be immensely helpful in cases of arrhythmia.

B & E Points and Neurotransmitter Production

In order for the body to produce the appropriate neurotransmitters the biochemical pathways involved in making them must be complete. If there is a nutrient missing in the chain, chemical conversion cannot take place satisfactorily. Ensure that nutrients are in place to facilitate this pathway.

You can check the B & E points in the clear as a stand-alone technique or before commencing this protocol. If you found nutrition to be involved, i.e. the set point showed in the clear, it is beneficial to make the correction whilst the nutritional reward is included in the circuit.

1. CL each B & E point **Fig. 119** in the clear. If any point shows (unlock), this indicates a need for nutrition.

2. Go to **Tables 22 & 23** overleaf and test the nutrients listed for each point. After identifying the nutrient (lock) Test for modality (unlock) and check that it raises vital force.

B & E Points as a Correction in its Own Right

Example

Find the hypothalamic set point on the head that two-points to the ICV.

Have your client place two hands over the valve (body point) while you simultaneously tap the set point 75 - 100 times. If the treatment still does not hold, look for the supporting nutrient **listed in Table 22 overleaf.**

GV 20 as a Master B & E Point (Deal)

Governing vessel 20 **(Fig. 21 on page 28)** is used in a number of ways. One idea is that it acts as a master hypothalamic set point and Dr Deal comments that some people say that tapping it clears all the individual B & E head point imbalances in one go. GV 20 is also a test for cranial faults, therefore if this point CL's he comments that it's important to ensure that the practitioner is clear about what it is that they are picking up when testing.

Yang – Neurotransmitter Deficiency - Schmitt (Will show under biochemical finger mode) – Table 22			
NEUROTRANSMITTER	**MERIDIAN**	**FORMATION**	**COMMENTS**
Acetylcholine	GB1	Choline, B5, B1, Mg, Mn, Vit E, B12	For Metabolism
Aspartate Glutamate	TW 23	Aspartate (Aspartic Acid) Glutamate (Glutamic Acid)	Low metabolic function, Low thyroid
Serotonin (5HT)	BI 1	Tryptophan, B6, B3, Mg, Fe, Folic Acid, 5-HT, Vit C, B1	Reduced elimination of water soluble toxins and toxic metals
GABA	LI 20	GABA, B6, Zn	Gut dysbiosis, Parasites
Glycine	LI 20	Glycine, B6, Folic, B3, B2, Fe, S	Gut dysbiosis, Parasites
Taurine	LI20	Taurine, B6, B3, Vit A	Gut dysbiosis, Parasites
Noradrenaline	SI19	Tyrosine, B6, B3, B1, Mg, Fe, Cu, Folic Acid, Vit C, Phosphatidyl choline	Inadequate sympathetic activity leading to food allergy
Histamine	ST1	Histidine, B6, Fe, Vit E	Hypochlorhydria, Low immune system
Dopamine	CV24	Tyrosine, B6, B3, B1, Mg, Fe, Cu, Folic Acid, Vit C, Phosphatidyl choline	Low oestrogen activity

Yin – Neurotransmitter Excess (Astill-Smith) Table 23			
NEUROTRANSMITTER	**MERIDIAN**	**METABOLISM**	**COMMENTS**
Acetylcholine	LIV14	B2, B3, Zn, Betaine	
Aspartate Glutamate Cysteine Homocysteine	CX1	B6, Mg, B3, NAC, Pyruvate, Vit C, Zn B6, B12, Folic Acid, Betaine, DMG (Dimethylglycine), B2	Effects of high excitatory neurotransmitters and effects on CNS & peripheral effects
Serotonin (5HT)	KID27	Methionine, B12, Folic Acid, Betaine, DMG (Dimethylglycine), S, Mg, Vit C, Zn, Cr, B2, Turmeric, Ginger, Bromelain	High serotonin Elimination of soluble toxins e.g. toxic metals
GABA	LU1	B6, B3	Oxygenation
Glycine	LU1	B6, Folic, B3	Oxygenation
Taurine	LU1	Vit C, Cu	Oxygenation
Noradrenaline	HT1	Methionine, B12, Folic Acid, Betaine, DMG (Dimethylglycine), Mg, B2, Zn, Cr, Cu	Excess sympathetic activity
Histamine	SP21	Vit C, Methionine, B12, Folic Acid, Betaine, DMG (Dimethylglycine), Mg, B2, Zn, Cr, Mo, Vit E, B6, B3, Fe, S, Bioflavonoid	Over reactive immune system caused by unresolved infection or allergy
Dopamine	GV27	Methionine, B12, Folic Acid, Betaine, DMG (Dimethylglycine), Mg, B2, Zn, Cr, Cu	High oestrogen or oestrogen derivative activity

B & E Points, Injury Recall Technique and Emotions

This quick fix seems to work as well as more elaborate emotional techniques IF the emotion is a priority/modality. Also, you don't need the person to share the emotional thought with you if they don't wish to.

Have the client think of the stressor. An IM will unlock. Check if it is a priority or modality.

1. Put the stressor into pause lock (circuit retaining mode). The IM should remain unlocked.

2. Whilst testing the unlocked IM, look for a hypothalamic set point/s (B & E Point) that lock the indicator.

3. Whilst the client touches these points with a neutral touch (2 fingers), carry out injury recall by placing your thumb in the mortice joint of each ankle and giving each a sharp tug in an inferior direction, see page 206.

4. Close the lock and retest the stressor using an accurate indicator muscle (AIM).

B & E Points for Reducing Pain

Nociceptors in tissue only respond to pressure, damage, A **nociceptor** ("pain receptor") is a sensory neuron that responds to damaging or potentially damaging stimuli by sending "possible threat" signals to the spinal cord and the brain. If the brain perceives the threat as credible, it creates the sensation of pain to direct attention to the body part, so the threat can hopefully be mitigated; this process is called nociception.

The signal from these receptors is transmitted through the spinal tract then translated in the brain. This means that whenever touch is involved, the brain knows about it.

When we experience pain, rubbing often helps because the receptors associated with rubbing are faster acting than those of pain hence the rubbing sensation overrides the messages from the nociceptors. Additionally, it has been noted that if a pain reduces when rubbed this is an indication for injury recall technique, see page 205.

The following technique prevents swelling and inflammation after injury and turns down the pain receptors. It can be used for any pain, recent or long-standing, and can also be applied in a situation where there is emotional hurt. So not only is it useful in clinic, but it can be used as a 'first aid' measure for anyone in pain. The recipient should receive immediate benefit.

1. Ask the person to TL the area of pain (you could ask them to evaluate their pain level from 1-10 SUD (subjective units of discomfort scale), test an AIM and enter into circuit retaining mode (unlock).

   If the pain does not TL use high gain techniques such as Pre-Stressing (Page 203) or placing the neck into extension. Also, it may show when using a gamma II muscle test.

2. CL the B & E yang points on the face. Note any that two-point (lock).

3. While the person keeps contact with the are that TL's, tap the relevant B & E point 100 times.

4. Repeat step 1 and ask the person to re-evaluate their SUD scale.

The Memory and Quality of Pain

When we mentally process what is involved with the experience of pain, the somatosensory cortex is activated. The sensation travels to the brain from the mechanoreceptors at the injury site, up the spinal cord to the post central gyrus which is part of the cortex. What is interesting is that it seems that the prefrontal area of the brain, involved in the generation and regulation of emotions, can assign value to other non-emotional inputs which involve the parts of the brain that interpret pain signals. If an IM unlocks it indicates that there is a problem with the neural circuitry which will show up when your client thinks about the pain.

This protocol is a way of thoroughly treating the root of pain, and taking it a stage further, when used in addition to the technique previously described. You will discover that different B & E points two-point when addressing the Location, the Quality, and the Memory (LQM) of the pain as opposed to TL'ing the pain itself (Deal).

Carry out the test and correction in steps 1-4

Cranial faults could act as a smokescreen because they will weaken any muscle when picturing anything, so check for these before continuing. The short cut corrections for cranial faults will be fine in this instance. (See page 171)

5. This time, your client does not TL the pain but thinks about:

    a. The Location of the pain – then test an AIM.

    b. The Quality of the pain i.e. the kind of pain (whether sharp, aching, throbbing etc.) – then test an AIM.

    c. The Memory of the pain – how it happened – then test an AIM.

6. If the IM unlocks to any of the LQM, enter the thought into circuit retaining mode (unlock).

7. Find the B & E point that two-points to the LQM (lock) and tap 100 times.

8. Cancel the lock and to anchor the treatment repeat step 5.

My arm really aches

Its really throbbing

What did I do?

Lateral Sway

Structural and Nutritional

Many clients complain of pain, tightness or burning between the scapulae, particularly when standing for any period. Athletes or body builders also can suffer from this.

Usually this is due to tight rhomboids. Stretching these will help. When the rhomboids and cervical spine musculature is tight, this causes an uneven lateral sway. This is addressed by administering B12 and performing a fascial flush on the rhomboids (B12 is the nutritional reward for fascial flush). This is a great party trick for anyone watching!

1. Ask your client to stand with their back to you with their feet apart approximately shoulder width.

2. Direct a laser pointer onto the spine between the shoulder blades.

3. Ask them to put their weight onto their left, then onto their right foot. Keeping the laser still, note how far the person sways in each direction. The pointer should be equidistant from the centre line when bearing their weight on each leg.

4. If there is an uneven sway, ask your client to chew a B12 tablet and then retest as in 1-3. You should now observe that the lateral sway becomes equidistant from the spine. For adults, give 500 micrograms daily.

5. Fascial flush is easy to apply. Deeply massage the rhomboid muscles. The drawing in **Fig. 120** shows the scapulae stretched out to reveal the muscle. In reality the muscle is in the small gap between the scapula and the spine on each side. The idea of this is to break up any adhesions between the fascial layers of the muscle so the direction of the massage in relationship to its fibres is not important.

6. When fascial release is applied to any muscle, the NL and NV should also be treated.

7. Consider testing and balancing the neck muscles.

Other Signs

Check for lateral sway if the client is lying on the couch and one foot is turned out more than the other. B12 supplementation will also help babies who have this issue. Vitamin B12 drops are available from some suppliers but first check with their nutritionist for suitability.

Lateral sway seems to be more prevalent in women. Addressing this imbalance can help PMS, amenorrhea (absent periods), menorrhagia (heavy periods), and dysmenorrhea (painful periods).

Rhomboids Major & Minor – Figure 120

Peripheral Vision Technique

This technique is rather strange. I used to use it a lot in clinic and had a particularly spectacular result with one client suffering from post-viral fatigue syndrome. It was significantly instrumental in turning her health around. Now I'm writing about it, I shall dust the cobwebs off this protocol and start to use it again because it's well worth including in your 'toolbox'!

This procedure is helpful for reducing pain and has been seen to improve self-esteem. It seems that forcing people to use their peripheral vision whilst touching the painful area is therapeutic.

Dr Sheldon Deal developed this protocol as a result of discussions with a brilliant scientist, Patrick Flannagan, about the benefits of night walking. In the U.S. there are actually courses that teach this skill. Just 80% of the optic nerve fibres go to the vision centres of the brain leaving 20% serving other brain locations. Therefore, there seems to be an element of vision that could, for example, affect motor skills.

In the night walking course, developing peripheral vision to the fullest extent takes practice and involves having a bead suspended from the peak of a baseball cap. Participants go out walking and focus only on the bead, not allowing their eyes to wander from it. When confident, course participants do the same thing in the desert during new moon and with no light pollution. They would find that they were able to avoid tripping on large stones, they automatically ducked under branches and unconsciously walked around bushes, none of which they could see with the naked eye. They had developed their peripheral vision to such an extent that their brain sensed obstacles that they could not see. Peripheral vision is described as our etheric vision. We have all experienced seeing something 'out of the corner of our eye' with our peripheral vision. Advocates of night walking also reported a reduction in aches and pains and a heightened sense of wellbeing. This led Dr Deal to develop this technique.

1. Find an AIM an upper body muscle works best for this test. Using a sustained muscle test (a continual gentle pressure), ask your client to watch your finger as you move it through their full vertical gaze. The muscle will unlock at some point along their vertical line of vision. This is a normal response.

2. Ask them to keep their focus on this point, i.e. the point at which the muscle unlocks, but also become aware of their periphery while you carry out the next step. Note their eye position.

3. Place your finger(s) in the edge of their visual field (make sure they can see your finger) and test the IM one quadrant at a time. The IM will lock when you reach their therapeutic quadrant.

4. Ask your client to remember their eye position found in step 2 and relax their eyes.

5. Have them touch the area of pain and give you a SUD (subjective unit of discomfort). If the area cannot be touched easily the practitioner can CL the point and place it in circuit retaining mode.

6. Maintaining the TL, help them find their focus point found in step 2 and soften their gaze and become aware of their peripheral vision in their therapeutic quadrant. Moving your fingers in this quadrant at the edge of their visual field will help them.

7. Now ask your client to turn their eyes towards their therapeutic quadrant and again let their gaze soften and become aware of their periphery whist you move your fingers around all quadrants of their peripheral vision.

8. Retake a SUD to see if there is any reduction in pain. If there is only a slight improvement, check that the pain area is a priority and carry out other procedures for it as needed.

This technique can be done for general health and wellbeing. If this is the case omit step 5.

Vision – Far and Near Sightedness

Sometimes we have clients say to us, "my eyesight is changing quickly, can you do anything about that?"

Eye exercises can certainly be helpful. Good nutrition can help prevent or delay problems such as macular degeneration and the formation of cataracts. This protocol helps identify long-term nutritional assistance for people with hyperopia (long/far sight) and myopia (short/near sight). (Deal)

Test for Hyperopia

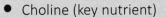

1. Ask your client to focus on the ceiling and test an AIM. It will usually remain locked.
2. Now alter their focus to near sight by then asking them to look at your finger placed a few inches away from their eyes and quickly test the IM. If the IM unlocks their vision cannot accommodate from far to near.

Test for Myopia

1. Ask your client to focus on your finger placed a few inches away from their eyes and test an AIM. It will usually remain locked.
2. Now ask them to focus on the ceiling and quickly test the IM. If the IM unlocks their vision cannot accommodate from near to far.

The nutrients for nutritional support help to produce the neurotransmitters that are involved in the relaxation and contraction of the eye muscles which gives us the ability to adjust our sight from near to far and vice versa.

3. Enter the result of step 2 into circuit retaining mode (**unlock**).
4. Test each of the nutrients from the following lists (**lock**). Any or all the nutrients in the list may show. Test for priority (**unlock**), then 'Raise Vital Force' (**unlock**). The nutrients need to be taken long-term.

Hyperopia

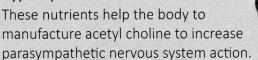

These nutrients help the body to manufacture acetyl choline to increase parasympathetic nervous system action.

- Choline (key nutrient)
- Pantothenic acid (B5)
- Organic minerals
- B Complex (I recommend enzyme activated)

Myopia

These nutrients help the body manufacture noradrenaline which stimulates the sympathetic nervous system. This helps to relax ligaments that the eye muscle is attached to, which allows better accommodation from near to far.

- Tyrosine (key nutrient)
- Folic Acid, B6 and B3, B complex
- Vitamin C
- Phosphoric acid
- Adrenal support

Blood Pressure Balance

If you have a blood pressure reading device, you could check the client's readings before and after carrying out this procedure.

For this procedure you will need two magnets. The magnets should not be a mix of north and south poles on the same side. They should be north pole only on one side and south pole only on the other side.

Please check that the person does not have any electrical device in their chest first!! The magnets for this procedure is contraindicated for anyone with a pacemaker. If anyone has stents, these are usually made of stainless steel or a cobalt material, which are not affected by magnets, but just use caution when using this procedure when anyone has ANYTHING foreign in their chest.

1. Firstly, to ensure that there is not an existing neck issue, your client places one hand over the back of the neck at C7/T1 (supine). The IM should be locked in the clear. If the indicator unlocks, address this first (see section on spinal misalignments, on page 142).

2. Have them remove their hand from C7/T1 and place the other hand over their heart area over the inferior part of the sternum and towards the left side. The IM should remain locked. The IM unlocks, correct first by placing the area of TL into circuit retaining mode (CRM) and identify a correction using the four finger modes.

3. Your client now places one hand over C7/T1 and the other over the heart area simultaneously. A quadriceps or piriformis are good indicators to use at this stage. If they two-point (unlock), there is a blood pressure imbalance. Before entering this into CRM you can check if this imbalance is okay to correct by activating modality or priority finger modes (lock).

4. Enter these two points into CRM (unlock).

5. Place one magnet under C7/T1 and the other over the heart. Find the combinations of north and south pole sides that locks your indicator again e.g. north pole over C7/T1 and south pole over heart area. If more than one combination shows (doubtful but a possibility), check for modality.

6. Leave this combination of magnets in place for a few minutes.

7. Remove the magnets and repeat step 3. The IM should now be locked.

8. To check if the magnets have been on the points long enough, activate the 'complete' mode, see page xxii. The IM will **unlock** if it is complete and you can cancel the lock. If the IM doesn't change (stays locked), apply the magnets for longer and repeat step 3 and 8 once more.

9. Your client could use the magnets in the same combination and positions at home.

Universal Application of Sagittal Suture Spread and Tap

This quick technique helps to reinforce the treatments you make so that the treatment holds.

Research happens in a strange way sometimes. Dr Sheldon Deal talks about how Dr Goodheart discovered that tapping the vertex of the head corrected imbalances that were seemingly unrelated to the shortcut challenge he used for identifying cervical disc problems. When one of his clients returned to say that tapping on his head had fixed his knee, Goodheart asked the question – why did that work?

It turned out that he had discovered that the sagittal suture is very therapeutic to the rest of the body. AK researchers found that if the sagittal suture two-pointed to any lesion, then correcting the sagittal suture after making the correction would be of benefit.

1. At the beginning of the session check whether there is a sagittal suture cranial fault in the clear, (see section on Cranial Faults for details on how to do this on page 175) and correct if necessary.

2. Using an AIM, identify the lesion that you are pursuing (unlock).

3. Ask your client to TL the sagittal suture at the same time. If the sagittal suture two-points to the lesion (lock) it shows relevance. You will see this even if your client does not present with the cranial fault at the start of the session.

4. Correct the lesion and then spread the sagittal suture 3 or 4 times on inspiration and then tap it a few times. Chewing just one tablet/capsule of magnesium whilst the suture is being treated can also be beneficial in helping the treatment to hold.

In my own clinic I tend to routinely test and correct the sagittal suture at the end of the session before my client gets down from the table.

Notes

List of Protocol in Categories

This quick referral list also includes protocols learned during a Foundation Kinesiology Course.

When a finger mode shows during treatment, the following techniques can be checked for and may show under these headings.

Electromagnetics

Centring - (Hyoid, gait, cloacals)	Aura Leaks
Switching Ionisation	Chakras
Dehydration	Auricular Lock (Ear unfurling)
Blood Chemistry	Ocular lock (Eye positions)
Acupuncture Meridians	Making corrections with sound and colour
Resetting the Biological Clock	Scar Tissue (affecting meridian flow)
Alarm Points	Tibetan Energies (Figure of Eight Energies)
Cross Crawl	Walking Gait (Also structural)
Pitch Roll, Yaw and Tilt	

Emotional

Goal setting with clients	Brain integration techniques
Alarm Points and Emotions	Psychological Conflict
Bach Flower Remedies (or other flower essences)	Fears & Phobias
Emotional Bruising	Emotional Stress Release
Temporal Tap	Spondylogenic Reflex
Eye Rotations	STO

Biochemical/Personal Ecology

Ileocecal valve (also structural)	Parasites
Ridler's Reflexes	Food intolerance
Heavy Metal Toxicity	Hypoglycaemia
Candida Albicans	Hypochlorhydria
B & E Points and Nutrition for Neurotransmitters	Digestive Insufficiency
Vitamins and Minerals in foods	Endocrine System Nutrition
Hypoglycaemia	

Structural	
Ileocaecal Valve	Neuro-vasculars
Houston's Valve	Origin & Insertion techniques
Chronic Valves	Spindle cell technique
Ileal Brake Challenge	Dural torque
Gastro-colic Reflex	Spinal Torque
Hiatal Hernia	Manual correction for 'Cystitis'
Lateral Atlas	Reactive Muscles
Fixations	Ligament Interlink
Temporomandibular Joint (TMJ)	Hypertonic muscles
Cranial Faults	Pelvic Categories
Retrograde Lymphatics	Uterine Lift and Functional Short Leg
Lovett brothers	Structural Corrections for Endocrine Glands
Spinal Misalignment Techniques	Walking gait
Retrograde and Anterograde Lymphatics	Shock Absorbers
Neuro-lymphatics	Cystitis Technique

General, or Mixed Category	
Injury Recall	Pre- stressing
Evaluating the Endocrine System	Pulse Synchronisation
Beginning and End Points	Sagittal Suture (Universal Application)
Lateral Sway	Past Trauma Resolution
Peripheral Vision Technique	Blood Pressure Balance
Vision (Far and Near Sightedness)	

List of Suggested Procedures

This is NOT a definitive list and is designed to help you at times when your mind goes blank.

Allergies	Atlas	Candida	ICV & Houston
	Nutrition (particularly Zinc)	Hypoglycaemia	Emotional
	Adrenals	TMJ	Digestive Insufficiency
	Food intolerances	Dural Torque	Metal Toxicity
		Blood Chemistry	

Back Problems	Injury Recall	Fixations	Emotional Bruising
	ICV	Reactive Muscles	Hypoglycaemia
	Atlas	Gait	Adrenals
	Lovett Brothers	Cross Crawl	B & E Points for Pain
	Dural Torque	Cloacals	Cranial Faults
	TMJ	Nutrition	Pelvic Categories
	All Muscle Techniques	STO	Fixations

Constipation	ICV & Houston	Food Intolerance	Candida
	Chronic Valves	Stress	Parasites
	Peristalsis Techniques	Fibre Deficiency	HCL & Enzyme Deficiency
	TMJ		Diet

Depression and Anxiety	Food Intolerance	Candida	Heavy Metal Toxicity
	Blood Sugar Handling	Parasites	Atlas
	Spondylogenic Reflex	Liver Toxicity	Ionisation
	Cross Crawl	Emotional Techniques	Blood Chemistry
	Emotional Techniques		

Diarrhoea	ICV & Houston	Food intolerance	Candida
	TMJ	Stress	Parasites
	Diet	Fibre Deficiency	HCL & Enzyme Deficiency
	Chronic Valves	Peristalsis Techniques	

Digestive	Sub-Clinical Hiatal hernia	ICV & Houston	Nutrition
	HCL deficiency	Spondylogenic Reflex	Adrenal Stress
	Enzymes	Chronic Valves	Emotional
	Dural Torque	Vagus	Thoracic Spinal Misalignments

Fatigue	Nutrition	Endocrine	Ionisation
	Food Intolerance	Emotional Techniques	Eight Energy (Tibetan Energy)
	Candida, Parasites	Blood chemistry	Aura Leaks
	Hypoglycaemia	Meridian Work	Chakras
	Retrograde Lymphatics	Cross Crawl	Modality Mode
	Digestion	Dural Torque	TMJ
	Ionisation	Metal Toxicity	Scar Tissue

Headaches-Persistent	Neck Muscles Atlas Dural Torque TMJ	Walking Gait Cranial Faults Postural Analysis Reactive Muscles	Blood Sugar Handling Endocrine Checks Blood Chemistry Liver Toxicity
Irritable Bowel	ICV & Houston Chronic valves Nutritional Deficiencies	Emotional Techniques Food intolerances Spondylogenic Reflex	Candida Parasites Chakras
Joint Problems	Ligament Interlink Muscles Food intolerance	Reactive Muscles Fixations Nutrition Candida	Injury Recall Cloacals Gait Parasites
Limb Pain	Reactive Muscles B & E Points Injury Recall Nutrition	Spindle Cell, O & I Fixations PRYT Spinal Misalignment	Ridler's Reflexes Food intolerance Candida Shock Absorbers
Muscle Weakness or Tightness (Persistent)	Allergies Lack of Nutrition Posture Check Emotional Stress PRYT	B & E Points Reactive Muscles TMJ Walking Gait Muscle Techniques	Chakras STO Cranial Faults Injury Recall Technique
Neck Problems	As for back problems Auricular Lock Spinal Torque	Hyoid Ionisation Cloacals	Walking gait Cranial Faults
Menopause	Endocrine Adrenal Stress Nutrition	Hypoglycaemia Candida Emotional	Food Intolerances Liver Dysfunction
PMS	See Menopause	Uterine Lift	
Migraine	Food intolerance Hypoglycaemia Candida TMJ Dural Torque	Spinal Misalignments Cranial Faults Walking Gait Pelvic categories	Endocrine Nutrition Adrenal stress ICV
Skin Problems	Nutrition Atlas Correction Candida & Parasites Endocrine Checks	Liver & Kidneys ICV Metal Toxicity Emotional Techniques	Liver Dysfunction Kidney Dysfunction Allergies and Intolerances

References

Beardall, A. (1988). Cloacal Synchronisation. In D. Walther, *Applied Kinesiology Synopsis* (p. 164).

Biological Mercury - Free Dentistry (with references). (n.d.). Retrieved from Educate- Yourself: http://educate-yourself.org/cn/mercuryfreedentristy2000.shtml

Burr-Madsen, A. (1990). Polarity Reflex Nutritional Analysis (PRANA).

Callahan, R. (n.d.). *Thought Field Therapy Course Manual.*

Chaitow, L. (1996). *Candida - Could Yeast be Your Problem?*

Deal, S. (1987-2000). In *Dr. Sheldon Deal Seminars 1987 - 2000 London, UK.*

Diamond, J. (1997). *Life Energy & The Emotions.* Eden Grove Editions.

DNFT Chiropractic. (1987). *An Interview with Dr Richard VanRumpt.* Retrieved from DNFT Chiropractic: www.dnftchiropractic.com

Feinberg, L. S. (2014). Dr. *NMT Seminar Introduction Part 1 (YouTube).*

Ferreri, C. (1996). In *Neural Organization Technique Basic Procedures.*

Goddard, G. (1991). *TMJ - The Jaw Connection - The Overlooked Diagnosis.* Santa Fe: Aurora Press.

Green, J. (2002). The Herbal Medicine-Maker's Handbook. In J. Green, *The Herbal Medicine-Maker's Handbook.* Berkeley: Crossing Press .

Guyton. (1991). *Textbook of Medical Physiology 8th edition.* Philadelphia: Saunders.

Ionization (n.d.) Retrieved from Wikipedia

Institute of Functional Medicine. (2005). *Textbook of Functional Medicine.* Gig Harbor: Institute of Functional Medicine.

Kenyon, J. (1984). *Modern Techniques in Acupuncture.*

Knowlative, W. (n.d.). Retrieved from *www.knowlative.com.*

Kumamoto, C., Romo, J. (2019, December). Clues about a deadly new fungus from one we know only too well. *ICHAN*, p. 22.

Leadbeater, C. W. (1927). *The Chakras, Madras (India).* The Theosophical Publishing House.

Macoicia, G. (1989). *The Foundations of Chinese Medicine .* Churchill Livingstone.

Pert, C. (1997). *Molecules of Emotion.* Touchstone - Simon & Schuster.

Prestwich, S. (circa 2008). DSK module 1 notes.

Sales, A. (2003). *Cyberkinetics Level 1.*

Sarno, J. E. (1999). *The Mindbody Prescrition - Healing the Body, Healing the Pain.* Wellness Central.

Schmitt, W. (n.d.). *How Injury Recall Technique Can Relieve Persistent Pain & Dysfunction.* Retrieved from Quintessential Applications.

Tal E., et al (1976). Effect of air ionization on blood serotonin in vitro. *Experientia*, Volume 32, Number 3 P. 326. Retrieved from SpringerCitations.

Thie, J. (2005). *Touch For Health.*

Tsu, C. et al. *Pathogeneis of Candida Albicans Biofilm.* Pathogens and Disease 2016 Jun.

Walther, D. S. (1988). *Applied Kinesiology Synopsis.* Pueblo Colorado: Systems DC.

Wikipedia. (2019). *Transverse Folds of Rectum*. Retrieved from Wikipedia.

Williams, D., Lewis, (2011). *Pathogenesis & Treatment of Oral Candidosis.* J.Oral Microbiol 2011 v. 3

Williams, L. L. (2011). *Radical Medicine.* Rochester: Healing Arts Press.

Index

List of Tables

List of Figures

Notes